I Left My Tent in San Francisco

D0293474

I Left My Tent in San Francisco

A tale of breathtaking ineptitude

EMMA KENNEDY

EBURY
PRESS

3 5 7 9 10 8 6 4

First published in 2011 by Ebury Press, an imprint of Ebury Publishing
A Random House Group company

The Random House Group Limited Reg. No. 954009

Addresses for companies within the Random House Group can be found at
www.randomhouse.co.uk

A CIP catalogue record for this book is available from the British Library

The Random House Group Limited supports the Forest Stewardship
Council® (FSC®), the leading international forest certification
organisation. All our titles that are printed on Greenpeace approved
FSC® certified paper carry the FSC® logo. Our paper procurement policy
can be found at www.randomhouse.co.uk/environment

Designed and set by seagulls.net

Printed in the UK by CPI Mackays, Chatham, ME5 8TD

ISBN 9780091935955

To buy books by your favourite authors and register for offers visit
www.randomhouse.co.uk

For Mouse and Mikey. I love them so.

Contents

Chapter One: Up, Up and Away   1

Chapter Two: So Good They Named it Twice   34

Chapter Three: If You're Going to San Francisco   53

Chapter Four: Got To Have a J.O.B If You Want
To Be With Me   78

Chapter Five: You Gotta Fight. For the Right.
To Paaaaaaaaaarty.   93

Chapter Six: Working Nine to Five   125

Chapter Seven: Oops, I Did it Again   147

Chapter Eight: Wherever I Lay My Hat   154

Chapter Nine: Hello! I Must Be Going!   191

Chapter Ten: And All That Jazz   209

Chapter Eleven: One Day at a Time, Sweet Jesus   229

Chapter Twelve: We Are Family   262

Chapter Thirteen: The Long Way Home   300

Epilogue   309

Acknowledgements   311

Chapter One

Up, Up and Away

$0

I was crouched in a bush, a stolen sign tucked under my arm, I was drunk and a police car was prowling. My bike was abandoned in the road and my best friend Dee was hunched next to me. 'Do you think they've gone?' she whispered, tugging at my sleeve.

'Definitely gone,' I said, words slurring. 'Let's get out of the hedge.'

I pushed my way onto the pavement, a broken twig in my fringe, and crawled on all fours towards my bike.

But they weren't gone. As Dee and I stumbled over each other to pick up our bikes, there was a screech ahead of us. The patrol car that had passed us at a slow creep moments earlier had made a loop at the top of the street and come back. I blinked and looked up. The car came to a crunching halt, at an angle, and two police officers leapt out and bore down upon us.

'Sorry...' I began, 'our lights aren't working. I think they must need new batteries,' but the burly officer before me wasn't interested.

'What's that?' he asked, pointing at the small plastic sign still tucked under my arm.

I looked down at it and swallowed. Twenty minutes earlier, in a moment of end-of-term high jinx, Dee and I had unhooked it from the top of a used Lexus on a garage forecourt. 'It's a prop?' I asked, looking over at Dee for some assistance.

'For a play?' she chipped in, eyebrows raised in hope.

'No,' answered the police officer. 'It's not a prop for a play. You've stolen that from a garage in Summertown, haven't you?'

'Oh yes,' I nodded. ' I forgot.'

The police officer gestured to his colleague, a short woman with an intense face, who came towards me, reaching for her handcuffs. She looked as if she might punch concrete for fun and, if anything, seemed vaguely thrilled. A small injection of hilarity shot through me. Here I was, slightly worse for wear, about to be taken down for nicking a small plastic sign that read USED CARS. GREAT DEALS.

'I am arresting you,' she began, coming closer, 'on suspicion of theft. You do not have to say anything, but it may harm your defence if you do not mention when questioned something which you may later rely on in court. Anything you do say may be given in evidence. Do you understand?'

I shot a quick, incredulous stare in Dee's direction.

'Can't we just take it back?' Dee asked, pointing towards the offending sign. 'It's only up the road. We can cycle there and put it back.'

'No, you can't.' said the female officer, still coming at me with the cuffs. As she took my right hand, I did something that many might have thought foolish. I looked up, threw her a cheeky grin and adopting a cod, 1950s' mockney accent said the one phrase I had been longing to say all of my life. 'It's all right, officer,' I said, holding up my other hand in supplication. 'I'll come quietly!'

Dee rolled her eyes. We were bundled into the back of the police car. We had to be at Heathrow in five hours. This was not the start to the rest of my life I'd been hoping for.

It had been something of a personal struggle to get in to the university of my choice. Nobody thought I could do it. My teachers said things like 'We're just concerned that you're going to feel terribly let down,' while my parents pulled anxious faces and made thin, whistling noises along the lines of, 'You can only do your best.' The message was loud and clear. Not a single person thought I would ever be accepted at Oxford.

I was from a state school and hadn't had the advantage of tuck boxes, ridiculous school mascots or science blocks donated by a passing prince in a barouche. All we had were slightly mouldy netball bibs and lunches so dense it was a mystery they didn't appear on the periodic table. Nevertheless, I was determined and nothing and nobody was going to stop me having a crack. Occasionally, I would meet up with my History teacher in a small cupboard of a room normally reserved for sacking members of staff but other than that, a pat on the back and a wave from my parents, I was flying solo.

My first brush with the university I was so obsessed with came on a damp Saturday morning in 1984. My teachers had urged me to apply to a college called St Catherine's on the sole basis that they'd taken someone from my school six years previously and they 'might remember'. One thing was troubling me greatly. Not my impending interview, for which I was considerably nervous, but the college itself. It was modern, built in 1962, and despite its relaxed location on the banks of the Cherwell, the glass and concrete buildings were reminiscent of a New Town shopping centre. This was not the Oxford I had dreamed of in my bedroom: the glorious spires, oak-lined rooms with sash windows, and packed with old leather sofas that eminent writers and poets and politicians had once sat on. This was somewhere you might find yourself if you were looking for an unappetising cheese pasty or getting a boil lanced. Still, beggars can't be choosers. I was at the Findus Crispy pancake college and I had to do my best to try and get in.

I was interviewed by two men wearing tweed jackets. They both sat in high-backed padded armchairs. The room smelled of coffee, and sitting on a low table in front of me there was a plate with a half-eaten biscuit on it. I stared at it. It was a custard cream. I perched on the end of the wooden chair that had been presented to me, clutching my knees, my heart thumping in my chest. If I did well, I thought to myself, then my life would take a magical course. The world, I naively dreamed, would be a generous hamper of opportunity from which I could pick things at will. The possibilities seemed endless – I could be an eccentric philanthropist, a radical philosopher or I might end up ruling the Universe – a bit like Ming the Merciless, but with considerably shorter fingernails.

We discussed the Treaty of Versailles, the rise of Nazism and the miners' strike that had been raging through the latter part of that year. Twenty pits faced closure and the Thatcher government, determined to crush the unions once and for all had stock-piled coal and converted power stations on the quiet. The miners were doomed, the unions would be destroyed and Britain's workforce would never be the same again. I talked about it eloquently, repeating word for word a conversation I had had with my Communist grandfather a week before over half a Guinness in a pub in Battersea. The fellows nodded and occasionally raised their eyebrows. I nodded and raised my eyebrows back at them. This felt *good*.

Two weeks later, I had a letter in which I was offered a place to read History, conditional on me getting two As and a B. Everyone around me was wide-eyed with disbelief. As moments go, it was right up there, pipping the previous top spot winner – the rain-soaked netball match where my school, Hitchin Girls' School, locally known as the Whorehouse on the Hill, had finally beaten the hated Dame Alice Harper, or Posh Twat High as we liked to call them. Every single time we encountered them, they thrashed us and in five long years we had never come close to equalising, let alone winning. It was galling. They would swan in, beat us and then waft off in their air-conditioned coach, stuffing their faces with just-baked iced finger buns. We fucking hated them.

But one soaking Saturday in November 1983, we were facing them again and suddenly, somewhere in the early moments of the second half, we took the lead. It was a bit like an overweight, asthmatic pub team going one up against Manchester United. Sensing our moment of destiny had finally come our blood was up. Our PE teacher, Miss Nettell, the prettiest and most glamorous teacher at our school, then almost threw a spanner in the works by inexplicably attempting to abandon the match because the rain was ruining her new hair-do, but we flat refused and carried on. We held on by the skin of our teeth and as the final whistle blew, we were a goal ahead. Victory was ours. It was a triumph for the comprehensive schooling system and to celebrate, we went crazy on lemon squash and jammy dodgers. I never thought a greater moment would come. But, with the arrival of this letter, it had.

And then disaster struck.

*

It was March 1985, and a milky sun was peeping out behind the dull, grey clouds that had lingered for much of that week. I was in the middle of a Latin lesson, sitting at the desk in front of my teacher, a small, well-presented woman with kind eyes and a hairstyle that hadn't budged a millimetre in six years. I had a terrible headache and my throat was tight. I was sweating and a sudden dizziness sent me slumping forward, head in hands, across my desk. My teacher took one concerned look at me and sent me home.

Hours later I was found by my parents, crouching in the corner of my bedroom, half crazed with hallucinations. I thought I was a sparrow, my mother thought I was dying. I had been struck down by the curse of the sixth former, glandular fever, and it was so bad it cast a shadow over the rest of the year. Extremely unwell, I ended up having to take a month off school. Reports from teachers came home, practically tear-stained, bewailing my condition and saying things like 'the most important thing is that Emma gets better' and 'I do not know if Emma's health can withstand the next few months. It will be tragic if it doesn't.' It was all rather alarming. My parents would huddle conspiratorially and I would have a go at walking down the garden and back again.

My main problem was simply staying awake. My dad would help me downstairs, proffer some toast that I would stare at, light a fire and go off to work. He'd return at lunchtime, toss the uneaten toast in the bin, wake me up and present some soup. I'd push a spoon through it. Occasionally I'd try and watch television. I could just about manage the opening credits of *Dogtanian and the Three Muskehounds* but as soon as anything approaching a plot kicked in, I was drifting off again. It was like being slowly preserved in amber.

To go to Oxford I had to get two As and a B, grades that before my illness, while challenging, felt achievable but, as the exams approached, I was still so weak and shattered that people around me began to whisper whether I should be taking them at all. I was having nothing of it, of course. It was inconceivable that I wouldn't sit my A Levels and my stubborn streak kicked in once more.

But this time, my determination was to be my undoing. During my British History paper I fell asleep and had to be nudged awake by the invigilator; during one Latin translation paper I spent most of it staring out of the window, my mind swirling like an empty void. I had nothing left to give. I was a husk. My grades fell accordingly. Oxford wrote me a polite but firm letter. I would not be reading History that year but, given my condition, if I would like to reapply then they would consider seeing me again.

I was bitterly disappointed. I was asked if I wanted to enter the university Clearing system, the mop-up net for the disenchanted, but I didn't have the heart to do it. Instead, I spent that summer washing dishes at a local hotel and being taught how to drink alcohol without throwing up by a 45-year-old Irish mother of four called Noreen. After six weeks I was promoted to vegetable peeler. I was earning £120 a week. I could afford skirts from Jigsaw. I was doing *well*.

Without noticing, thoughts of Oxford slipped away.

Mrs Graebe had been my English teacher. She had retired after my O Levels and I hadn't seen her in over two years. I had never been particularly fond of her, probably because she was one of the older teachers and although she commanded a calm authority had a dusty demeanour that fell short of instilling a sense of excitement. I had bumped into her outside a small shop in Hitchin where sixth-form girls liked to hang out and buy joss sticks that smelled of petunia oil. She was pleased to see me; I felt a little embarrassed. There was always something excruciating about bumping into your teachers in town. Especially ones who'd left. You might have to call them by their *first name*.

'Are you off to university in September next year?' she asked me, smiling gently, assuming I was still in Hitchin because I was taking a year off before plunging into higher education.

I stared past her. It's never pleasant having to confess to failure and so I shook my head and explained my predicament. Mrs Graebe frowned and thought for a moment. She placed a hand, softly, on my shoulder. 'Emma,' she began, 'I don't understand why you wanted to read History at university. You were one of the best English students I ever had. And as for not going to university at all – are you *quite* mad? You've got a brain – use it! Here,' she added, handing me a card with her address on it. 'If you decide to have another go and you want to try for English, I want you to come and see me. Don't give up. *Never* give up.'

She strode off, her words ringing in my ears. A surge of regret coursed through me. I had lost sight of the one goal I had ever given myself. I felt the stirrings of my old determination rattling somewhere behind my ribcage. Mrs Graebe was right. *Never* give up.

Spurred on, I spent the next eight weeks travelling on the bus to Mrs Graebe's house, a rectory in the village of Kimpton, where she would give me tea and cake and we would sit discussing poetry and plays and the great novelists of the nineteenth century. I would not be re-taking my A levels, we decided, but instead I would take the Oxford entrance exam and hope that that would be enough to secure me a place. She charged me not one penny and didn't make me call her Barbara. Her reward, she constantly told me, would be when I got in to Oxford.

As I stood in an ancient stairwell of St Edmund Hall waiting to be interviewed for a place in the English faculty, small battered leather briefcase in hand, I thought of nothing but Mrs Graebe and not letting her down. It was quite something to have somebody believe in me and after the months of illness I had endured, I had a point to prove. This time, I was interviewed by three people: two ancient fellows – Reggie Alton, a mischievous-looking chap and Bruce Mitchell, the renowned Anglo-Saxon scholar – and a beaming blue-eyed woman called Lucy Newlyn, the youngster in the pack. The walls were lined with books and an old oak table stood to one side with a set of tea things laid on a tray. I was offered a sherry. I politely declined but instead opened my tiny leather suitcase and pulled out five essays I'd written and handed them to Bruce. 'You can read those,' I said, 'to help you make up your mind. I haven't applied anywhere else.'

Bruce seemed quite taken aback with this and, fixing me with an almost baffled stare, asked, 'And what will you do if you don't get in?'

I returned his gaze and without a moment's hesitation threw down my intent. 'I shall re-apply next year,' I declared. I was back.

A week later a heavy envelope embossed with the college crest tumbled onto our doormat. The journey to this moment had been long and arduous. It had been a roller coaster: everyone around me doubting me, the incredible joy of getting a place only to have it snatched away because of illness, the random encounter with Mrs Graebe, the switch to English, the crawl back to good health. I sat, alone, on my bed staring at the envelope in my hands. It felt as if I was about to jump off a precipice and, depending on what lay within, I would either fly or fall. I turned it over, ran my forefinger under the seal and took out the letter from inside.

'I am very glad to be able to tell you,' it began, 'that the college has decided to offer you a place to come into residence in October 1986 to read English.'

My chest swelled, my eyes filled with tears and as my parents tumbled in through my door I was overwhelmed with emotion. It was, and still is, the greatest achievement of my life. The best bit, of course, was getting to tell Mrs Graebe. I rang her and broke the news, laughing as she hooted with joy.

A few days later, I received a volume of poems by Wendy Cope called *Making Cocoa for Kingsley Amis*. It was from Mrs Graebe and a short inscription had been written on the inside cover.

'Dear Emma,' it read. 'Anyone can give up. That's easy. But you didn't. Never stop persevering. Yours, Barbara Graebe.'

It was advice I was going to need.

My parents, Brenda and Tony, while proud as punch that I was going to Oxford, were, at the same time, worried I was going to struggle to fit in. My mother, concerned that I was going to be persecuted for coming from humble stock, took me to one side.

'There are a lot of people,' she began, forehead knitting itself into a frown, 'who don't like the Welsh.'

I stared at her.

'They won't give them a chance. So don't tell anyone at Oxford that your father's from Wales. Or they'll all think you're a coal hewer. And a belcher.'

My father, despite being delighted for me, was also wracked with the sort of sorrow reserved for the only surviving relative of a drive-by shooting. His only child was leaving the nest and he didn't seem to be coping. We had been to buy a bicycle for me to take to university and had gone to a small second-hand shop tucked down a side street near the railway station. It was filled with the flotsam and jetsam of a slightly bygone age. There was an old Decca record player, faded green with a chunky white plastic trim (which I purchased on the spot), a table heaped with a dusty tea set, old chairs piled high and, leaning along the walls, framed pictures stacked against each other. Sitting in the window was a bicycle painted a deep, resonant purple with a white leather seat and a fulsome wicker basket on the front. When I saw her, something clicked. She was perfect. I grinned. 'We should give her a name,' I said, patting the saddle. 'She'll be my constant companion for the next three years. She needs a great name, something noble and true.'

'You could call her Myfanwy or Gwendolyn,' said my father, clearing his throat.

I screwed my mouth sideways. 'Mum says I shouldn't tell anyone about the Welsh thing. In case I get picked on by posh people. And they think I have flatulence.'

My father looked purposeful. 'Don't ever be ashamed of where you've come from, Emma. Welsh people DO have a lot of wind. That's true. It's the mountain air. But as my mother used to say, we all shit out the same hole.'

At this point, the shopkeeper, who had been readying himself for a sale, grimaced a little and moved away. But my dad was right.

'Well that's that then,' I added, with a nod. 'I hereby name this bike Gwendolyn!'

The car was packed to bursting. My mother had given me her old grey trunk that we'd packed with books and things I'd need for term. On top of it my father had Sellotaped a list so that we could cross off things as they went in. It read

Mugs – 4
Cutlery
A few plates
Fruit bowl
One saucepan
Tin Opener
Bottle Opener
A vase
Box of tissues
A couple of files

And that was it. These were the basics with which I needed to survive the university jungle. My mother had, at one point, toyed with the idea of getting me a sandwich maker but had quickly decided against it, arguing that 'If everyone knows you've got facilities to provide hot cheese toasties you'll never get *any* work done.'

So with Gwendolyn strapped upside down to the roof of

the car I heaved a small suitcase of clothes onto the back seat next to me and decamped to Oxford.

It was a beautifully sunny day and as we drove I stared out the window watching the long reflection of my bicycle's wheels as they spun in the wind. No one said much. For the past 19 years we had been together through thick and thin and here we were, about to be parted. Being an only child, I was incredibly close to my parents and, as much as I was longing to go to university, this was a terrible emotional wrench. Things would never be the same again. And we all knew it.

My room was in a modern annex tucked behind the sort of picturesque front quad that makes parents ooh and then aah. My living quarters were not, as my mother had assumed, the stuff of *Brideshead Revisited* but instead were an anonymous 1970s' rectangle with a pervading aroma of warm glue. There was a small tinge of disappointment that I would not be living in the romantic surrounds of an oak-lined suite but I was so excited to be there they could have shown me to a cardboard box at the back of some bins and I wouldn't have cared. Together we unpacked the contents of the trunk and set about covering the walls with posters I felt were a declaration of my intent. There was a Gerald Scarfe RSC poster of Macbeth, an enormous red and yellow Lenin, arm aloft as if he had all the answers and a large black-and-white poster of the Woody Allen film *Manhattan*, celebrating the island's magnificent outline. I stood with my hands on my hips and nodded. 'What do you think?' I asked, looking about me.

Dad was standing at my window and staring down into the dining hall opposite. 'Looks nice,' he said, giving a small nod and after a pause, 'You know you can come home anytime. I can make you cakes.'

My mother placed a hand on the flat of my back. 'Don't let anyone make you feel inferior, Emma. You got in, just the same as they did. If anything, you're cleverer because you did it on your own without loads of money. You're as good as anyone here. And don't forget it.'

I gave them both a weak smile. I *was* a bit worried about mixing with the public-school crowd. My only brush with a posh lot had been playing netball against Dame Alice Harper. 'And try not to overdo it,' my mother added. 'You've only just got yourself better.' She stopped and sniffed the air. 'That smell,' she began, nose scrunching upwards, 'heady brew. Slightly giving me a headache. Well. You're all unpacked. I suppose we should leave you to it.'

We all stared at each other. My mother, realising that my father was on the brink of an emotional collapse, took the brisk plaster-pulling approach, clasped me to her quickly and said 'Right, come on Tony, off we go!' and marched towards the door. Dad, bottom lip trembling, staggered towards me, reached into his pocket and pressed a twenty-pound note into my hand.

'In case of emergencies,' he gargled then, after a swift, python-like grip, he let out a small, strangled wail and stumbled out of the door, the strains of his tears carrying all the way down the corridor. I stood, alone, and blinked. My parents had left the building.

I was absolutely terrified.

Fear was preying heavily on my parents' minds too. My mother, for all her bravado, was convinced that Oxford would transform me into an objectionable braying Hooray Henry and that I would return to Hitchin at Christmas ashamed of the pair of them and bemoaning the fact we didn't live in a castle. She returned home only to clamber up the stairs in a state of abject despair where she collapsed at the top of the landing and lay, face down on the carpet, wailing into the crook of her elbow. My father, after trying to pull her up and failing, had similarly fallen into a deep morass of gloom and had crawled, desolated, into my bedroom where he sat on my bed with one hand on his forehead and the other on his only child's abandoned pillow. A period of considerable and unfettered wailing then took place, after which my mother, wiping her tear-stained face, raised herself merely to shout, 'We need to get drunk!' Needing no further encouragement, my father trudged downstairs and opened the only bottle in the house, a concentrated dessert wine left by an obscure relative one Christmas that was so strong, it actually had a skull on its label. Twenty minutes later and the whole lot was gone.

As luck would have it, all students taking English had been set a small exam to see how much of the reading list we'd done over the summer so I didn't have much time to feel miserable. I had been joined by two of my stable mates – Doug, a quiet unassuming fellow who was on an Army scholarship and Andy, a thoroughly loveable young man with a penchant for heavy-knit jumpers. We had been sitting, for an hour, reading out the entries from *The Oxford Companion to English Literature* of the books that had eluded us, drinking coffee and generally marvelling at our newly conferred student status. We had just got to the more obscure writings of Daniel Defoe when a figure appeared in my open doorway. I looked up. A girl wearing a battered brown leather jacket, blue striped skirt and Doc Marten shoes was leaning against the doorframe. Over her shoulder was slung a drawstring bag covered in cartoon dinosaurs. Her hair was cut into a light bob, out of which poked one errant ear, and her features were delicate: slightly pouting lips, chiselled cheekbones and bright blue eyes that had a spark of mischief about them. I stared at her. She stared at me. 'Is this your room?' she asked, walking in uninvited and perching herself on the arm of a chair in front of me. I nodded. She looked round and raised an eyebrow. 'Are you a Communist?' she asked, gazing up at Lenin.

I shook my head. 'No. But I went to Moscow when I was in the sixth form. Our school librarian fell down a staircase and broke her arm.'

'Did you push her?'

A small grin fleeted across my lips but I didn't reply. There was something quite arresting about this confident creature that had waltzed in uninvited. She hadn't even bothered to tell me her name and she certainly hadn't asked for mine. 'What's that?' she asked, gesturing towards a strange plaster-of-Paris figure in flowery dungarees Blu-tacked to my wall.

'That's Master Hemulin,' I replied. 'You know, like the Moomins? But actually not like the Moomins at all. I made him with a friend from school after my mother reversed into a tree in front of my school gates. She was having a driving lesson. I was mortified. So my friend, Alison Macaulay, suggested we make a small man, to take my mind off it. It took hours.'

'Was Hemulin the one that's forever wandering off and going on adventures?'

I nodded. 'He was the wild card in the pack.'

'Yes. I liked him. I like his dungarees,' she added, fingering their hem. 'Very snappy. Did you make them?'

'No,' I said, shaking my head. 'Alison Macaulay did.'

'Did you make his carrier bag?'

'No, Alison Macaulay did that as well. It's supposed to be a Sainsbury bag. Alison Macaulay didn't think Master Hemulin was sophisticated enough to shop at Waitrose.'

'Alison Macaulay sounds very capable. Which bits did you make or did Alison Macaulay do everything?'

'I drew on the face. That was all I was trusted with.'

The girl leaned back and considered it. 'Bit lop-sided, that eye there,' she mumbled, pointing. 'And the mouth slopes. Master Hemulin looks like he's had a stroke.'

I stared at Master Hemulin's pale white face. He was bald and looked a bit stoved in on one side as if someone had smashed him about the face with a large frying pan. The girl was quite right. He looked very unwell. I screwed my mouth sideways and scratched my neck. Perhaps I'd take Master Hemulin down later, when everyone was gone? Tippex his eyes out and have another go? The girl pushed herself off the chair arm and slung her bag back over her shoulder. 'Anyway, I live down the hall,' she added, heading back towards the door. 'I'm from Kent. We often have terrible snow.'

'Who was that?' asked Andy, as we watched her go.

'No idea,' said Doug. 'But she's very pretty.'

'*Really* pretty,' agreed Andy, mouth slightly hanging open. 'Gorgeous, actually.'

'I think I might make friends with her,' I added. 'Do you think she'll want to be friends with me?'

Andy and Doug both looked at me. I was wearing white trousers with blue stripes, a granddad shirt, an old chunky cream cardigan with bulbous brown buttons and some faded deck shoes. I looked like someone who had failed the audition to get into Haircut 100. They said nothing. The gauntlet was down.

I didn't see her again for four days. It was the morning of Matriculation, the ceremony during which all Freshers are inducted into the university. Dressed in my black gown and mortarboard, I found myself at the back of a long crocodile of hopeful faces. We were waiting for our official photo and the photographer, a thin man in a brown jacket that was too big for him, was organising people in height order. I looked about me. This photo would probably hang in my toilet for ever and I felt a stab of anxiety that I wasn't anywhere near someone I wanted to be immortalised with.

I stepped out from the line and looked down it. There she was: the one sticky out ear, the quizzical expression, and the air of just suppressed monkey business. I grinned and waved. 'Hello,' I smiled. 'You came in my room the other day. Quick, come here,' I said. 'Come and stand next to me for the photo.' She shot me a quizzical glance as if she couldn't quite place me. I blinked. 'I was the one with Master Hemulin.'

Her head cocked slightly to one side then, unfolding her arms, she walked out of the line towards me. 'Oh yes. The one who likes adventures. The wild card in the pack.'

'That's right,' I nodded.

The photographer, seeing her break ranks, shouted over, 'No! Stay where you are, thank you! Keep the line!'

'I'm fine here, thank you,' she said, looking at him defiantly, then, turning to me, added 'My name's Dee. What's yours?'

'Emma,' I said. And that was that. We were off.

*

After the ceremony we hung out together, rattling through the preliminaries – she was reading Medicine, had gone to a posh school and had two sisters, one older, one younger. Her parents were still married and alive and she had a dog, a King Charles Spaniel, called Monty. She spoke easily and calmly and it struck me straight away that in any given circumstance, she would never lose her temper. She knew who she was and where she was going. She was, in every respect, the exact opposite of me. I was a little intimidated by her, to be honest. She was beautiful, cool and ever so slightly aloof, in the way a cat is, and as that first evening together wore on, I was slightly concerned that we had no business being friends whatsoever. And then a man in black tie came up to us.

We had gone to a post-Matriculation drinks party that was being held for Freshers in the Oxford Union, that bastion of debate where political careers aplenty had been launched. We were standing, pints in hand and still in our sub-fusc, chatting about the boys in our year. There was a foppish young man at our college reading French called Mark who we'd both noticed. He was extremely good-looking, had an ice-cream swirl of blond hair and dressed like a dandy. The only problem was that he had set his store out from the off and had been seen wandering round college carrying a teddy bear. 'Do you think he has any idea how ridiculous he looks?' I was saying. 'I mean we all loved *Brideshead Revisited* but actually carrying a teddy bear? Really?'

'Hello, ladies,' boomed a voice from behind me. I turned round. A tall, muscular man with no neck was looming over me. He grinned, displaying a set of mismatched teeth. 'What college are you from? I'm at Queens.'

'Teddy Hall,' I replied.

Ignoring me and slightly muscling me out of the way so he could have easier access to Dee, he moved forward. 'What school did you go to?'

Dee stared up at him and didn't reply. He was clearly drunk and she didn't want to engage in a conversation with him. I chipped in. 'Hitchin Girls' School,' I said, proudly.

The bloke curled up his lip. 'Never heard of it.'

'No, I don't suppose you would. It's a state school.'

His forehead furrowed and, taking a large gulp of beer, he turned to me and said, 'Do you realise my parents paid for your education?'

'I'm not sure your parents paid for it entirely,' I replied, frowning. 'I don't think my local authority showed them a photograph of me and asked them for a cheque. I think you're confusing me with African orphans. I come from Hertfordshire. My father's Welsh. My grandfather was a coal miner. We all enjoy belching.'

A small, wry smile was building on Dee's lips. The drunken boy, sensing he was being made fun of, blustered on. 'I think it's a disgrace that you people should be educated for free. My parents have to pay for me. So why shouldn't your parents pay for you? My parents had to pay a fortune for my education. And they did it to make sure I got here. And not only that, but their taxes paid for you too.'

'Sorry,' I replied, shaking my head a little. 'Are you saying I'm not entitled to be here because I had a free education?'

'I'm saying you should be *grateful*.'

I gazed in disbelief. Here, staring me in the face, was exactly the kind of person that my mother had warned me about.

Dee gently put down her pint glass and took me by the elbow, then, smiling up at the drunk said, incredibly politely,

'I'd be *grateful* if you fucked off. Given that my friend here managed to get into Oxford without any of your advantages that makes her vastly brighter than you. Goodbye.' And with that, she swept me effortlessly from the room.

'Arsehole,' she whispered as she walked me away from trouble. 'Probably the first time he's spoken to a girl. One that's not inflated, anyhow.'

I laughed. Dee laughed back.

From Matriculation onwards, Dee and I became inseparable. It was a friendship that was to last, through thick and thin, for the next three years. Boys came and went but Dee and I had an unbreakable bond. We had gone to balls dressed in black tie after realising that posh frocks had no practical purpose from 2 a.m. onwards. We had wandered in on my then boyfriend as he cavorted with another naked man, only to purse our lips and withdraw without saying a word. We had found a rowing boat at midnight and spent the night travelling the Isis in it. We had fought off geese during a solar eclipse. We had developed a mutual and inexplicable obsession with the Australian soap *Neighbours*, so much so, that I had physically wet myself with excitement on being taken to see one of the stars at the Oxford Christmas Panto. We had cycled to Blenheim on May morning to fill our bicycle baskets with pink cherry blossoms: I had a near-broken ankle and we ended up sleeping in a ditch in a rape field but we had hitched a ride back into the city on the back of a truck and at 6 a.m. had sat, hanging out of a window overlooking the high street where we scattered our pickings over the May Day crowds below. It was a love affair, pure and simple, a deep yet totally uncomplicated mutual adoration. We were the very best of friends. But our perfect life was about to come to a crashing halt. At the end of May 1989, Finals loomed and before you could say Jiminy Crickets, our three years at Oxford would be up.

The goldfish bowl of university life had kept me cocooned as if life did not exist beyond the Ring Road but with Finals only days away, I knew that decisions needed to be made. Dee, who was studying Medicine, was in no such quandary. Her life was mapped out. She would be heading to London in October to take up the clinical part of her studies. The only thing I had been interested in up to that point was comedy, but for some reason, it never crossed my mind that I could leave university and make a career of it. I had spent the previous summer committed to what turned out to be a rather miserable run with the Oxford Revue at the Edinburgh Festival and my love for comedy had turned sour. I would have to knuckle down and think about what I actually wanted to do with my life. Sensible friends around me had spent the tail end of our final term going to Milk Rounds and attending career conferences. I had rode around on Gwendolyn, face upturned, flying over speed bumps pretending she was a horse. I didn't feel ready for the working world. I needed something to segue me gently from academia and youth to my adult life. Not just a holiday, something else, something more defining, and something that would give me breathing space to work out what I wanted to do.

Two weeks before the end of Finals, Dee came up with an idea. 'What about that?' she said, pointing at the poster pinned to our college Notice Board. 'Work America. It's like Camp America but with no children involved. Which is a good thing.'

'I don't think we'd be allowed to work with children,' I pondered.

'Not if we were going to have any sort of influence over them, no,' agreed Dee. 'Meeting tonight. At the National History Museum over by Keble. Shall we go? It's got a dodo.'

The Oxford University National History Museum was, as most of the city was, an impressive structure, and as we walked towards it I found my eye drawn upwards to the swifts darting in and around its neo-gothic tower. May had been unseasonably warm that year and given the hours we were putting in at the library revising for our Finals, the walk through the early evening heat was a welcome treat. Blossom was still lingering on a few of the trees and the low, golden sun was casting the city in its most flattering light. I would miss all this. It is a great and cruel trick that your final term is spent in such abject misery and then, as Finals finish and you are overwhelmed with relief, you're asked to leave. It's like a sudden bereavement. Every last moment had to be savoured.

We were both exhausted from working so hard, sallow-eyed and yellow-skinned, and as we entered the museum and walked past the famous Oxfordshire dinosaur, the collections of butterflies and that infamous dodo I had a sense that I could just lie down and become one of the preserved exhibits. Pieces of A4 paper with scrawled arrows were directing us to a small meeting room towards the back of the main hall. There were about twenty plastic chairs laid out in rows in front of a desk on top of which sat a young fellow in a light blue T-shirt. Beside him was another boy with a mop of black hair that looked as if it hadn't seen a comb in years and a girl in neatly pressed three-quarter-length trousers and a vest top.

Her hair was tied back into a tight ponytail and she was holding a clipboard, giving her an air of smug efficiency that
instantly made me suspicious. About us were various inquisi-
tive students, some were sporting late spring tans, others,
obviously finalists, carried a vaguely haunted stare. 'There's
that bloke from Balliol,' whispered Dee, giving me a nudge.
'The one that keeps trying to get off with you.'

I glanced over my shoulder to see a lanky young man in
a grey-white T-shirt and khaki shorts. I grimaced, turned
around quickly and sank a little into my chair. But it was too
late. He'd seen me. There was a tap on my shoulder and a hot
breath gushed into my ear. 'Hello,' said Guy, taking the seat
immediately behind me. 'Haven't seen you around. Been
revising I expect.'

I nodded. Guy raised his eyebrows; his hand fell onto
my shoulder.

'I know someone who did this last year. Did Camp
America. Got Lyme disease.'

'Isn't that Necrotizing fasciitis?' asked Dee, turning to
stare at him. 'The flesh-eating thing?'

'Think so,' mumbled Guy, eyes ablaze, 'and he went
all paralysed.'

Dee and I stared, our faces contorted into horrified
revulsion.

'So, want to come for a drink later?' said Guy, looking at
me. I caught Dee's eye. She looked away.

'Can't,' I answered, with a faux-reluctant shrug. 'Got to
look over my Restoration essays.'

Guy looked disappointed. There was no way I was going
for a drink with him. He had followed me about all term,
popping up wherever I was, leaving notes pinned to my door,
invites in my cubbyhole, it had been relentless but I wasn't

interested and what had started out as mildly flattering had actually turned into a grand irritant.

'I think everyone's here who's coming,' started the fellow in blue at the front, looking at his watch. 'Welcome to BUNAC. We're a non-profit organisation that helps students work abroad. Today we're talking about working in North America. There are two ways you can go to the US and work – with the Camp America programme, which Suzy will tell you about and with the Work America programme which Mike will talk about. For both programmes, BUNAC will help you find cheap flights, help you get your visa and explain how you go about getting your social security card...'

The boy, called James, was an affable fellow, bright eyed and enthusiastic with a line of leather strings tied around his wrists and a casual air that suggested someone who was nowhere near ready to hang up his shorts and flip-flops. He talked about the practicalities of going to work in America, accommodation options, the benefits of the BUNAC system, about the opportunities it presented and the genuine confidence-building benefits of working abroad. I slightly glazed over. Not because I wasn't interested but because my Finals-diverted brain kept dragging my sub-conscious back towards Coleridge and Alexander Pope and where, exactly, I'd put that long essay I did on Chaucer.

'So now I'll hand over to Suzy, who'll tell you about Camp America.'

The girl stepped forward. Everything about her said 'Venture Scout'. I looked at her clean-pressed lemon trousers, the neat belt, the impeccably clean espadrilles and then cast an eye over myself. I was in a pair of faded soft cotton shorts with a large hole across one thigh, my Aertex top, with a smell of the poor house about it, had seen much better days and I was wearing a pair of black-and-white battered Converse baseball boots. I don't think I'd washed my hair in a week. I looked back up again. I suspected, in a one-to-one scenario, we wouldn't have much to talk about.

'The most important thing,' she began with a grin, 'is that you like children!'

Dee and I exchanged a quick glance. She cleared her throat and scratched her neck. I shifted in my chair. 'Camp America is a great summer programme whether you have coaching skills or teaching skills, you're going to find your time well spent...' My mind trailed off to Jonathan Swift. I stifled a small yawn. The warm evening sun was pouring in through a few open windows and the smell of a distant barbecue was wafting on the air. I unfolded my arms and sat up a little. I was in grave danger of nodding off.

'We're not doing that,' muttered Dee, from the corner of her mouth. 'Over my dead body.'

'Although she said if you do coaching you get a whistle. You get a *whistle*, Dee.'

I leant sideways, resting my face in the palm of my hand. Perhaps this wasn't such a good idea, I thought to myself. I hadn't really paid much attention during the important bits so even if I did want to go, I reasoned, I wasn't entirely clear on how to do it. Then Mike stood up. Jocular Mike. Mike with the big mop of hair and the bouncy knees. 'Work America,' he yelled, 'is BRILLIANT!' My eyes popped open. 'You can do what you want and go where you want! You can do ANYTHING! You can work for a bank! You can work in a theme park! You can work for a jet-set executive! You can work in New York! You can work in Chicago! You can work in California! You can work ANYWHERE! And the great thing is, it's SO easy to get work. If you don't sort something out before you go, don't worry! Because you can get bar work or restaurant work like THAT. They LOVE an English accent. Go CRAZY for it! And here's the best bit – because you've got an English accent, you'll make a FORTUNE in tips!' Dee and I looked at each other, our eyebrows slightly rising. We'd both worked as waitresses. This was sounding like a tasty prospect.

We signed our names on a slip of paper and took a bundle of forms to fill in. Having arrived in a sluggish state, we were now buzzing. 'This is going to be great!' enthused Dee as we scampered back to college. 'We can get a job the day we get there, work for two months, fill our pockets with gold and then spend the last month travelling across America! It'll be incredible. Like an amazing road trip!'

'And we'll be as rich as Croesus!' I yelled, jumping into the air a little. 'And I can buy as many whistles as I want! Land of the Free, here we come!'

The decision was made. We were off to America. The rest of my life could now happily be postponed. I was electrified with excitement. Not only were we going to have the time of our lives, but we were going to get rich too. Like a badly coiffured Dick Whittington with sudden access to air travel, I was going to the Big City to make my fortune. I would be set up for life, and would return, glorious, in a suit made of silver dollars where I would promptly buy London and re-invent the wheel. My optimism was unfettered and like the swifts that darted in and out of the Museum's Tower, the summer was mine for the taking. There was only one minor matter to be dealt with. I had to tell my parents.

My father's head slumped forward onto his knuckles. His shoulders were heaving and he was crying. My mother, shocked to her core, had shifted backwards, physically recoiling, and was sitting, frowning, with her mouth open. I sat perched on a small wooden stool in front of them, in my hand a half drunk pint of lager. We were in the Turf Tavern in Oxford, a low-beamed inn filled with requisite nooks and crannies. I had finished my Finals and now all that remained was to pack up my things and say farewell to being a student. My parents, who had driven to pick me up in a state of unbridled joy, had been expecting to fill the car with everything I owned and return to the familial home in triumph where, my father hoped, I might 'build a house at the bottom of the garden' and live with them for ever. My father had been waiting for this day for three years. But I had different ideas and I'd broken it to them gently. I was not going home.

'What do you mean you're going to America?' asked my mother, with a small puzzled shake of her head.

'She's not going to come back, Brenda,' sobbed my father, shoulders juddering. 'It'll be like my sister Marion. She met that GI, he took her dancing and then he sent her a parcel with chewing gum in it. Next thing we know, we never saw her again.'

My mother shot my father a small irritated glance. 'Everyone can get chewing gum nowadays. It's no longer a valid reason for emigrating.'

'I'm not emigrating,' I explained. 'I'm just going for four months. And I've got a loan from the bank.'

'You've got a loan?' quizzed my mother. 'How much for?'

'Three hundred and fifty dollars,' I said, taking a sip of my beer. 'Dee suggested it, so we've got a stop-gap fund. For emergencies. It'll tide us over until we get a job.'

In fact, both Dee and I had secured a small loan of $350 each from our relevant banks. We had assured them that, even though we were saddled with enormous post university over-drafts, America would be a magnanimous benefactor. We were coming home rich, we had told them. It was the safest loan they would ever make. My $350 loan had been granted by a man from Nat West with a crop of strawberry-blond hair and a dimpled chin. 'What are you going to do when you get back from America?' he had asked me.

I had been momentarily stumped but after a significant silence I had picked up a pen, twirled it in my fingers and said, 'Something thrilling.'

'Something thrilling that involves being paid wages?' he asked, undeterred.

'Yes.'

And that was that. I got my loan.

'Have you got a job?' continued my mother.

'No. But they said we didn't need to have anything sorted out before we go because we'll be able to get work in a restaurant or bar like THAT. And apparently the tips will be massive. Because we're English. They love the accent. We're going to make a lot of money, Mum.'

My mother leaned forward and heaved a sigh. 'Well,' she said, eyebrows raising, 'Dee *does* have a lovely speaking voice...'

'Yes,' I nodded, vigorously, 'she *really* does.'

'But where are you going to stay?' asked my father, wiping at this eyes.

'Our flight takes us to New York,' I rattled on, 'and we'll be there one night.'

'Oh God,' said my mother, hand clamping to her forehead.

'And then we'll fly on to San Francisco because last year we had an exchange student from Stanford so we can probably stay with her. And then we'll get jobs, work for two months and then travel back to New York.'

'But where will you stay when you're travelling back?' asked Dad.

'Not sure. Maybe we'll camp.'

My parents glanced at each other. Camping was a slightly dirty word in our family. My early childhood had been blighted by it. Yet here I was, ready to pick up the baton of damp canvas and run with it once more. My mother blinked, grabbed my forearm and said, 'You're thinking of camping? Are you *insane*?'

Having helped my parents pack everything into the car I was left with nothing more than the clothes I stood up in and Gwendolyn, my trusty bike, who, after much deliberation, I had decided was going to remain in Oxford for ever. I was going to leave her, as dawn rose, on the corner of Queen's Lane, unlocked, in the hope that someone would find her and make the most of her. It broke my heart but it felt like the right and noble thing to do.

The evening's itinerary ran thus. Dee and I were going to have a last, delicious take-away burger from Peppers, an organic establishment dishing out the finest beef patties in Oxford, drink the bottle of champagne that I had been given for finishing Finals and then bike to Summertown where there was an end-of-term party where we would drink too much, smoke too much, talk rubbish and then get the first bus out of Oxford in the morning and meet our parents at Heathrow for the big send off. At least that was the plan. But nine hours later, when I should have been tucked up in bed,

I was in custody, sitting in a police interview room being questioned by a female constable who looked like a bulldog. Gwendolyn had been seized for having no lights and I was staring down the barrel of a theft charge.

'So what,' asked the constable again, tapping at a pad with a chewed biro, 'were you intending to do with the used car sign?'

'Don't know,' I answered. 'I haven't even got a car.'

'So did you take it because you wished you did?'

I was in a dull grey room illuminated by a strip light that was flickering every now and again and making low fizzing noises. The constable, I noticed, had a light fuzz of hair on her upper lip that in normal lighting wouldn't have been noticeable but in this scorching and unattractive gloom, every hair sat upright asking to be stared at. I had been questioned for well over an hour: why had I been in Summertown, what had I been doing, why had I gone to the garage forecourt, why had we taken the sign and how had we taken it? It had been relentless. I had no idea where Dee was, we had been separated the moment we had entered the police station and as she was led off one way I was led off in another. I had managed a quick, over-my-shoulder glance in her direction and she had thrown a small, baffled shrug back. A fleeting moment of tomfoolery had drawn our end-of-university celebration to an abrupt end but more importantly, I thought, as I glanced anxiously up at the clock, this turn of events was jeopardising our plans. We had a plane to catch.

'Can you just give me my punishment now?' I asked, 'because I'm going to America in five hours. And I've got to meet my mum.'

The constable looked at me with withering scorn. 'No. We can't give you your punishment now. This isn't the Wild

West. We'll decide if you're to be charged. If you're lucky you'll get a caution. I'm not entirely convinced you're taking this seriously.'

'I am taking it seriously,' I replied, trying to sneak a look at my watch. 'I'm ever-so sorry.'

'I'm going to read your statement back to you. And then if you agree with it, you're going to sign it. All right?' I nodded. 'Right then.' She cleared her throat. '"We were trav-elling down the Banbury Road having been at a party in a friend's house. We had quite a bit to drink at the party because it was our last day at university. Normally I don't drink much and this may have been a contributory factor to what happened next. I may have had as much as a whole bottle of wine. I was drunk but not so drunk that I couldn't ride a bike. Because I was in high spirits I thought it would be funny to take one of the plastic used car signs from the top of one of the cars on the forecourt of the garage in Summertown. I have no idea why I thought this was funny. It seemed quite funny at the time. Obviously it is massively less funny now. In fact, it isn't funny at all. I have no idea what I was going to do with the sign. It may have sat in my room for a bit. Although I haven't got a room now so I might have just left it hanging round college somewhere. I might have left it in a toilet. I am pretty certain that after some sleep I would have reflected on my actions and returned the sign to the man who owns the garage in Summertown. I am very sorry if he is upset by the removal of one of his plastic used car signs."'

'Don't forget we offered to take it back when you arrested us. Don't forget that bit.'

'We haven't got to that bit yet,' she said, shooting me an irritated glance. '"We then decided to head back to college.

When we saw the police car coming towards us we thought they were going to stop us because we didn't have lights on our bicycles which I am aware is an offence. I have got a light but its batteries are dead. I forgot to replace them. So when I saw the police car I thought I had better get off my bicycle but ended up crashing into my friend's bicycle and we ended up lying on the road. This may have been to do with how much alcohol we had consumed. I do not know why I crawled into the bush. When we came out of the bush we were happy to cooperate with the police officers. My friend offered to return the stolen sign. But we were arrested instead."' The constable stopped and spun the statement across the table towards me. 'So if you're happy with that,' she added, 'then you can sign that.'

'And then will I be allowed to go?' I asked.

'Yes, you'll be allowed to go.'

Five minutes later I was being walked to the back of the police station where, I noticed, Dee was sitting waiting. 'Did you get questioned for ages?' I whispered as we were processed towards the door.

'No,' replied Dee, serenely. 'I just told them it was all your idea and then they gave me coffee and biscuits.'

A quick look at my watch told us we had half an hour to get to the bus station. The sun was coming up, bathing the city in a soft, pink light, and as we ran through the empty streets it was if we had the place to ourselves for a few fleeting moments. Oxford had been everything I had wanted it to be. Now it was America's turn. And all we had to do was turn up, right?

Right?

Chapter Two

So Good They Named it Twice

$700

Heathrow! The gateway to dreams! The portal to all things exciting but, above all, very, very bright. Terrible hangovers and artificial lighting have never been the happiest bedfellows and as we wandered, crumpled like a pair of burst balloons, the prospect of having to entertain two sets of parents was as bleak as death itself. Exhausted, overwrought and with eyes gluey with tiredness we had tried to lie on the floor of a dimly lit McDonalds only to find ourselves being swept up with a broom by an indignant cleaner. 'You cannot sleep here!' he snapped at us as we stared up at him from the carpet. 'This is a restaurant! Not a motel!'

'I think "restaurant" is a bit of an exaggeration,' mumbled Dee, pushing herself up onto her knees.

I lay, mouth slightly agape, tongue lolling, arms stuck underneath me like a useless rag doll.

'Get up!' barked the cleaner, shoving at my legs with his broom. 'Cannot sleep here.'

'I think,' I groaned, one eye un-sticking itself open, 'I might have brain damage.' I lifted my head and, looking upwards towards the unforgiving blaze of the main concourse, saw a figure loom before me.

'Oh, Emma,' I heard it say. It was my mother. We were discovered. A hand came down and took me by the upper arm. 'Look at the state of you.' Having been helped up I stood, dirty with shame, swallowed and stared at my feet. 'Is that vomit on your shirt?' asked my mother, pointing.

I looked down at my chest. There was an unpleasant and unaccountable stain. 'I don't think it's mine,' I murmured before adding, 'I'm very ill.'

My mother, who was slowly coming into focus, tightened her lips and turned to another blurry figure that, I had to assume, was my father. 'Get her rucksack,' she said, gesturing with her hand. 'She can't sit on a plane for five hours looking and smelling like that. Someone will try and hijack it just to get off. Pass me a clean shirt.'

'Oh, hello Emma,' said another voice, to my left. 'I thought you were a tramp.'

It was Dee's mother. I stared into the middle distance. This was already the worst airport send off imaginable.

Having been frog-marched to the nearest toilet to get changed I had to accept that I was not looking my best. I flinched as I caught sight of myself in the bathroom mirror. My skin was a wretched yellow, my hair lank and lifeless. I leaned forwards and pushed my tongue out – it was like looking at a rancid prosciutto.

'Shall I chuck this shirt?' asked Dee, holding my stained top between two fingers. I nodded. Somehow, Dee had managed to preserve an air of fragrance. Probably because she'd been given coffee and biscuits at the police station but mostly because she was, and always would be, a lady.

I was going away for four months and all I was taking was a rucksack that I had packed in a panic the previous day. As I watched it slide gently away on the check-in conveyor belt, my sleep-deprived mind rumbled over what I may or may not have forgotten: pair of shorts, yes, they were in; T-shirts, obviously; some cotton trousers, folded not scrunched; swimming costume? No. But then I don't think I even had a swimming costume. Smart clothes for interviews? Don't be ridiculous. Towel? Yes. Though it wasn't washed because there hadn't been time. And it was a bit damp. I'd have to remember to get that out when we got to America; if I didn't everything would smell like a wet dog. Money, passport, social security card and, most importantly, our ticket home again on 1 October – all safely tucked into a bumbag that my father clipped round me while telling me to 'never let that out of your sight'. Of that he had no need to worry. Like tortoises, we would be carrying everything we possessed.

We still had an hour and a half to kill before boarding and given the early hour and the fact that our parents were desperate to hang on to us for as long as possible, we all headed over to a buffet-style breakfast bar where they were serving every permutation of a full English possible and, mysteriously, chicken tikka masala. 'Who eats curry for break- fast?' asked my mother, pointing at the livid red mass bubbling quietly in front of her. 'Or is it like when we found out it was all right to eat cheese and salami for breakfast on bread that wasn't even toasted? Is it like that?'

'It's probably for people who've been up all night,' offered my father. 'You know, truckers. So it's their supper- time. It's not even breakfast.'

As they spoke a bald-headed man with a fat neck sniffed and pointed towards the curry. 'Chicken tikka please,' he said, shuffling his tray along the metal rail.

My mother, nudging my father, turned to the man and said, 'Have you been up all night? Trucking?' She beamed at him and gestured towards the curry.

He looked at her blankly and blinked. 'No,' he replied, puzzled. 'I'm going to Belgium.'

Everybody stared. 'Well,' said my mother, breaking the silence, '*someone* has to. Now then, Emma. Breakfast. Come on. What do you want? Sausage? Bacon? Beans? Egg? Tomatoes? They've got tomatoes. Toast? Hash browns? Mushrooms?'

'I don't know if I'm that hungry, Mum,' I replied, staring bleakly into the food counter.

'She'll have everything,' she told the pimpled youth poised with a large serving spoon. 'Except the fried bread. And extra tomatoes please. For vitamins.'

I thought about protesting but there was little if no point and so I stood, arms hanging by my sides, shoulders slightly rounded, giving off the faint whiff of despair.

Dee, startlingly bright-eyed, was contemplating the food with a finger poised on her lower lip. 'Can I help you?' asked a woman in a green tabard and paper hat.

'No, thank you,' Dee replied, with impeccable manners. 'I'm just browsing.'

I had been pushing a small lump of sausage around my plate for the past fifteen minutes; my head slumped into the palm of my hand. Here I was, on the brink of an adventure of a lifetime, and all I wanted to do was lie on the floor, sleep and hope the dull fog swirling between my ears would evaporate. My mother had taken it upon herself to warn me of every possible pitfall she could imagine, presumably in the hope that by mentioning drive-by shootings, becoming accidentally addicted to crack cocaine and befriending serial killers they became statistically less likely to happen. Though my eyes were open, I was drifting in and out of consciousness, my mother's words muffling away in the background. Mum shook my forearm and said, 'Did you hear that? Your father and I are going to go round Europe. While you're away. Like sixth formers do. Except we'll have better shoes.'

I looked up. 'What do you mean?' I asked, frowning.

'We've decided,' she added, shooting a nod towards my father, 'that as you're off we might as well be too. So we're going to travel round Europe. Like a gap year for grown ups.'

'You're going for a YEAR?' I said, sitting up.

'No,' said my mother, with a tut, 'just for the summer. I'll send you letters.'

I didn't quite know how I felt about this. My parents' previous attempts at travelling were a minefield strewn with crushed and broken souls. They were hopeless at it. And here they were, happily declaring they were off on a gadabout.

'What with your bad luck and my lack of any discernible practical skills there's a genuine risk that our holidaying simultaneously across two continents might bring about the end of civilisation,' I said.

'We'll be fine,' said Dad. And then we all stared at each other because we all knew he was lying.

The farewells were awful. Clasping turned to clinging and gentle weeping transformed into open wailing. Dee's parents told me to look after Dee and my mother, who had a more accurate assessment of the situation, just told Dee to look after herself. I was to be trusted with nothing. All I could bring to the table was a vague sense of misplaced optimism.

In 1989 I had been to four countries: France, Italy, Greece and Russia. France and Italy had been on family holidays where we were beset with disaster year in, year out. Greece was a three-week scrape around some islands with pals from

Oxford, during which I had been cornered by the village elders and shown round a fishing boat rendering me technically engaged to a young man in spectacles whom I'd never met. Russia was a school trip to Moscow and Leningrad where I had run away from the official guide with my friend Sam Vaughan and ended up having to give my coat *and* trainers to some heavy-set gentlemen in an alley. In short, I was no travel expert. Having said that, I knew where I was with Europe but America was a different prospect and going there was a big deal. In 1989, the world was still a place with a proper sense of distance. Email and mobile phones were something common folk could only dream about. I hadn't even heard of the Internet. Not only that but neither Dee nor I possessed a credit card. The traveller's cheques in our bumbags were all we had. We may as well have been in crinolines and bonnets.

The sensible thing, of course, would have been to sleep on the plane but I'd only flown twice in my life and was experiencing levels of excitement reserved for children under the age of ten who discover not only that Santa is real but that he's also letting you drive the sleigh. 'Can you believe this?' I asked, bug-eyed, waving the courtesy pack of eye mask, miniature toothpaste and comb in Dee's face. 'And we can watch films. Actual films.'

Dee gazed at me with a resigned indulgence, pulled her eye mask down over her forehead and said, 'Wake me up when we're in Manhattan.'

It was a glowing inferno of a day as we approached New York. Nose pressed against the window, I stared down at the sprawl of speedboats leaving white trails through the Hudson. Sparkling blue rectangles were peppered everywhere. I frowned, not being able to work out what they were but then realised, after some brain bending, that they were swimming pools. Only footballers and chat-show hosts had swimming pools in Britain. It all seemed incredibly glamorous: sun blazed off the top of skyscrapers; the Statue of Liberty, arm aloft, waved us in to land. It felt as if a golden curtain to a secret garden was being lifted back and we'd been invited to step inside. I was genuinely thrilled to be in America. In 1989, it still held a cache of wonder and seemed untroubled and on top. The Cold War was creaking to an end and capitalism's tendrils were spreading like ivy. We were at the birth of a new world order and America was the Captain.

'Apparently,' said Dee, who had just woken up and was thumbing through an in-flight magazine, 'they have frozen yoghurt in America.'

I blinked. 'Why would you freeze yoghurt?' I asked. 'That's like freezing *cheese*.'

Dee shrugged as we descended into JFK. 'We're not in Kansas anymore, Toto.'

The journey from the airport took at least an hour. We'd jumped into a cab and crept towards Manhattan in heavy traffic. The lack of urgency was of no concern. I was mesmerised by every traffic light, every road sign, the way the cars seemed to bounce, the combs sticking out of magnificent afros, the baseball shirts, the size of things, the relentless advertising hoardings that towered along the roadside, everything and anything that was almost the same but fundamentally different from back home. Even the roads *sounded* different, and as we crossed the Brooklyn Bridge, I wound down the window and listened to the steady thump-thud of the wheels as they rolled over ridges. As we passed the bridge's peak and I caught my first glimpse of the glorious upwards hallelujah of Manhattan itself, I felt quite emotional. I thought about the poster that I had stuck on my college wall all those years ago. I had stared at the island's silhouetted outline every day and here I was, seeing it for real. I turned to Dee and we smiled at each other.

We were staying, for one night only, at the Sloane House YMCA at 356 West 34th Street and 9th. Red bricked with a fancy white trim, it looked for all the world like a rather overambitious cake that might fizz to life with fairy lights at any given moment but its impressive exterior belied its fallen glories. Once a home for transient young fellows and men from the armed services, its 1,493 rooms had once included such luxuries as a barbershop and a tailor's room. It had held lectures, arranged sightseeing trips and even entertained Bible study breakfasts but now it was a shadow of its former self. Like all places on their last legs, the air of caring was long gone and as we walked into the entrance hall a smell of light depression wafted towards us. Given the blazing day, the dark gloom of the reception area was all the more oppressive, the overhead strip lighting doing nothing to alleviate the dreary aspect. A battered-looking desk was inset to our left and, having heaved our rucksacks to the floor, we wandered over.

'Can you see a bell?' said Dee, hooking her top teeth over her bottom lip. I didn't reply. My attention was elsewhere. An incredibly tall black man in a cream flared trouser suit and matching Stetson had just drifted into my eyeline. He looked glorious. I couldn't take my eyes off him. 'Ahh,' Dee added, pointing towards a buzzer and a small sign next to it. 'Ring for service. No guns,' she read, then paused before adding, 'That last bit's in brackets.' She pressed her finger downwards. A thick, raspy rattle jangled out.

Beyond the desk, a dark wooden door opened and a short man in his forties, unshaven with darkly ringed deep-set eyes appeared. His skin had a greasy, unhealthy hue as if the gloom of his surroundings had taken a physical toll. He was wearing a black vest top, slightly grubby, and was holding an enormous sandwich that dripped mayonnaise and had salami sticking from its end. He was chewing and as he looked up at us, he wiped the side of his mouth with a napkin. 'Yeah?' he asked. 'You new?'

'Yes,' replied Dee, with a smile. 'We *are* new. We'd like two rooms for one night, please. And we've got no guns,' she added, pointing towards the sign.

The fellow blinked and swallowed. He put his sandwich down onto a pile of unopened envelopes, wiped a hand on the bottom of his vest top and opening a cupboard, pulled out two keys. 'Twenty-Two-Fourteen and Twenty-Two-Fifteen,' he said, slapping the keys on the counter in front of us. 'Sign the book over there. Payment in advance. Twenty bucks each. Elevator's down the hall. Twenty-second floor, turn right.' He picked up his sandwich and took another bite as we fumbled in our bumbags for the money. His sandwich had left a grease mark on the corner of one of the envelopes.

'We haven't got any cash yet,' explained Dee, pulling out a traveller's cheque and her passport. 'Do you take these?'

The man groaned a little. 'I'd prefer cash but if you ain't got none then it'll have to do. Make sure you fill in your passport numbers right. I don't want to be ripped off. You know you can use them to get cash right?'

'Really?' I asked. 'I didn't know that.'

He nodded. 'I don't do it. But some people will take them for cash. Just sayin'.'

Picking up our keys and throwing our rucksacks over our shoulders, we made our way to the lift, an ancient contraption with a lattice door that required heaving open from left to right. A discarded soda can lay crumpled in one corner and the bare light bulb on the ceiling had blown so that our journey up to the twenty-second floor was a succession of blackouts interspersed with sudden dingy flashes. The man I'd seen earlier in the cream suit and Stetson had followed us and as the lift creaked upwards he turned to us and said, 'You want some stuff? Drugs stuff? Pot, pills, heroin?'

'No, thank you,' I replied, with a small smile. 'I *love* your hat.'

'Umm,' interrupted Dee. 'Do you take traveller's cheques?'

I turned and shot her a small stare. Dee was the poshest person I knew. She was a vision of quiet refinement, the sort of woman who always orders fish in a restaurant. She was dainty, precise, her skin was flawless. Her nails were forever trimmed to perfection; she was beneficent, gave off an aura of permanent capability and was the person most likely to be canonised within my lifetime. 'What are you doing?' I mumbled, trying to flick my eyes back in the direction of the drug dealer we were trapped in a lift with. She held out her hand to stop me; she knew what she was doing.

'I don't want any drugs, thank you,' she continued. 'But we haven't any cash. We've only got traveller's cheques and I was wondering if we could give you a traveller's cheque for some cash?'

The man's face contorted in a vision of befuddlement. 'Traveller's cheques?' he guffawed. 'Now I heard it all. Wow.

First time in New York?' Dee nodded. 'Man. Good luck, girls. You gonna need it. How much you want?'

Dee pursed her lips. 'Would fifty dollars be okay?'

'Sure thing,' he replied, reaching into his waistcoat pocket. He pulled out a tight roll of dollars, unclipped them and flicked out one fifty-dollar bill. Dee wrote out the traveller's cheque on the wall of the lift and they made the exchange. I stood, doing nothing. This was the sort of scenario my mother would have intense concerns about. We'd been in New York for less than an hour and here we were doing business with a drug dealer in a grimy elevator.

Much to my relief, he got out at the next floor.

My room, if you could call it that, was tiny. Rectangular and narrow, it was undecorated apart from a dirty square on one wall where clearly a long-gone picture had once hung. All that remained was the unused hook and a pattern of mouldy swirls that was a work of art in itself. The bed, shoved hard up against the wall, was as single as they came and as I threw my rucksack onto it, it let out a thin rattle in protest. I sat down to test the mattress. I could feel the thick wire mesh of the bed frame beneath it. There was a starched top sheet pulled tight that was rough to the touch and gave off a slightly pungent chemical odour. I shoved my rucksack to the top of the bed and, resting my head against it, lifted my legs and stretched out. I looked about me. There were only two other things in the room: a white metal chair, bolted to the floor, and a bedside cabinet that doubled up as a safe. The metal around the lock was scoured with deep gouge marks. The cabinet, I noticed, was also bolted to the floor and, on a whim; I rolled over and dropped my head over the edge of the bed. I let out a small, incredulous laugh. The bed was bolted down too.

There was a short, gentle rap on my door. Dee's face appeared.

'I don't think my sheets are clean,' she said, with a grimace. 'They're crumpled. And they smell suspicious.'

'Do you want me to swap rooms with you?' I asked.

'Don't be silly,' she replied. 'You can't sleep in dirty sheets.'

'Why not? I do it all the time at home.'

'No. It's fine. I'll mention it to the man when we go out and ask him to change them. Have you seen the view? It's amazing.' She inched her way past the chair and cabinet towards the window.

'Let's have a look.' I hopped off the bed and squeezed next to Dee as she pushed the window upwards. Shoulder to shoulder, we stuck our heads out and looked out over the tangle of rooftops and cables and water coolers. I pulled a packet of cigarettes from my back pocket. 'Want one?' I offered. Dee nodded. Noise was rushing up at us from the avenue below, yellow taxis poking up like dandelions while the occasional blue light weaved through the snarl of traffic, sirens blaring. Looking down it was like casually wandering onto the lip of a volcano just as it was about to blow.

'That road goes on for ever,' I said, puffing smoke from the corner of my mouth as I took in the enormity of the avenue. 'Is that the Empire State Building?' I added, pointing out a familiar silhouette in the distance.

'Looks like it,' said Dee. 'Come on. Let's go out. We're only here tonight. And I don't know how much longer I can stay awake. What shall we do?'

'I suppose we ought to go and see the Statue of Liberty. I think you can get a boat out to it or something? Or have I imagined that? What does your book say?'

The book on which we would be relying for the next four months was not the usual fare. Dee, determined to plough her own furrow, had refused, point blank, to get the tried and tested *Rough Guide to the USA*. Instead, she was pinning all her hopes on a pale blue book with a road on its cover that snaked off into the horizon. It was called *Crossing America*, which was precisely what we were intending to do. She fetched it from her room and handed it to me to scan. On the inside cover there was a brilliant advert for the Pony Express, which exclaimed,

WANTED
YOUNG, SKINNY, WIRY FELLOWS
Not over eighteen. Must be expert riders,
willing to risk death daily.
Orphans preferred.
Wages $25 a week
Apply Pony Express Stables
St Joseph Missouri

Its introduction boldly claimed that travelling across America was 'as much about the journey as about a series of destinations'. It was a clarion call to adventure.

'Hmm,' I said, flicking through the New York pages, 'it doesn't actually tell us what to do or how to do anything in the city. It just tells you how and where to leave it.'

'It can't be that difficult,' Dee replied, stubbing out her cigarette on the window ledge. 'Everybody on Manhattan knows where the Statue of Liberty is.'

'I'm positive there's a ferry you can get to it. You know, like the one in *Working Girl*.'

'Are you doing that thing again where you believe things just because they've been in a film?'

'No. This isn't like the *Harry and the Hendersons* debacle. It's true. There is definitely a ferry to the Statue of Liberty. Let's get a bus.'

'No,' said the driver, shaking his head. 'You cannot pay for a bus ticket with a fifty-dollar bill *or* a traveller's cheque. How many times do I have to explain? The fare is fifty cents. Look at the sign.' He gestured towards a small sign bolted just below him that read: LOOSE CHANGE ONLY.

'But we haven't got any loose change,' explained Dee. 'We've only just arrived.'

'No shit,' said a man sitting immediately to our left.

I looked down the bus. A sea of scowling faces looked back. 'We only want to go to the Statue of Liberty,' I said, turning back to the driver. 'And we have to leave New York tomorrow. It's our one chance.'

The driver, a neatly presented fellow with a thick nose and a moustache, sighed and let his head fall to one side. 'Take these,' he said, unexpectedly handing us two tickets. 'I'll tell you when to get off.'

My eyes widened. 'Really?' I said, my mouth falling open.

'Thanks so so much,' added Dee. 'Really thanks so much.'

'Yeah, yeah,' mumbled the driver, waving us towards the seats. 'And stand clear of the doors. No change. Jesus. Who comes to New York with no change?'

Nobody on the bus looked particularly pleased with this turn of events and as I offered a small, conciliatory smile to the man who had spoken up moments earlier I received nothing but a furiously chewing jaw in return. We sat down. The seats were plastic and faced inwards rather than towards the front of the bus. I twisted myself around so I could look out the window. New York seemed a glori-ous, maddening bustle, a heave of bodies speeding down every street. Nobody was ambling but pacing as if their life depended on it as if dawdling, like jaywalking, was strictly forbidden. Women with massive hair strode in smart suits with trainers and white socks over their tights, something I'd never seen before. High heels got you nowhere and this town moved fast.

'Look Dee,' I said, tugging at her sleeve and pointing at a road sign as we passed it, 'Broadway.' I grinned. It felt magic: the names in lights, the air of pizzazz. Suddenly, it felt like we were *really* in America. I was so happy to be there, so pleased to have sidestepped the immediate grief of leaving university and the uncertainty of my future. Maybe, I thought, as I stared out at all the go-getters and achievers, I might, one day, get to be like them too? Maybe *I'd* be a high-flying career woman, pacing down streets in a sharp suit and trainers? Maybe *I* would have high-stacked important-looking hair, commanding the respect of my peers and driving fear into the hearts of my enemies? Perhaps this was my destiny – to let America show me the way and possibly, if all went well, I could end up with a career that involved owning a Filofax? I blinked. 'Oh brave new world, that has such people in it,' I mumbled. The possibil-ities were *endless.*

The entrance to the Staten Island Ferry was like a vast, concrete anthill. People poured in and out of it in a swarm. Dusk was settling and a low-lying sun cast a golden glow over the Hudson, the tips of the glassy crop of skyscrapers sparkling in the last soft rays of the day. As we stared up at a departure board, bodies bustling past us, there seemed a lot to choose from. This was a surprise. I had assumed that there would only be one boat.

'Ferry number three,' I said, with an air of confidence. 'That's the one we need.'

'Are you sure, Emma?' Dee replied, looking around. 'I can't see anything about the Statue of Liberty.'

'This was definitely the ferry Melanie Griffith got on in *Working Girl*.'

'And was she going to the Statue of Liberty?'

'No. She was going to work for Sigourney Weaver.'

'Right.'

We stared at each other for a brief moment. I think it's fair to say that we both knew full well that we were in entirely the wrong place.

'Oh well,' said I, with a shrug. 'We're here now.'

'We've got another problem,' said Dee, pointing at the passenger gates. 'We need twenty-five cents each.'

'We've got no change.'

'Yes. I know we've got no change.'

There was a short silence. This had been my idea and, being the first thing we'd done since arriving, it brought with it a sense of a grave responsibility, not least, because it was going to be the only thing we did in New York before we left. 'I'm going to ask people who look nice if they'll give us some change,' I said.

Dee looked at her watch. 'We've been in America for three hours and we're already begging.'

With a positive nod I strode into the crowd and started asking strangers for money.

'Look at that,' I said proudly fifteen minutes later as I returned with a dollar in change, 'that's our first American wages. It's true. They *do* love the English.'

The boat we found ourselves on was a vivid orange hulk of practicality called the *Andrew J. Barberi*. We had no idea who Andrew J. Barberi was but on asking one of the ferry workers, we found out he was a high school football coach. I wondered if a cross-channel ferry would ever be named after my PE teacher, Miss Nettell. It was doubtful. There were three levels with two outside observation decks towards the rear and it was to one of these that we made our way and stood, elbows resting on the handrail, as the boat pulled away from Manhattan. The view was glorious: the skyscrapers, the World Trade Center and the first lady of freedom, her verdigris hues glinting in the dying sun, all of it was a wonderful sight, iconic and resplendent.

'Hasn't she got huge forearms,' I said, pointing to the statue. 'To be honest, she looks like a man in drag.'

'Did you know that the insides were made by the same man who made the Eiffel Tower?' said Dee.

'Mr Eiffel?'

'Yes. Him. And that it was a gift from the French to celebrate the Declaration of Independence.'

'The French hate us.'

'Yes. They do. But we make terrible cheese so you can't blame them.'

'Cheddar is good.'

'Yes. Cheddar *is* good.'

'And Double Gloucester. And Sage Derby. And Yarg. Don't forget Yarg.'

'Are you just going to say every English cheese you can think of?'

'No,' I protested. 'Cheshire. That's it. I can't think of any more.'

'Precisely. And *that* is why the French despise us,' said Dee as the Statue of Liberty got smaller and smaller.

We had, of course, got on the wrong boat. The boat we were on was a working commuter shuttle between Staten Island and Manhattan, so I had been right in one respect: it *was* the boat Melanie Griffiths used to get to work which, I suppose, was a small moral victory. As it pulled in to dock, we looked askance at the now distant Ellis and Liberty islands and instead turned our attentions to where we had ended up. While there was no doubt that the working commercial ports of New York were certainly worth a visit, I hadn't imagined that my first-ever sightseeing trip in America would involve staring at thousands of roll-on roll-off containers. We tried to show willing by taking a few pictures of some cranes. I stood with my hands on my hips and nodded appreciatively at a tall stack of wooden crates. Dee marvelled at a big rope. 'That's a big rope,' she said, pointing. It got dark quite rapidly and both of us, jet-lagged and still hung-over, made the return trip in relative silence. Despite our fatigue, there was an air of contentment. We had arrived, that was the important thing. Tomorrow we would fly to San Francisco, set up home, and begin the search for employment. Everything felt possible.

As we arrived back in Manhattan and began to walk back to the hostel, a glowering murk began to gather in the skies. The air had assumed a treacle-thick quality and a dark canopy of clouds was creeping over the peaks of the skyscrapers above us. Heavy drops of rain started to fall and we ran, backs of T-shirts pulled over our heads, as we tried to make it back to the Y before the storm kicked in. By the time we got up to our rooms, a dense curtain of rain was crashing downwards. We crouched round my still-open window, drying our hair with towels and watched as lightning bolts blazed across the skies. Down below, the city had come to a standstill, the storm drowning out the hopeless blares of the horns. Dee stuck her head out of the window and upturned her face into the rain. I lit a cigarette and sat, shattered, on my flimsy mattress. Across the street, on a gantry, a man appeared, arms outstretched. He was totally naked. Fire and water. We had been baptised. Welcome to America.

Chapter Three

If You're Going to San Francisco $611.50

The plan was breathtakingly simple: fly to San Francisco, get picked up by an obscure distant relative called Jerry, track down Joplin, a friend from college, move to a flat somewhere, find a job, become rich beyond our wildest dreams. The end. I had been incredibly efficient and rung Jerry *before* we left England. It was the sort of go-getting initiative I hoped would stand me in good stead for the job-hunting to come. I had left a message saying, 'Hello! It's Emma! Your third cousin twice removed! We're getting the lunchtime flight. See you at the airport!'

That was it.

I had failed to tell him:

a) what airport we were flying from
b) which airline we were flying with
c) the departure and arrival times of our flight

For all Jerry knew we were coming from Hong Kong in a hot air balloon.

As we sat on the plane, Dee thumbed through a copy of *Cosmopolitan* she'd brought with her from England. I let my head fall backwards onto my headrest and loll to one side so I could gaze out the window. Men in oversized gloves were throwing luggage from open racks into the hold. They were in short-sleeved shirts, wore sunglasses and chewed gum like professionals. A box of doughnuts sat perched on the seat of a small forklift truck and one of the men, climbing into the cab, moved the box to a space in front of the steering wheel, took a doughnut and bit into it. With the doughnut pinched between his lips, he reversed the truck towards the open hold. Just out of his line of vision a rack, emptied of luggage, had drifted sideways. There was a small crunch. Suddenly all the men stopped what they were doing and looked up.

I sat forward, pressing my nose up against the window but I couldn't quite see what had happened. The truck driver, taking the doughnut from his mouth, twisted his head round to see what he had hit. I couldn't hear what they were saying but another man appeared and was gesturing with a thumb over one shoulder towards an area underneath the airplane. The man with the doughnut scraped a hand down his face and pulled the truck forwards away from the fuselage. The others left the bags where they lay and together walked towards the point of impact. I could tell from their body language that something had gone very badly wrong.

'Dee,' I said, nonchalantly, 'do they let planes take off after they've been crashed into by a forklift truck?'

'Probably not, no,' she muttered, engrossed. 'Look at that,' she added, tapping the front cover, '"If you want to *dazzle* at work – develop your career charisma." We should read that. And memorise it.'

I looked back out the window. One of the men, in a Grateful Dead T-shirt, was waving towards someone in a fluorescent yellow jacket holding a clipboard. The others had given up loading the luggage and were leaning against the racks. The truck driver was handing round the box of doughnuts. This was not the hustling urgency of a ground crew anxious to get a plane up and away. The man in the yellow jacket ducked away from view and then reappeared from under the fuselage with a deep scowl on his face. I watched as he climbed the stairs into the aircraft, his face set like stone. I shifted and craned to see over the seat in front. He appeared at the top end of the aircraft and, after a quick chat to one of the air stewards, was shown towards the cockpit. I looked back out the window. A pack of cards had emerged. None of this looked good. There was a crackle of static above me.

'Ladies and gentlemen,' began the voice, 'this is the captain.' Dee lowered her magazine and looked off into the middle distance. 'I'm very sorry to have to tell you that during luggage loading one of the ground crew accidentally drove into the plane. It's nothing too serious but it has damaged the navigational equipment. Obviously we can't take off with the plane in its current state and we're going to have to wait for this to be fixed. I've been told that an engineer has already been called and as soon as I have any further information I'll let you know. I'm not allowed to let you disembark so I'm afraid it's going to be a question of sitting tight until the problem is dealt with. Please accept our apologies and rest assured we'll be on our way as soon as possible.'

A tide of groans rippled through the plane. Dee turned to me and raised an eyebrow. 'Was this anything to do with you?' she asked.

'No,' I said, pointing out the window, 'it was down to a doughnut.' I leant towards her so I could have a look at *Cosmopolitan*. 'Is that the agony page?' I asked. 'Give me one to solve. I'll be good at this.'

I was a great fan of Agony Aunts. My first experience of
them had been Cathy and Claire, the elder sister figures in
teen must-have magazine *Jackie*. Despite the vast majority of
readers being well under 16, their column was always dispro-
portionately preoccupied with sex and we would huddle
round it at school gasping and giggling. 'Can I get pregnant
by a pillow?' was one that stuck in my mind. A girl had woken
up with a pillow between her legs and was concerned that she
may now be expecting. 'But expecting what?' I had asked,
aged 13. 'Bean bags?' *Cosmopolitan* was, in many ways, the
grown-up version of the same thing. 'Come on,' I said,
giving Dee a nudge. 'Read one out.'

Dee cleared her throat, 'Riddle me out of this conundrum
– "I am a fairly attractive twenty-three-year-old woman who
has never had a decent boyfriend. Every man I have gone out
with has used me – for sex, money or convenience. Although
I knew I was being used, I always let the relationship continue,
as I didn't want to be alone. I am well educated and interesting and have close friends who don't understand why I am still
single. I am becoming very depressed about my situation and
long to experience the physical and emotional closeness of a
relationship. How can I face each day knowing I may never
find someone? What can I do?"...That's it.'

I sat back in deep thought. It's always very important, in
the role of Agony Aunt, to give sensible but honest advice.
Sometimes, I had learned from Cathy and Claire, you had to
say things that a person didn't necessarily want to hear. It's
the Agony Aunt's job to be lucid and open. The Agony Aunt
had to tell it like it is. I began. 'Are you *quite* sure you're
interesting?' I said. 'Because you sound a bit moany and dull.
Lighten up! Why not take up an unusual hobby? Like
taphophilia or noodling?'

'What are they?' Dee laughed.

'Taphophilia is the love of a cemetery. Noodling is fishing with your bare hands. Both of which would make her fascinating beyond belief. "Hello. I am a noodler." See? Hooked from the off.'

Dee consulted the official Agony Aunt's verdict. 'That's not what Irma Kurtz suggests. She says the lady shouldn't consider herself to be an object on a shelf waiting to be chosen by any old passer-by. And that she needs to stop spoiling people or trying to buy people and that desperation is never an attractive quality. That's what she says.'

I shrugged. 'I think mine is better.'

'Good grief,' said Dee, turning the page. 'Look at that. It's an advert for a sanitary towel that comes with a pair of 3-D glasses.' She detached the cardboard spectacles and stared through them at the red and green image on the advert.

'And it works: 3-D sanitary towels. They look very bouncy.'

'Can we do the questionnaire please? I love the *Cosmo* questionnaire. What's it on?'

Dee flicked to the relevant page. '"Don't let a poor self-image cramp your style – How do you see yourself?"'

'Can I make up my own answers? Rather than the ones in the magazine?'

Dee nodded and pulled a pen from her bumbag. 'Number one. In terms of physical attractiveness you are...'

'A shambles.'

'I'll tick "Rather unappealing". Number two. Your intelligence is...'

'Artificial.'

'I'll tick "You're bright enough". Number three. In your career you expect to become...'

I stopped. This was the million-dollar question. What *would* I become? A teacher? Someone working in middle-management in a fax-machine company? A mime artist? I heaved a sigh. 'No idea.'

Dee totted up the answers. 'Having a quick look at the results, you're unemployable. Congratulations. Talking of careers, we should have a look at that article that was on the front. The one about career charisma.'

I stared out the window as Dee flicked backwards. There was quite a commotion going on underneath the plane. Cones had appeared; yellow flashing lights were beating at intervals and the luggage handlers had all decamped to a large luggage rack where they were sitting playing cards. I turned back.

'Go on then,' I said with a small sniff. 'I probably need to pay attention to this bit.'

Dee scanned the article quickly. There was a picture of a woman in spectacles and a tight pencil skirt. She was holding a pen to her mouth with one hand and had the other on her hip. She was in high heels, wore pearls and clearly meant business, while still retaining her sexual identity. Obviously.

'Apparently, ' Dee began, 'to have a bright career we need to have a combination of personal magnetism, social skills, body language, attitudes, knowledge and "extra sparkle".'

'What does "extra sparkle" entail?' I asked.

'I'm not sure,' replied Dee, peering hard at the magazine. 'It's not clear on that point. But it does say that forty per cent of every assessment is made on first sight.'

'Oh dear,' I mumbled, thinking about what I'd packed in my rucksack.

'We need to look "executive" and not "secretarial". We also need a "steady look, a quiet voice, a firm handshake and a sense of purpose and resolve".'

I bunched my lips into a tight, concerned knot. 'While we're at it – what's the horoscope for Gemini?'

Dee flicked forwards. 'Gemini – "You'll find yourself flying off the handle a lot this month. It's left you insecure, in chaos and in debt. Borrow money if you have to."'

'Oh.'

We had been sitting in a slowly roasting tube for six hours. Everyone around us was red-faced and sweltering. Women were fanning themselves, men had taken off their ties, undone their top buttons and rolled up their sleeves. We had remained, languishing quietly, with nothing but *Cosmopolitan* to keep us amused. We had read about sex discrimination, man hopping, hitting out at hay fever, the life of Elizabeth Barrett Browning, how to tame the most volatile relationship you'll ever have (with your hair) and an interview with the dreamy Paul McGann. We had read it all. About three times. Below us we had listened to bangs, sawing and at one point, I'd seen a man going under the fuselage wearing a face shield and carrying an industrial-sized blowtorch. I wasn't entirely sure I wanted this plane to fly me to San Francisco. It would be just my luck if it crashed and I was killed. Not only would I be prevented from making my fortune, but I owed the bank $350. There'd be no paying it back if I was dead.

As far as sustenance was concerned, all we'd been given in six long hours was one small plastic cup of lemon squash that had been handed out, free of charge, three hours ago. The chief steward had made much of the free drink, as if they were really going out of their way to help us when technically they didn't have to do one damn thing until we were in the air. Dee, a proper lady who set high store on basic human decency, was as livid as I had ever seen her. 'I am surprised,' she said, caustically, as she was handed the weak, watery drink, 'that they didn't get a herald with a horn to go before the tray. Anyone would think they'd given us all a free trip to Barbados. Look at it. My urine's stronger than that.'

I looked about me. All human joy had abandoned ship.

'Let's play the Moral Maze,' I said, tapping Dee lightly on the forearm. The Moral Maze was a game Dee and I used to play when we were in long queues for gallery exhibits or sitting waiting in doctors' surgeries. The object of the game was to present a dilemma so catastrophic and dreadful that it would require proper and considered thought. It was a brilliant way to fend off boredom.

'They're not going to be as awful as they were last time are they?' said Dee, picking at a loose thread on her skirt. 'Because I don't think you're ever going to beat the one where I had to choose between cutting my leg off or killing my dog.'

'That was an extreme Moral Maze,' I nodded.

'Yes, it was.'

'Okay. So Moral Maze me this. You find a manuscript.'

'What of?'

'Of a book.'

'What sort of book?'

'It's a brilliant crime thriller. The protagonist is a troubled, divorced detective. He lives in the French Alps. He makes his own liqueurs from the mountain flowers and he keeps hens.'

'I like it.'

'So you read it and it's amazing. It's going to make millions. Do you leave it where it is or send it to a publisher and pretend you wrote it?'

'Hang on,' said Dee, thinking. 'Where did I find it? Because the author could be in the vicinity. And they've probably got another copy.'

'You have found it at the scene of a car crash in which the author and all his family have died. They're all dead. Everyone who could say you didn't write it is totally and utterly dead.'

'Hmm. That changes things.'

'Not only that, but there is a letter with the manuscript that says "One and only copy".'

'This is too easy. Of course I'm going to pretend I wrote it.'

'But wait!' I cried, hand rising to my mouth. 'Something amidst the carnage stirs! It's the author's baby! Who, lest we forget,' I added, gripping Dee's arm to increase the tension, 'is now an ORPHAN and who will live in penury in an ORPHANAGE all its life UNLESS you come clean and tell the publisher that the baby's father was the author. NOW WHAT DO YOU DO? Start the Moral Maze!'

'Hmm.' Dee stared upwards and bit on her bottom lip. 'Okay. Well, there is an issue here. If I take the manuscript to the publisher and come clean then it's not immediately apparent that the child will benefit. There may be a lot of paperwork involved. The publisher may be untrustworthy. No. I think what I would have to do, for my own piece of mind, would be to take the manuscript to the publisher, tell them I wrote it, become a multi-millionaire while at the same time *adopting* the author's baby.'

I raised an eyebrow. 'What if the publisher asks you to write a follow-up blockbuster?' I asked.

'I'll tell them I have a terminal repetitive strain injury. They'll trust me. I'm a doctor.'

I sighed and looked at my watch. 'God. It's past seven. I hope Jerry knows we're delayed.'

Dee picked *Cosmo* out of the pocket in front of her. 'I've read this five times now. And I'm still none the wiser about getting lovelier legs.'

'Ladies and gentlemen,' came a crackle above us. 'I am pleased to be able to tell you that we have now been given permission to leave. Cabin crew, prepare for take off.'

A massive cheer rang through the cabin. The plane was fixed. We were heading west.

We arrived in San Francisco at one in the morning. I could see palm trees from the window and, despite the late hour, I was thrilled. California was blue bleached skies, long-legged girls on roller skates, boys playing beach-ball; it was a hands behind your head, stretched out on the sand, eyes shut in the sunshine kind of state. It was deckchairs and hammocks, crystal clear waters, birds high in the sky and not a cloud to be seen. I hadn't just come to California for the summer, California *was* summer. Or at least it would be, when the sun came up.

'What does Jerry look like?' yawned Dee, as we approached the doors into Arrivals.

'I've seen a picture of him when he was ten,' I said, humping my rucksack to adjust it on my shoulders. 'He was wearing shorts and had glasses.'

As we poured into the Arrivals concourse, we stopped and stared into the crowd waiting. People behind us peeled off to be embraced by family members or had their suitcases taken by limo drivers in suits. I scanned the throng in front of me, squinting for a glimmer of recognition or a sign with my name on. But there was nothing. We silently looked from left to right hoping that, at any moment, someone would step forward to claim us. Twenty minutes later, everybody else had gone. We looked at each other. 'I don't think he's here,' I said, letting my rucksack drift to the floor. 'Now what do we do?'

'Have you got his number? We could ring him.'

There was a row of telephones across the concourse to our left and so, picking my rucksack up and slinging it over my shoulder, we wandered over. Telephones in any country other than your own have an air of mystery to them. While it is safe to assume that using them involves money and dialling, the order in which those things happen is not automatically clear. We stared at the blue and grey contraption in front of us. 'We've got two twenty-five-cent pieces,' said Dee, opening up her bumbag. 'That's all the change we have. What do you think? Money first?'

'Try it,' I said, with a nod.

Dee picked up the receiver and dropped our first quarter into the machine. Nothing happened. 'There's not even a dial tone,' she said, with a shrug.

'Oh wait,' I added, suddenly noticing a small sign hanging from the bottom of the telephone. 'Out of Order. Do you think it's a clue?'

'How annoying. Now we've only got this.' She held up the small silver quarter. George Washington, stern and filled with purpose, shone out at me. I took it. 'Be careful, Ems, that's our last coin.'

'What do you think?' I asked. 'Dial first, then put the money in? Or money, then dial?'

Dee gave a small grimace and shook her head. 'I really don't know. Toss the coin. Heads dial first, Tails money first.'

I threw the quarter into the air and caught it as it descended. I flipped it onto the back of my left hand and held it out. It was Heads.

'Oh God,' said Dee, crossing her fingers.

Taking the scrap of paper with Jerry's number on that I had stuffed into my trouser pocket I began to dial. 'No! Wait!' cried Dee, pressing her finger down on the receiver. 'That's the full number with international code. It'll be a local number from here.'

It was a close call. My eyes widened with relief. 'Oh, well spotted, Dee,' I muttered, as I held the paper up again to dial.

I tapped in the last number and stood, with the coin poised, ready to be dropped. 'It's ringing.'

'Hello?' said a sleepy voice. I shoved the quarter into the telephone.

'Jerry?' I said. 'It's me, Emma. We're at the airport. Did you get our message? Our plane was delayed. A man eating a doughnut broke the navigation equipment and...oh,' I added, holding the receiver away from my ear and looking at it, 'it's gone dead.'

We stared at each other for what felt like an eternity. Very, very slowly, I placed the telephone down and swallowed deeply. 'Okay,' said Dee, hands on hips. 'This is very simple. We'll just get a cab to Jerry's house. It'll be expensive but we can use the stop-gap fund. It'll be fine.'

'No, Dee,' I said quietly, chewing my lip. 'We can't do that. Because I *don't know where he lives.*'

Dee blinked and said nothing. I turned from her and looked about the airport. I was vaguely hoping that, by some miracle, my parents had followed us and were hiding behind a pillar. But they weren't.

'Perhaps we could try phoning Joplin?' I suggested, my voice trailing into a defeated mumble.

'We've run out of change,' said Dee, rooting round in her bumbag in the vain hope that somewhere, at the bottom of it, there'd be a hidden coin. 'I wish they'd told us how much change we'd need in America. This is a woeful oversight. Did anybody tell us about the change thing? No. They did not.'

'What are we going to do?' I whined. 'Maybe we can sleep at the airport?'

'No,' said Dee, shaking her head and looking purposeful. 'We're not doing that again. Look,' she added pointing at a big board of local adverts, 'there are loads of motels and hotels. We can phone one of them and see if they'll send someone to get us.'

'But we can't phone them,' I wailed. 'We've got no change.'

'Emma,' said Dee, gripping me by the arms. 'See that security guard over there? By the doors?' I looked over my shoulder and nodded. 'Go over to him, pretend you're fourteen and that your mother has sent you unaccompanied to stay with your useless father who hasn't bothered to come and pick you up. Then cry a bit. And then ask for a quarter. You can do this! Now GO!'

Shoving me in his direction, Dee shooed me towards the guard. 'But I don't look fourteen,' I complained, looking back towards her. She looked me up and down.

'Yes, Emma,' she said, with an encouraging nod. 'You *do*.'

Well this was awful. We'd been in America for two days and I'd been sent begging on both of them. Still, the horoscope had told me to ask for a loan if I needed one and who was I to fool with the cosmos? The security guard was a bald black man, rotund of belly with an impressive handlebar moustache. He was standing, with his arms folded, and had clearly been watching our every move. As I meandered towards him, he fixed me in his beams and hooked his bottom lip over his upper.

'Excuse me,' I began, 'I was supposed to be picked up. By my dad. But he hasn't turned up. And I haven't got any change to use the telephone. And I was wondering if you could lend me a quarter? So I can use the phone? And show me how to use it actually because I'm not quite sure whether it's coins or dialling first...I'm fourteen.'

I stopped, a weak smile crumbling across my face. The security guard, caressing his moustache with his bottom lip, looked me up and down. 'The payphone for the motels is free,' he said, and then, unfolding his arms and pointing behind me, added, 'it's over there. Where your friend is.'

'Did you get it?' whispered Dee, as I marched back towards her, head down.

'Don't say another word,' I muttered. 'I am embarrassed beyond LIFE.'

We had chosen the Best Western El Rancho Inn from the wall of hotels on offer, mostly because it had a large yellow crown at the top of its logo, which Dee took as a good sign. 'It looks as if it may have paid host to the Queen. I know that's unlikely. But that's the impression it gives.'

There was no doubt about it; it was certainly better than lying on the floor of a fast-food restaurant. Two miles from the airport, the Best Western El Rancho had the look of a Spanish haçienda and, from the moment we walked in, it was obvious that it was way beyond our budget. 'I can give you a queen room for a hundred dollars,' said the receptionist, throwing us a hopeful look. Dee nudged me. A *queen* room. That was a good omen. A hundred dollars was clearly beyond what we could afford, but we were shattered and past caring and, even though it was taking a significant dent out of our stop-gap fund, we'd reasoned it would be fine because tomorrow we'd get a job. This, we convinced ourselves, was precisely what the emergency fund was for. And so we checked in.

The following morning sunshine was pouring through the window, bird song was twittering on the breeze and as I woke, I smiled and let out a small sigh. We were in California. I was amazed. It was all so *thrilling*.

Breakfast, we discovered, was a buffet of pastries on a table in reception. 'How much are the croissants?' asked Dee, taking a plate.

'They're complimentary,' said the receptionist, a bright-faced girl with her hair tied back into a silky ponytail.

Dee shot me a glance. 'Go mental. It's free,' she mouthed, taking a croissant. And a pain au chocolat. And an apple Danish.

'You're never going to be able to eat all that,' I said, nudging her in the arm.

'I'm going to spare nothing,' she said, a look of defiance and determination flashing through her eyes. 'See if I don't.'

As we sat, munching pastries and sipping our cups of coffee, we took the opportunity to assess our financial situation. We had decided to pool our funds and, having both brought $350 each, our starting pot was a grand $700. The cab from New York airport had cost us $30, accommodation had cost us $40, we'd blagged bus tickets, begged for the ferry but had spent another $18.50 on hamburgers. In San

Francisco, 50 cents had been lost to the telephone system and the El Rancho had set us back a pricey $100. Breakfast was free. Which meant that our Stop Gap account was now, two days into the adventure, sitting at $510. 'It's gone down a lot quicker than I'd anticipated,' said Dee, totting up the total. 'But we took a hit with this place. We should make the most of it.'

'I don't think I can eat a hundred dollars' worth of Danish pastries,' I said, trying to stuff another mouthful of sticky almond croissant into my mouth.

Refreshed, we tried again to make contact with Jerry and, with the help of the receptionist, we succeeded. The plan was to meet him at a diner, The Frazzler, in a suburb of San Francisco called San Ramon. 'So you get on the BART at Montgomery,' explained the girl on reception, laying out a map in front of us. 'That's on Market. Which is the main through road in the city. You take that to Walnut Creek. Get off there and pick up a DXI bus. That'll take you to San Ramon. And remember, in California, you queue for the subway but you don't queue for the bus. There you go,' she added, handing us the map with a smile. 'And good luck!'

'Oh,' added Dee, proffering a $10 traveller's cheque, 'can you turn this into change please. All coins. Thanks.'

'Good thinking,' I said, with a firm and impressed nod.

The Bay Area Rapid Transit was so clean you could eat your dinner off it. Large pristine halls transformed into spacious airy platforms dotted with polite lines of people standing patiently between designated tramlines painted on the floor at 15-yard intervals. It made the London Underground look like a dead dog. A hum, like a sound from the future, filled the air as a beautiful, aluminium brushed tube train, emblazoned with sharp blue stripes and tinted windows, glided into the station. The journey to Walnut Creek was straightforward, the bus stop we needed easily located and before we knew it, we were standing at an intersection called, rather wonderfully, Crow Canyon. The Frazzler was directly opposite the bus stop, a generic sparkling diner with a large neon sign that declared itself open. Away from the centre of San Francisco with its persistent cooling bay breeze, the temperature had risen considerably and, for the first time since arriving, we experienced the full scorch of the Californian heat. 'God,' declared Dee, with a small puff, 'It's unbelievably hot.'

Dumping our rucksacks on the floor, we slid into a red leather booth. The only other people in the diner were a man and two children, one boy, one girl, both of whom had a shock of tangled red hair. They were struggling with enormous hamburgers and the little girl, in pigtails and a gingham pinafore, was holding a chip and flying it through the air. I caught her eye and smiled. She stuck her tongue out at me.

'Hi!' said a blond, tanned woman who had glided to the side of our table. 'I'm Cindy. I'm your waitress. What can I get ya?'

'I think we're just going to have coffee please,' said Dee, smiling.

'Caff, de-caff? Black? White? Cream? Half-fat? Non-fat? Non-dairy? Froth? No froth? Large? Regular? You have to choose.'

'Definitely caff,' I proffered.

'With...half-fat?' added Dee, suggestively. 'No froth? Regular?' I nodded.

Cindy scribbled down our order, scooped up our menus and glided off.

We both sat, gazing out the window, sipping our coffees and waiting for Jerry to arrive. A large white pick-up pulled into the parking lot. I sat up a little and tapped Dee on the forearm. 'This could be him.' The windows of the pick-up were tinted so as it sat, a heat haze dancing over the bonnet, I was unable to see who was driving. The front door opened and a man appeared. 'I don't believe it,' I said, shooting an incredulous stare in Dee's direction.

'Shorts and glasses,' confirmed Dee. 'We have our lift.'

I didn't think it was possible for a grown man not to have changed much in twenty years but Jerry was the living proof. Scrawny arms and legs, pale beyond belief, polished trainers, white shorts with creases pressed down the centre, buck-teeth, frosted glasses and a moustache. He looked like a nerd who'd gone to a Comic-Con dressed as Burt Reynolds. 'Wow,' I half whispered as Dee threw down a handful of change to cover the coffee. 'Do you think he lives underground? He's the colour of Nosferatu.'

He was standing, hands on hips and legs slightly apart as we heaved our rucksacks through the double doors of The Frazzler. I gazed towards him. He looked like a luminous pair of scissors.

'Hello!' I called out. 'Are you Jerry?'

'Yeah!' he exclaimed, in a flat, nasal drawl. 'You Emma? I thought you were in your twenties? How old are you? Fifteen?'

Dee snorted. I stared. 'No,' I replied. 'I'm twenty-two.'

'You're shitting me?' answered Jerry, shaking his head and letting his mouth drop open.

'Five lousy cents?' a voice shouted from behind us. We looked back over our shoulders. 'You leave a five-cent tip?' It was Cindy, our waitress, who had followed us outside. 'Here!' she shouted, throwing the offending coin in our direction. 'Take your lousy, stinking money and shove it up your ass!' whereupon she extended the middle digit of her right hand and thrust it violently in our direction.

I bent down and picked up the offending coin. 'Here,' I said, handing it to Dee, 'can't let that go to waste. That's *change*.'

'You gotta tip, girls,' chided Jerry, opening the back of his pick-up for our rucksacks. 'Fifteen per cent. Basic. You can stick your packs in here. And mind the paintwork.'

Jerry's truck was immaculate. There wasn't a speck of dirt anywhere, no heaps of scrunched-up sweet wrappers, no piles of scrawled directions and no hardened boluses of chewing gum sticking proudly from every available surface. It was clutter-free. 'This is a bit different from your car, Emma,' said Dee, as she slid into the front passenger seat. 'Do you remember that time there was that mysterious smell?'

'I thought it was a figment of my imagination,' I nodded, climbing in behind her. 'But it wasn't. It was a goat's cheese. It was three weeks before I found it.'

'Never smelled anything like it,' said Dee, shaking her head. 'It was like the concentrated essence of a million teenage boy's feet.'

'Although the upside of that was that nobody wanted a lift.'

'Ooooh,' said Dee, pressing a button on the arm of the door, 'electric windows.'

'No,' complained Jerry, leaning across Dee and pressing

the button so the window glided back upwards, 'don't open the windows. It ruins the air conditioning.'

Dee and I exchanged a quick look.

San Ramon, as far as we were concerned, was to be a very temporary stop over until we found something more central but all the same, we were treated to a grand tour that took in the AT&T building, the front gates of a fancy Country Club and a small row of shops. Jerry's apartment was a good 20-minute drive from Crow Canyon, a gated complex that had the feel of an upgraded hall of residence. Entry into it was via an electronic key card that Jerry kept in a small leather pouch that hung from the rear view mirror. 'Have you got a spare one of those?' asked Dee, pointing. 'That we can use?'

'Nope,' he said, driving into the parking area. 'Oh MAN! Someone took my spot!'

I looked up. The car park was empty apart from one small delivery van. 'Can you go there?' suggested Dee, pointing towards a row of empty parking spaces. 'Or there?' pointing across to another empty line. 'Or what about there?' she added, trying to be helpful, gesturing to another host of vacant slots.

'That's *my* spot,' Jerry grumbled, drawing the truck to a halt by the delivery van. '*My* spot.' I caught Dee's eye again and stared away again quickly. 'I'm gonna leave him a note. MAN. You don't park in another guy's spot. You just don't.'

'So,' I chipped in, to change the subject, 'is it okay if I phone my mum? To let her know we've got here safe?'

'Yeah, but I'll want cash up front,' said Jerry, still scowling in the direction of the delivery van. 'And I'm gonna order in pizzas, so give me twenty bucks and that'll cover the two.'

'Do you take traveller's cheques?' asked Dee, smiling. 'It's that or a bag full of change I'm afraid. Although I would like to hold on to the change. It seems to be quite important.'

Jerry blew a short, sharp, rankled sigh from the side of his mouth. 'That all you got? You got no notes? I'll have to take a cheque to the bank. Get it cashed. Kind of a pain in the ass.'

'That's it I'm afraid. Unless we get some cash later today or tomorrow. If you're happy to wait?'

Jerry's head lolled to one side as if he was experiencing a sudden and inconveniencing pain. 'Okay. I'll take the cheque,' he said, reluctantly. 'But it's a pain in the ass.'

I suspected that Jerry didn't really want two English girls staying in his apartment. We would have to tread very carefully, I thought to myself.

The apartment was small: there was one bedroom, a compact shower room and a cramped kitchen-diner that tripled up into a sitting room. We were going to be on the couch that pulled out to serve as a guest bed. There was a large wooden shelving unit opposite the sofa upon which sat the most enormous television I'd ever seen but as I looked around I realised there were no photos or pictures hanging on the walls, no books, in fact there was nothing to declare that anyone actually lived there. It was a bare shell of a home and it was immediately apparent that thrusting ourselves upon a distant relative was not necessarily a welcome arrangement for anyone. We slumped our rucksacks into a corner and stood looking awkward. 'I'd offer to wash up,' I said, throwing my hands in the air. 'But there's nothing to wash up.' Dee shot me a look. I fell silent.

'I'll order the pizza,' said Jerry, tossing his car keys into a small bowl by the microwave. 'You like meat?' We both nodded.

We sat, in virtual silence, eating large slices of pizza smothered with cheese and indeterminate lumps of what may have been beef. A programme called *America's Most Wanted* blared from the television, a modern-day lynch mob of a show that seemed much taken with the crash zoom into traumatised faces of hysterical women and weeping children. A man with the thickest neck in America had been driving around the state of Nevada robbing banks blind. He'd even hit someone on the upper arm with the butt of his gun. 'I couldn't use it for a week!' wailed the victim. It was hypnotic.

Given that our first few days in America had been less than auspicious I was slightly dreading the obligatory phone call home to my mother. Like a divining rod of disaster, she would be able to detect the merest trickle of trouble and I was going to have to have my wits about me. 'Don't tell her about the begging bits,' advised Dee, as I dialled the number. 'Or the wrong ferry bit. Or the plane bit. Or the airport bit. Or the hit to the stop-gap fund bit. Actually, don't tell her anything. Just tell her the weather's lovely.' I nodded.

'Mum!' I yelled, 'We're here! We're at Jerry's!'

There was a scream down the receiver. They were clearly very excited to hear from me.

'The weather is really lovely,' I began, sticking an upward thumb in Dee's direction. 'Really nice. Hot. Not a cloud in the sky.'

'Did anyone steal your luggage in New York?'

'No.'

'Or offer you drugs?'

'So you wouldn't believe how hot it is.'

'And you're managing your money all right? You're being careful?'

'I think it must be in the nineties. At least. Anyway, how are you?'

'I've got terrible wind,' said my mother, matter of factly.

'It's been awful!' shouted my father in the background.

'I think it was Jerusalem artichokes. Won't be having those again. I'm glad you called today. We're off on *our* adventure tomorrow morning,' replied my mother. 'If we die then all the papers you need are in the red box.'

'You're not going to die.'

'Well, we might, your father is making me go to Marseille. You know what that's like. I'll try and send you a letter a week. I've got Jerry's address. If you move you'll have to let me know where you are. Have you got a job yet?'

'No, we've only just arrived, Mum. We'll start looking tomorrow.'

'What's the parking like?' shouted Dad.

'Nobody cares what the parking is like in America, Tony,' chided my mother.

'Well,' I chipped in, 'you say that but Jerry cares about the parking!'

Jerry shot me a glance. I smiled. He didn't smile back.

'He had his parking place taken by a delivery van. It was quite the commotion.' An awkward, bristling silence filled the room. I cleared my throat. 'Anyhoo. Doesn't matter.'

'Are you eating properly?' rattled on my mother, ignoring me.

'Yes, we just had pizza. Dee says hello,' I added, as she waved towards the phone.

'So we're off to France tomorrow. Then we'll go to Switzerland. We're going to travel round Italy too. And your father wants to go to Germany, to Berlin. He wants to see the Wall. I said to Tony, I bet there isn't a person in Germany who wouldn't be thrilled to see that thing come down. Although I did read an article in the paper about a woman who'll be devastated if it went. Utterly devastated. Because she's married to it.'

'Excuse me?' I asked. 'How can you be married to a wall?'

'She is,' my mother explained. 'She's married to the Berlin Wall. She's an Objectum Sexual. They're people who fall in love with inanimate objects. And she's married to the Berlin Wall. And if it came down, she'll be distraught, because they'll be killing her husband.'

'Hang on a minute, Mum, I'm going to ask Dee about this.' I held the phone away from my ear. 'Have you heard of Objectum Sexuals?' I asked Dee, who shook her head. 'They fall in love with walls and things. This woman got married to the Berlin Wall.'

'Was their best man the Wall of China?' quipped Dee.

'Dee wants to know if the best man was the Wall of China,' I relayed.

My mother hooted.

It was so lovely to talk to Mum and Dad. Just hearing their voices made me feel secure as if I was for ever tied to them, a safety rope that would always prevent me from falling. As we said our goodbyes, a small tinge of sadness rippled at my edges. I was about to have the adventure of my life and, in a way, it was a shame that my parents weren't there to share it too but it was right and proper that they were not. This trip would be the making of me. And I had to do it without them.

I turned to Dee and smiled. 'Good tip about the weather. That held many a storm at bay. Thanks for that, Jerry. I think that put their minds at rest.'

Jerry jerked his head in acknowledgement and stood up. 'Right then,' he announced, picking up the TV remote. 'I'm going to bed. If you wanna read then you can use that side lamp but no loud talking or nothing. And no TV.' He flicked the remote towards the television, clicking it off then, waving it in our direction, he wandered into the other room.

'Did he really just take the TV remote with him so we can't watch television?' I whispered.

Dee looked at me and nodded, 'We need to leave here as soon as is humanly possible. We need to get a job.'

Chapter Four

Got To Have a J.O.B.
If You Want To Be
With Me
$485.00

Our first problem was how to get out of the gated apartment complex. Jerry had driven off to work and as we stood, staring up at the electronically locked gates, we realised that, with no door and no handy release mechanism, we were trapped. We had arranged to meet our friend, Joplin, who, it transpired, had organised a job interview for us with Frank S. Bishop, the human resources executive of a major bank in San Francisco. I was wearing shorts, a blue Aertex top and a pair of flip-flops. Dee had managed to throw on a flowery skirt and a yellow T-shirt. 'Do you think,' I began, looking down at my slightly dirty toes, 'that this outfit exudes extra sparkle?'

'Not really, no,' said Dee, pursing her lips. 'But it is very hot. We'll just have to ooze purpose and resolve using our teeth. I have crowns. They're excellent.'

Dee was entirely correct. The Americans were mad for teeth and here we were with our *English* teeth, English teeth with *crowns*. Surely, I thought, Frank S. Bishop would be overwhelmed. 'Yes,' I agreed. 'We must smile excessively at Frank S. Bishop. He'll like that. Mind you, if we can't work out how to get out of here, we're going to be smiling at no one.

'There's a number pad here,' said Dee, pointing towards a small silver square inset into a tall brick column flanking one side of the great gates. 'If we knew the correct number combination then we could key it in and we'd be freed.' She nodded encouragingly and then randomly tapped at some numbers with her forefinger. 'No. It's as I suspected. I don't know the combination. Let's just pretend we haven't seen it.'

I stood back and, with one hand on my hip, shaded my eyes with my other so as to examine our predicament more scientifically. There was no barbed wire on top of the wall. That was good. And it didn't seem to be electrified. Which was even better.

'If we find something to use as a leg up,' I proffered, 'we could climb over.'

'I could use you,' suggested Dee, staring upwards. 'If you bent over, I could stand on your back, pull myself up and slump over the top.'

I nodded in agreement. 'If you use me as a leg up,' I said, squinting into the sunlight, 'and you get over, who will I use as a leg up?'

'I'm not entirely sure,' said Dee. 'Bend over and we'll think about that later.'

Doubling over I braced my arms against the bottom of my thighs. Dee, hitching her skirt up and tucking it into her pants, put her hands either side of my shoulders and using her knee, hoisted herself onto my back. Using the rails of the gate to steady herself, she brought her trailing leg up and stood across me, legs slightly apart. Hooking her hands over the top of the gate, she pushed off and heaved herself upwards, swinging her right leg so that her ankle hooked itself over the rim. I stared up at her. She seemed to have come to a lumpen stop. 'I've lost momentum,' she said, her chest squashed against the gate. 'Give me a shove up.'

Lifting my hands up to her rump I shoved Dee towards the top of the gate. Throwing her right knee over the edge and using it as a leverage point, she scraped herself upwards so that she was lying prostrate across the flat lip of the gate's summit. 'Now just drop down,' I said, rotating a finger through the air. 'It's not that high up. Don't break your ankle.'

Dee blinked. 'All right then,' she said, setting her jaw with a sense of purpose. Hanging on to the top of the railings with her hands, Dee let her body slip off the rim but she couldn't let go. She was now hanging from her hands off the top of the gate, her skirt stuffed into her pants and her legs dangling akimbo. 'Dee,' I said, gesturing into the air, 'just let go. Everyone driving past can see your pants.'

She nodded, closed her eyes and relaxed her tight grip from the top of the railings. Landing with a small thud she seemed momentarily startled but realising nothing was broken, she got up, dusted herself off and pulled her skirt out from her pants. 'Good,' she said. 'Now its your turn.'

'But I've got no one to give *me* a leg up,' I said, screwing up my nose. 'We didn't really think this through.'

'What about that bin over there?' said Dee, pointing behind me to a corner of the parking lot. I glanced over my shoulder. A brown, malevolent-looking dumpster sat in front of a low hedge. It was chest height. If I wheeled it over to the gate I could climb onto it and use it to get over. As I approached, the sharp tang of warm, rotting food seeped into my nostrils. I wafted a hand and pulled a face. It smelled biblical.

'Wheel it to the edge, here,' encouraged Dee, pointing a

finger through the gate towards the brick column. 'That'll give it some stability.'

Steering the bin into position, I took hold of one of the gate railings with one hand. With the other, I pressed down on the top of the bin while at the same time jumping, knee first, onto it. But I hadn't checked that the lid was secured and as my weight fell downwards, the cover slid sideways and I found myself, slipping, knees first, into the dumpster. A pungent punch of rancid waste kicked me full in the face. I gagged and then, standing up, gagged again. I looked down. My lower legs were covered in various bits of shit. There was more gagging, then, eyes watering, I looked up at Dee and said, 'I've fallen in the bin.'

'I can see that,' said Dee, screwing her mouth sideways. 'Tell you what – if I hold onto it through the bars then perhaps you can push yourself onto the rim and use that to jump over the gate?' She stuck her hands through the rails and took a firm hold. 'Go on, try it now.'

Gripping the gate with both hands, I pulled myself out from the gooey maelstrom of half-chewed food and mouldy peelings. Placing one foot onto the top of the bin, I hopped upwards and, momentarily resting both feet on either side of the hole, kicked down and jumped onto the crest of the gate. The dumpster skidded backwards. It slewed left, then right and with one, magnificent wobble teetered sideways spewing its contents across the parking lot.

'You've got some carrot on your foot,' said Dee, as I dropped down next to her. 'And what's that?' she added, pointing at a large white globule on my shorts. 'Mayonnaise? Parsley sauce? Not sure. Look, there's a sprinkler over there. Go and stand in it for a bit.'

I stood, grim-faced, the swish swish tick tick tick of the

sprinkler dousing me down. As interview preparations go, I thought, this was severely lacking.

The last time I'd seen Joplin she'd been standing in the front quad of St Edmund Hall with a green Mohican, customised Doc Marten boots and her trademark red baseball jacket. She was the first American I'd properly got to know: she was obsessed with The Smiths, introduced me to brave new phrases such as 'Fear THAT' and 'Totally Bitchin'', had an acid tongue and generally presented a vision of New World exoticism that I found intoxicating. She had come over as an exchange student during my second year, stayed for three terms and then returned to the US. She was one of the coolest people I'd ever met. We were meeting her in the TransAmerica Redwood Park near the pyramid, San Francisco's most recognisable skyscraper. Dee and I sat waiting for her on a low wall, dangling our legs in the summer sunshine and sipping on some strawberry milkshakes. There was a small plaque on a wall behind us and as she sucked on her straw, Dee strolled over to read it.

'Who's it for?' I asked.

'Bummer and Lazarus,' replied Dee, thumbing towards it.

I blinked and got up to take a look. It was a bronze plaque, two dogs carved into the top.

BUMMER AND LAZARUS

Bummer and Lazarus were two stray dogs that roamed this part of San Francisco in the 1860s. Their devotion to each other endeared them to the citizenry and the newspapers reported their joint adventures, whether stealing a bone from another dog, uncovering a nest of rats or stopping a runaway horse.

Though authorities destroyed other strays on sight, the city permitted these two to run free. Indeed, they were welcomed regular customers at popular eating and drinking establishments on Montgomery Street. Contrary to common belief, they were not Emperor Norton's dogs. They belonged to no one person. They belonged to San Francisco. When Lazarus died in October of 1863 (followed by Bummer in November 1865) a reporter for the Bulletin described them thus 'Two dogs with but a single bark, two tails that wagged as one'.

We looked at each other. 'Who calls a dog Bummer?' I said. 'I mean, COME ON.'

'It probably didn't mean the same thing in 1860. Even if this is San Francisco. That's quite sweet. It's a bit like us isn't it? Strays wandering about.'

'We're not begging for scraps though,' I added.

'Yet,' replied Dee.

A coiffured woman in a beige skirt suit and court shoes was striding towards us. I turned and looked up at her. I did a double take. It was Joplin.

'Fear me,' she said, with a twinkle. 'I'm wearing a *blouse*! How do you like America so far?'

'Nobody smokes, there are health warnings on beer, TV is mostly adverts about cholesterol-free-miracle-whip or mild tranquillisers and there are a disproportionate amount of very small dogs,' said Dee, smiling.

'Why are you damp to the touch?' asked Joplin, giving me a hug.

'I fell in a bin and Dee made me stand in a sprinkler,' I explained.

'But you've got a change of clothes, right?'

I shook my head. Joplin stared. 'You've come for a job interview in flip-flops? What do you think they're going to offer you? A middle-management position in the sandcastle department?'

I raised a hand. 'It's fine. I'm planning to use my teeth to devastating effect. And Dee. She's got crowns.'

'Yes I have,' confirmed Dee, tapping her two front teeth with a forefinger.

'Oh. My. GOD,' said Joplin, shaking her head. 'Well, we can't do anything about it now. Frank's expecting you.'

The bank was swish with an imposing, draconian air. If I was a betting woman, I'd have placed an odds-on bet that it wasn't the sort of establishment that hired damp people who smelled of bins. We were wafted past a long avenue of faux marble columns and into a walnut-trimmed office where Frank S. Bishop was standing, thumbs tucked behind bright blue braces and surrounded by the accessories of a successful life: framed pictures of him on a yacht, a few shining trophies set in a glass cabinet, a gleaming set of golf clubs and a mobile phone, the first I'd ever seen. It was black, had a long antenna and a clamshell design. I stared at it. 'Like it?' asked Frank S. Bishop, stepping forward and gripping my hand firmly. 'It's a Motorola MicroTAC. Way better than the Ericsson Hotline. Mind you, at thirty-five hundred dollars, it *should* be better.'

I looked over at Dee. She was grinning wildly and showing her teeth to great effect.

'I understand you're looking for work in San Francisco?' said Frank S. Bishop, fixing us with a look that was textbook purpose *and* resolve. We nodded. He was standing with his hands on his hips. It was an executive stance, I thought, not remotely secretarial. He turned away from us and gazed out the window. 'I'm the vice president of this bank's Human Resources Division. I have to get it right. If I don't get it right then this bank doesn't work properly and if this bank doesn't work properly then a lot of people lose money. And it starts right here. With me. I'm the front line. Because at this bank, we want winners. Are you winners?' He spun round and looked at us.

Dee was still grinning so I took the initiative. 'I was the Runner-Up World Conker Champion once.'

'What the hell's a conker?'

'It's a horse chestnut. From a tree. We call them conkers. You put them on string and take it in turns to try and smash them. I would have won but I was let down in the final by a soft nut...never mind. It's not important.'

I mulled over the *Cosmopolitan* career charisma requirements in my mind: personal magnetism, knowledge, a steady look, extra sparkle. I wondered if my short anecdote on conkers had satisfied these necessities and quietly impressed Frank S. Bishop? I wasn't sure, so I decided to look at him. Steadily.

'It's my job to pick the winners,' Frank S. Bishop was saying. 'This bank needs one hundred and ten per cent commitment. There is nothing more important to our customers than their money. Nothing. And we need people who aren't just going to look after that money, we need people who are going to make *more* of it. Have either of you had any experience in the financial markets?'

We both shook our heads.

'Ever worked in a bank before?'

No.

'Ever worked for a big corporation?'

No.

'Ever worked in a high-pressure business environment?'

No.

'Oh wait,' said Dee, holding up a finger, 'I worked in a pub. Does that count?'

'And I washed dishes. But I was promoted *very* quickly.'

'Okay,' said Frank S. Bishop, sticking out his bottom lip. 'Well!' he declared, guiding us towards the door like a gentle sheepdog. 'It was real great to meet you. Joplin, help these ladies out. And have a great day!'

We were swept quietly from the room.

'He liked you,' said Joplin, with an encouraging nod. 'I could tell.'

'Really?' I replied, eyes widening. 'Do you think he'll offer us a job?'

'No.'

We spent the rest of that afternoon going in and out of every hotel we passed. We filled-out forms, shook hands with women wearing vast amounts of make-up and showed our teeth to their best advantage. The main problem was that nobody seemed to *have* any jobs. Or at least, that's what they were telling us. Our first day of job hunting had come to nothing. No matter. Tomorrow was another day.

We were not returning to San Ramon that evening but instead heading to Joplin's place, a cool little apartment on the edge of the up-market Marina District. Wide, tree-lined roads decorated rows of brightly coloured Edwardian houses with large bay windows. The mood was tranquil, the apartment glorious. Bathed in a clean white light, it overlooked the San Francisco Bay and had views of both the Golden Gate and Alcatraz. Bare, polished wooden floors were framed by summery yellow walls and Joplin had filled the place with contemporary minimalistic furniture. Given that we were the same age, I found it breathtaking that she had managed to a) get herself a proper job and b) had her own place. I was in awe. *This* was extra sparkle.

Joplin had arranged for a few friends to come over and meet us: there was Palmer, a slightly camp but straight red-haired Italian-American with a penchant for menthol cigarettes, Yogi, a fabulous big black woman with a laugh so deep it was practically seismic and Caroline, a preppy Harvard Business School graduate who was in the city for an internship but lived in constant fear of earthquakes and couldn't wait to leave. 'Hey, let's have a British drink to celebrate! Emma,' said Joplin, handing round a bowl of Japanese crackers, 'why don't you fix some gin and tonics? Gin's on the sideboard, tonic in the fridge, ice in the freezer, glasses in the cupboard next to the sink.'

I skipped off towards the kitchen and felt very cosmopolitan. Mixing drinks in a classy apartment in San Francisco was a lot better than opening a supermarket own-brand bottle of wine with my thumb or picking half-smoked fag butts out of bins. Proper jobs meant sophisticated aperitifs and fancy snacks. I could see that now. It was like being shown through the gates of Xanadu. All I had to do was nail my career charisma and blended cocktails were mine for the taking. Grinning, I pulled down a small phalanx of glasses and began measuring out the gin. Dee was holding forth about our attempts, earlier that day, to visit the 52nd floor of the Bank of America building. According to our guidebook, the Carnelian Room had views that were nothing short of stunning and so, after our fruitless day of job-hunting, we'd headed there for a morale boost. 'But the lift,' she was explaining, 'only went up to the thirty-first floor.'

'And we couldn't work out what to do next,' I chipped in, lemon in one hand, knife in the other.

'So we just wandered round for a bit. Because there was no other lift. But there must have been another lift because no skyscraper has fifty-two floors but only builds a lift for the first thirty-one. That would be insane.'

'So we went looking for it,' I added, poking my head out from the kitchen.

Dee nodded and raised an arm in my direction, 'Yes we did. But the thing was, there were no other lifts to be seen. And we were just meandering about, through this office...'

'And this woman came up to us,' I shouted, opening the tonic.

'Who looked quite fierce,' said Dee, 'and she asked us what we were doing and whether we had official business.'

'I told her we were on official sight-seeing business,' I shouted, opening the freezer compartment and reaching in for the ice tray nearest the door.

'Which didn't go down well,' explained Dee. 'And then, for no reason, she looked at us a bit funny, squinted and asked if we were Irish.'

'I told her my grandmother was Irish,' I yelled over my shoulder as I banged the ice cubes into the glasses. 'And then she went a bit mental.'

'She did. She went panicky. Like we were the IRA or something.'

'Fear that,' laughed Joplin. 'Maybe she thought you had a bomb?'

'We didn't. We had slightly soggy paper bags with half-eaten turkey sandwiches in them. Anyway, she called security.'

'No way,' said Palmer, shaking his head.

'Yes way,' I added, coming in with the tray of drinks. 'Escorted off the premises at gunpoint. Right. Gin and tonics for everyone. Cheers!'

We all picked up our glasses, clinked and gulped. Dee, who had taken a dainty sip, stared down into her glass and frowned. 'Umm, Joplin,' she said, tentatively, 'do you have a novelty ice-cube tray?' I crunched down on the ice cube in my mouth. It was an odd shape and felt very hard. I cracked down on it a little more.

'No, why?' Joplin answered, who then instinctively looked down into her own glass. 'Oh. My. GOD,' she screamed. 'Emma! You've used Sebastian's frozen mouse babies!'

'I've used what?' I asked, scrunching my nose up and chewing on my ice cube. 'Who's Sebastian?'

'Sebastian,' Joplin explained, pointing towards a hitherto unnoticed glass tank, 'is my snake. He's fed on dead mice babies. Which I keep frozen. In an ice tray. Emma, our gin and tonics all have floating dead mice babies in them.'

I spat the contents of my mouth into my hand. Staring up at me was the ice cube I had been chewing – a bald, bug-eyed dead mouse.

'Oh God,' said Caroline, and then promptly and very neatly vomited into her hand.

The following morning we found ourselves back in San Ramon and on the job hunt. It was a blazing day, well into the 90s, and with no mode of transport other than the feet Mother Nature gave us, our search for work had become a sweating trudge. We tried the Noga Corner coffee shop (no jobs available but they did persuade us to try one of their phenomenal burgers), The Original Hot Dog Place, American Speedy Printer Centers, Fur-N-Feather Pets and the San Ramon Community Center. We were told the same thing wherever we went: there were no jobs but if we wanted to fill in a form we could and they'd get back to us if an opening became available.

To be honest, this wasn't what I'd been expecting. Spurred on by Mike's rallying cries at the BUNAC meeting, I had rather naively hoped that America was waiting to welcome us with open arms. It hadn't crossed my mind it would be a *struggle*. Admittedly, we hadn't done ourselves many favours. Because of the heat, we were presenting ourselves to potential employers dressed like beach bums, we wore no make-up and people were having trouble believing that I was of a proper legal age. We were as far removed from the picture of the pencil skirt-clad executive go-getter as you could get.

The days dragged on. We were stuck in San Ramon with Jerry, who was now taking the TV remote to work with him so we couldn't sit and watch television during the day. We pounded the streets, left our details everywhere and waited. But nothing came. We'd been job-hunting for two weeks, morale was slowly slipping away and our stop-gap fund, originally intended for small but essential emergencies, was now our only means of survival. Things were serious.

As usual, we were out, walking the streets and going into every business we could find. We'd been wandering for a few hours, again with no luck and then I saw it – The Half Crown English Fish-n-Chips restaurant, Union Jack blazing and East

End classics tinkling out from its doorway. I gripped Dee's forearm. 'Look!' I said, pointing excitedly. 'They're bound to want us. We're actually English. And we know everything about fish and chips.'

Dee nodded, enthusiastically. 'We're *really* experienced in fish and chips. This is it, Emma. They're going to snap us up.'

'Purpose and resolve,' I mumbled, as we strode with considerable determination towards the door.

A small, gentle-faced woman ran the Half Crown English Fish-n-Chips restaurant. I liked her immediately. There was no need for us to remember about the teeth. We were already grinning from ear to ear.

'Hello!' I said, leaning over the counter. 'We're English!'

The woman smiled back. 'Great!' she replied. 'What can I get you?'

'Nothing!' answered Dee, throwing her arms in the air. 'We'd love to work here.'

'We would,' I nodded, enthusiastically. 'We'd *really* love to work here.'

The woman's face fell. 'Oh girls,' she began. 'I'm real sorry. I did have a couple of vacancies. But two British boys came in yesterday and I gave the positions to them.'

We stared, saying nothing. We'd missed the gig by a day. And not only that, but there were other English people looking for jobs? In San Ramon? What were the chances?

'Here,' said the woman, holding out a bowl of fortune cookies. 'Take one of these each. I'm sorry.'

We reached in and took a fortune cookie. Dee snapped hers open. '"You have great physical powers and an iron constitution",' she read. 'What's yours?'

I gazed down at the small, beige fortune cookie in the palm of my hand. I was feeling crestfallen and depressed.

I broke it in two, pulled out the thin paper strip and looked down. I said nothing. Without a single word, I handed it to Dee. She took it and read.

'"Bad luck and misfortune will haunt you for all eternity".'

Chapter Five

You Gotta Fight.
For the Right.
To Paaaaaaaaaarty.
$27.85

Dee turned and stared at me, her eyes widening. 'They can't make cookies with fortunes like that in them,' she said, glaring at the doom-laden scrap of paper in her hand. 'That's irresponsible.'

'For ALL ETERNITY, Dee,' I said, wearily pushing myself out through the door. 'Not a bit of it. ALL of it. And HAUNTED. Not dogged, not bothered by, not mildly irritated, HAUNTED.'

'I'm going to write to someone and complain,' said Dee, shaking the offending item between her fingers. 'This is outrageous. What if you had a weak mental constitution? This might have been the straw that broke the camel's back. You could be on suicide watch now. And all because of a biscuit.'

'Killed by a biscuit,' I nodded. 'They could carve that on my gravestone.'

Dee screwed her lips in a fury. 'Biscuits,' she announced, with some force, 'do not go around determining people's destinies. Did the Fates at Delphi bake biscuits? No. They did not.'

The Moirae of Delphi, the three women who weaved the metaphorical threads of all mortal's lives were Clotho,

Lachesis and Atropos. Clotho sat at her spindle and spun the individual threads, Lachesis measured out the length of each thread and Atropos, the hard-assed one, cut the thread, determining how long someone would live for and the means of their death. They were fucking bitches. But no, they did not bake biscuits. All the same, it was near impossible not to feel suspicious. Fate versus free will: the greatest philosophical debate of the ages and here I was, slap bang in the middle of it.

It was difficult not to feel rattled. I was in America, trying to make my way, and all I had experienced since arriving *was* bad luck and misfortune. Perhaps the cookie was right? Perhaps I *was* destined for a life of near misses and melancholy?

'How much money have we got left?' I asked, as we trudged our way back to the apartment.

'Twenty-seven dollars and eighty-five cents,' replied Dee, with a heavy sigh.

'How has this happened?' I said, throwing up my arms. 'That's not enough to get out of California, let alone to New York.'

'It's not enough to get us across San Francisco, Emma. And only then if we don't eat anything and drink water from grass sprinklers. I wouldn't mind if we had hunting skills but I can't even catch a spider.'

'I don't know what to do,' I said, quietly. 'We can either rob a bank or we're going to have to phone home and ask to be rescued. I'm not sure which is the worse option. It's so humiliating. Here we are, trying to make out we're independent and capable and our only hope is getting a bail out from our parents. Or committing a serious criminal offence. We may as well be seven years old.'

Dee stopped for a while in thought. She bent down and picked up a small stick that had fallen from a tree above and began methodically to peel the thin bark from it, revealing the light, slightly moist wood beneath. I stared out into the houses below us, expensive bungalows with pools and fancy cars in driveways. The sky, as ever, was a perfect azure blue, the grass, against all the odds, a green deeper than it deserved. We were surrounded by Californian affluence but it was a wall as impenetrable as the one that cut Germany in two. We were on the wrong side of it and we were desperate.

'I think we might *have* to phone home,' said Dee, breaking the silence. 'I'm not sure we've got any other option. But it's such an admission of failure, I don't know if I can bear it.'

I looked upwards. A solitary white cloud in the shape of a cotton ball was floating across the sky. It looked lost, as if it had taken a wrong turn. It was hard to know what to say or do. We were so far from home and, right at that moment, it would have been the easiest thing in the world to ask for a parental lifeline. But I also realised that growing up, properly growing up, meant taking responsibility for your own actions and destiny. Nobody was going to get me out of this mess except me. I turned and looked at Dee. 'You know, when I got into Oxford,' I began, 'my English teacher sent me a book and she wrote inside it, "Never stop persevering". That's what she said. If we phone home, we've given up. I don't want to give up. We've still got twenty seven dollars eighty five cents.'

'Yes,' smiled Dee, gently, 'you're right. We have. We've got twenty-seven eighty-five. It's not over yet. And fortunes can turn on a tuppence.'

'Or a quarter. This trip has been all about loose change. We've got this far. And we can turn it around. Let's make a pact. We keep looking for jobs and we only phone home when we're down to our last dime. Agreed?' I held out my hand. Dee took it and shook.

'Agreed. And if we haven't got enough change to phone home then we'll rob a bank.'

'How will we do that though? We haven't got any guns.'

'We can buy bananas, wait for them to turn black and improvise.'

'They'll call you Bunch Cassidy.'

'That joke doesn't really work.'

'I know. Just pretend I didn't say it.'

Despite our brave optimism we had been in America for a month and were still jobless. As our emergency fund had dwindled to nothing we were forced to spend increasingly more time at the apartment. We couldn't even afford to take buses so our daily search for jobs was restricted to a ten-mile radius. If we couldn't walk there, forget it. Not surprisingly, the arrangement with Jerry was at breaking point. He hated us and we loathed him but with no job and no funds to move out we were stuck.

It was a Tuesday and we were lying on the sofa bed, crushed after another day of fruitless job searching. I was staring up at the ceiling, Dee was reading a book she'd found in a cupboard called *Mission Earth: The Invaders Plan* by L. Ron Hubbard, the inventor of Scientology. She was frowning. 'So let me get this straight,' she said. 'This guy is supposed to have said the way to make money is to invent a religion. He then does that and actually gets people to believe it?'

'Well,' I said, turning to face her. 'As far as I am aware, Scientologists believe that aliens called Thetans came to earth on a spaceship and left bad vibes everywhere and to get rid of them you have to give the Scientologists all your money. It's amazing. Imagine that moment, when you stand in front of another human being with a functioning brain and tell them that all the world's ills are down to aliens called Thetans. That takes some brass. They have to do it with a straight face. It's like if George Lucas suddenly said, "Hey everyone, you know that Jedi stuff? It's TRUE." You have to admire him. L. Ron Hubbard must have had balls the size of China.'

'Perhaps we should come up with a religion?' Dee suggested. 'To make money? Although,' she added, with genuine rue, 'I'm not sure we give off a prophet aura.'

'No,' I agreed, shaking my head with some regret. 'Lepers, yes. Prophets, no.'

'Emma, if L. Ron Hubbard can get people to believe in Thetans then we can get a job. What we need,' Dee continued, staring upwards, 'is a plan. A plan of action. We've been walking in and out of shops aimlessly. We need struc ture. Let's get a piece of paper and a pen and make a list. A dynamic list.'

I hopped up and dug out a pad from my rucksack, returned and sat, cross-legged on the sofa bed.

'Okay,' I began, writing THE PLAN FOR TOMORROW'S JOB HUNT in capital letters at the top of the page.

Dee crossed her arms with purpose. 'So the first thing we're going to do is One: phone everyone we've already seen and check if they've now got some jobs. If that fails,

'Two: phone San Ramon local ads and see if they've got any jobs. If that fails,

'Three: go to Danville and Walnut Creek and see if there's anything there. If that fails,

'Four: go to San Francisco City Center Hostel. There may be adverts for jobs.'

'What about our money? That'll mean we use it all up on bus fares.'

'It's all or nothing now, Ems. All or nothing.'

'Okay. Then,' I added, looking up, 'if that fails…'

'If that fails then, Five: get a job in McDonalds. If that fails,

'Six: hitch a lift to another state and try again. If that fails,

'Seven: go home and cry.'

'That's an excellent list,' I said, with a small nod.

'Yes it is,' answered Dee, punching her pillow. 'And by GOD we're going to have a job by the end of the day if it kills me.'

We woke the following morning with a real sense of purpose. Enough was enough. It was time to draw a line in the sand and finish this battle once and for all. Between us, we now had $9.42. If we didn't find employment today, then it was game over. We would have to admit defeat and go cap in hand to our parents. As luck would have it, our day of destiny began with the gentle thud of an envelope landing on the hall carpet. 'Letter from your mum, I think,' said Dee, handing it to me. It was an air envelope and had French stamps on it, my mother's signature scrawl splattered across its front. 'Your mum's handwriting is extraordinary,' added Dee, resting her elbows on the counter of the breakfast bar. 'Don't know how you can read it.'

'I know,' I replied. 'It's like a woodlouse has got drunk, fallen into a pot of ink and run amok. Shall I read it out?'

'Yes, go on,' nodded Dee. 'I love your mum's letters.'

I cleared my throat.

'"Dear Emsy

'"First – the writing paper. It came wrapped in high-quality cellophane and cost £7. I wasn't wearing my glasses and couldn't see the price."'

'Ha!' laughed Dee. 'I bet your dad had something to say about that!'

I raised an eyebrow and continued. '"Second – we are currently in a very stylish house which provides certain stylish comforts. I was worried that it smelled of mice. Then I realised it was your father's socks."'

'Oh. So it runs in the family?'

Ignoring her, I continued, '"Third – something is wrong with this area of France. Had indescribable meal in a restaurant that cost nearly £30. At the next table were ten hunters plus their killing knives. One spent most of the meal lovingly cleaning it of rabbit's blood. Utterly terrifying. Feel as if I am on Lindisfarne. I will begin writing a novel. It is the only thing left to do."'

I stopped and looked up, grinning. 'Next bit's in my dad's handwriting – he says, "Mum was right about the cost of paper. With the envelopes it was almost 14 quid."'

'Knew it,' said Dee, resting her chin in the palm of her hand.

'Back to mum now. "I nearly bought you a winter coat. Tony prevented it. I do hope you've found yourself a job."' I stopped for a moment. '"We've been very worried. Hopefully, by the time you get this, you will have found something but if you haven't then we can help you come home. I would rather that than have you in danger or trouble. I'm sure I'm worrying unnecessarily and that you've found yourself something fabulous. Although your father has just pointed out he hopes you don't need to come home because if you do, you haven't got your keys and you won't be able to get in. Love you very much. Love to Dee. Mum and Dad."'

'That's true,' I added, looking up. 'I haven't brought my keys.'

'Well,' said Dee, with a determined nod. 'We'll just have to get a job then, won't we?'

I let the letter drift onto the breakfast counter. My parents were hard-working people. They had grafted all their lives. It was the final spur I needed. There was no way I was going back to England.

'This is the day,' I said, stabbing a purposeful finger downwards. 'This *is* the day! We are not coming back to this apartment without a job. Look at us. We're bright, friendly people. We've got brains. You're easy on the eye. You've got great teeth. Both my eyes point in the same direction. I'm an easy to get along with kind of gal. We're going to go out and we're going to ooze winning spirit. That's what we're going to do. We're going to *ooze* it.'

'You're right!' said Dee, getting to her feet and looking noble. 'Today we do what we came here to do. We are going to GET A JOB!'

Seven hours later and we were at Idea Number 5 on our Plan of Action. We had tried everything. We had phoned everyone, filled out application form after application form, we had even been to see a priest in the hope that divine intervention might kick-start our luck. He had smiled and nodded but having established that we weren't suitable as choristers it looked like even God couldn't help us. It was the same story everywhere: no current vacancies.

I felt hollow and anxious. 'Bad luck and misfortune will haunt you for all eternity.' The words rang in my ears. Here we were, Oxford graduates, once filled with blind hope, endless optimism and naïve arrogance, staring up at a McDonalds sign.

'Well,' I said, as we pushed open the doors. 'Nobody could say we haven't tried. How much is in our emergency fund?'

'Three dollars and seventy-five cents. That's it.'

'We may be flipping burgers, but we'll be employed. And while we're doing this, we can still look for something else.' Despite our useless and unsuccessful day, I was still grasping for positives. I turned and held the door open for Dee. There was something crushed and deflated about her. Working for McDonalds was not the pioneering life-enriching experience we'd envisaged when we arrived, brimful of possibility, in New York all those weeks ago. I thought about that first night, standing at my bedroom window, watching the rain slash down and the lightning scour the skies. I had been excited, filled with joyous anticipation and yet here we were. We were at the end of our rope. Beggars, it turns out, really can't be choosers.

The restaurant was busy with three queues of people loafing towards the counter. Ahead of them the minor cacophony of fast-food production was in full swing: bags were being hectically filled with fries, soda was being siphoned into large plastic tumblers and burgers, of every permutation, were being wrapped and stacked. We joined the end of the middle line but neither of us spoke, an air of defeated inevitability hanging heavy over us. As we reached the front, an overweight teenage boy with a beard of spots looked at me. 'What can I get you?'

I cleared my throat. 'Can we speak to the manager, please?'

'Was something wrong with your food? You wanna make a complaint?'

'No, we'd just like to…apply for a job.'

The boy blinked and raised his eyebrows in genuine surprise. 'You sure?' he said, leaning forward a little and whispering. I nodded. He shrugged. 'Delroy!' he shouted, turning to address a man at the back of the kitchen. 'These girls want to speak to you.'

A man, skinny and tall with dark rings under his eyes, came over. He looked extremely harassed and twitchy. His eyes, I noticed, were darting hither and thither, scanning the restaurant constantly for whatever the next problem might be: a tray of leftovers not stashed into a bin, a paucity of straws, a slick of ketchup on the floor. 'What's the problem?' he asked, his left eye twitching.

'We'd like to apply for a job please,' I said, mustering a smile from the dark side of my soul.

For a moment, I had his undivided attention. His wandering eyes locked on mine and he stared at me unblinkingly, as if his brain was scanning the pair of us for a sign of human intelligence. 'You Australian?' he asked, cocking his head slightly to catch my accent.

'No,' I replied. 'We're from England. We just graduated. We're doing Work America.'

'You're doing Work America and you want to work in McDonalds?'

I nodded and stared down at my shoes.

He shook his head. 'I don't think so,' he said, with a wave of his hand. 'Billy! Napkins! Dispensers!'

I stared back at him. 'We've got degrees from Oxford University,' I said, in desperation, and then, gesturing towards Dee, 'She's going to be a doctor. An actual doctor.'

Dee said nothing. Her shoulders were hunched.

'Listen, I appreciate your interest, but really, ladies, no. I'm not hiring. Okay. Thank you,' he said firmly and then, turning away from us, yelled, 'Wanda! We're running out of gherkins. Bring some up!'

The hustle of the restaurant hadn't stopped for a single second. The lines carried on creeping towards the counter and burgers continued to be flipped. Even here, in the most disposable environment possible, we were nothing. We made our way out of the restaurant in a daze. This was it, the nadir of our desperation.

We couldn't even get a job at McDonalds.

Down to $3.75 between us, I didn't just feel depressed, I felt terrified. We had enough to last us no more than a few hours and despite the obvious and immediate problems like food and lodging, one massive predicament was staring us in the face. Without asking our parents for money, we couldn't even *get* home. Our flight back to England was from New York. We were on the *wrong* side of the continent.

As we made our way down the street, Dee, who, till this moment had been so strong, dependable and resilient, stopped suddenly and sat down on the edge of the kerb. She was crying. Not pathetic girly tears but the silent, heartfelt sobs of someone who has reached their personal breaking point. I sat next to her and stared into the gutter. I had no more ideas. We were on the verge of destitution. We'd have to hand ourselves in to the British Embassy and declare ourselves bankrupt. We'd be dispatched homewards in disgrace, our abject failure a source of gossip and laughter. I sat and thought about how we *could* hand ourselves in to the British Embassy and whether I'd have to break a leg or throw myself in front of a car just to take the edge off the embarrassment. At least if I was maimed it wouldn't be so mortifying.

Because we were in the city, we had arranged to meet Joplin at six and with heavy hearts and tired legs; we wandered over to the plaza near her office, the plaque for the two stray dogs now slightly more resonant. We had barely spoken since McDonalds, our heads hung down, our shoulders rounded. We were, in every sense, broken. It had never occurred to me that we'd come to America and not find any work. The idea had been preposterous. Yet here we were, about to be on our uppers, sitting on a brick wall and half tempted to start begging for real.

'Hey!' shouted Joplin, as she bounced towards us. 'God! Who *died?*'

'We tried to get a job at McDonalds,' I said, miserably. 'They didn't want us. We've got less than four dollars to live on. I don't know what to do.'

'Ladies,' she began, reaching into her pocket and pulling out a leaflet. 'I have the answer to all your problems. Look at this.' She unfolded an A4 poster and handed it to me. 'They're called Voter Revolt. They're like a consumer action group. It's door-to-door canvassing. Nobody wants to be a door-to-door canvasser. Nobody. They'll be desperate. Seriously, you'd have to turn up for the interview naked while jacking up *and* sexually abusing a child not to get it. They're hiring tonight. And their building is right round the corner.'

*

Thirty minutes later we were sitting in front of Stacey, a small intense-looking woman, who held our fate in her hands. Voter Revolt was a non-profit consumer watchdog organisation set up in 1987 by two altruistic visionaries, Harvey Rosenfield and Ralph Nader. Their funding relied heavily on donations from Californian consumers collected via mail-out appeals or door-to-door canvassing. We sat in silence as Stacey stared down at our application forms. She was tapping a pen up and down in her right hand. She looked up. 'Great. Can you start tomorrow?'

Dee and I looked at each other. 'YES!' we shouted.

We had done it. We had finally secured employment. Beside ourselves with relief, we ran, arms in the air and jumping back to the plaza where Joplin was still waiting for us. To celebrate, Joplin kindly took us out for some supper and then, as if things weren't brilliant enough, delivered the wondrous news that Palmer, the friend of hers we'd met at the disastrous drinks, now had a spare room. His flatmate was going to be away for the rest of the summer and he wanted to know if we'd like to move in. He didn't even want any rent from us; it was too good to be true. Dee and I sat, shaking our heads in disbelief. We had been snatched from the jaws of despair. This was our tuppence. Our fortunes had turned. Suddenly, everything felt glorious.

The Voter Revolt orientation session took place the following afternoon and was held in a small grey meeting room where a row of chairs were laid out in front of a wooden table. On it was perched Stacey, arms and legs folded. As we sat down, smiling shyly at our soon-to-be colleagues, I realised that other than knowing I was going to be knocking on doors asking for donations, I had not the first clue what cause I'd be collecting for. 'I hope it's cancer or whales,' I whispered, 'because we'll do quite well if it is.'

'Especially if its whale cancer,' nodded Dee. 'That would be ideal.'

'Car insurance,' began Stacey, 'in the state of California is out of control!'

Dee and I exchanged a quick sideways glance.

'Do you want to spend the rest of your life being unable to drive a car unless you can insure it for double its value?'

I looked around. A couple of people shook their heads.

'Now as you know, the Supreme Court upheld Prop 103 but the current insurance commissioner is failing to implement it. We need funds to keep the pressure up and ensure that consumers in California are getting the insurance deal they deserve.'

Stacey was a scrap of a thing with the permanently hounded look of someone dedicated to making things better. She was the first Californian woman I'd met who looked as bad as we did. For this alone, she had my respect.

'Now I'm going to hand round some sheets that'll give you the basic canvass rap you'll need to deliver on a door-to-door basis,' she continued. 'Remember the goal is to get twenty-five-dollar sponsors. We'll do some role-play – the winner gets a slice of pizza – and then we'll head out. Okay. Who wants to go first?' She looked around the room. 'How about you?' said Stacey, finger pointing firmly at Dee.

'Oh,' said Dee, grimacing. 'Oh dear.'

'Up you get. Okay. I'm the door. Give me your rap. You can use the sheet I just gave you, for now. That's fine.'

Dee pushed herself up from her chair reluctantly and cleared her throat. 'Hello,' she said, reading. 'My name is…Dee…hello. And you are?'

'No, it doesn't really matter what my name is,' said Stacey, with a shake of her head. 'Just stick to the sheet.'

'Right. Hello. My name is Dee. I represent Voter Revolt, the consumer group that passed Prop 103 for insurance reform.' She stopped and looked at Stacey. Stacey stared back. Dee, lowering her voice, leaned forward and whispered, 'Shall I just carry on? With the next paragraph? Or should I wait for questions there?'

'Just carry on.'

'Okay. Purpose…'

'No, don't read out the paragraph headings. Just read the paragraph.'

'We're in your neighbourhood tonight working to implement Prop 103 to get you the twenty per cent rate rollback in your liability insurance. Take a look at our statement of support. Hand over clipboard. Oh. I probably shouldn't have read that out either?'

'No,' said Stacey, then turning to face the rest of us, 'you'll all be given a clipboard with the statement of support on it. That's what you show to your doors. Okay. Carry on.'

'I'm sure you are aware,' continued Dee, frowning with concentration, 'the Supreme Court upheld Prop 103 but now the insurance commissioner is not implementing it. She is working with insurance companies to block the twenty per cent rollback we all voted for. Voter Revolt is completely citizen-backed. We're going door-to-door as we did to get Prop 103 passed and people in the neighbourhood are contributing twenty-five dollars or more to give us the resources to keep public pressure on the insurance commissioner and fight the insurance industry to lower our rates. The best way to fight for 103 is by cheque – this gives you a receipt and it's safer for me to carry.' Dee stopped and looked towards me, relieved that she'd finished.

'Okay,' said Stacey. 'What did everyone think?'

There was a wall of silence.

'I think she read it out really well,' I said, nodding enthu-siastically.

'Yes,' nodded Stacey, 'she did read it well. But when you come to do your doors for real, you'll need to engage. Eye to eye. So look at the rap, learn the facts, and then make it your own. Okay. Who's next? You, gentleman at the back...'

An hour later a black guy called Arnem had won the coveted slice of pizza. I watched him eat it, my mouth slightly salivating. Dee tapped me on the upper arm. 'You know when we're supposed to show the statement of support?' she whispered. 'How far away should we hold it? Because the print is quite small. But we're not supposed to hand the clipboard over. So that would mean thrusting it into their faces.'

'Or holding it at length if they're long-sighted,' I said.

'But even then, it's going to need to be quite close. Like this.' She propelled the clipboard towards me at speed.

'Ooh,' I said, flinching.

'Exactly,' said Dee, with a nod. 'This plunging and shov-ing is a potential minefield.'

'Give it to me,' I said, taking the clipboard. 'I'm going to stand over there. Tell me when you can see the statement of support.' I walked five paces away and then turned back to face her and held the clipboard up. 'Can you see it now?'

'No.'

I took a step towards her. 'Can you see it now?'

'No.'

I took another step towards her. 'Can you see it from here?'

'No.'

'What are you doing?' asked Stacey, frowning.

'We're trying to work out from what distance you can actually see the statement of support,' explained Dee, gesturing, 'because it's quite hard to read. But we can't shove it up people's nostrils.'

Stacey stared at us. 'Just get in the cars.'

We were being driven to Sausalito, a well-to-do suburb just over the Golden Gate Bridge. A large road sign welcomed us at the outskirt declaring the small, bay town to be a 'Cholesterol Free Zone'. Dee's eyebrows knitted in thought. 'But what does that mean? They don't eat eggs? Or kidneys?'

'Mayonnaise is banned in the state of California,' quipped Arnem, who was in the back seat with me. 'I ain't making that shit up.'

'You so are, Arnem,' I said, shooting him a quizzical look. 'They can't ban mayonnaise. Everyone is mental for it.'

'Mind you, no one in their right mind eats kidneys,' chipped in Dee. 'They may be delicious but they're full of toxins. A kidney stores poisons. Baffles me as to why anyone would ever want to eat one. And offal. Don't get me started on offal.'

'What the hell is offal?' asked Arnem, pushing his cap to the back of his head.

'Intestines,' I replied.

'Get the hell out!' he yelled, his face mutating into a vision of disgusted shock. 'Who the HELL eats intestines? They're just full of shit!'

'My grandmother made me eat tripe once,' I added. 'It was this plate of rubbery, grey, rough textured sorrow that smelled and tasted of dung. I may as well have eaten a plate of fried arseholes.'

Arnem shook his head, wound down his window and stared out. 'Man,' he muttered, 'that is *nasty*. I ain't *never* going to Europe.'

The car had stopped at a traffic light. I looked out towards the kerb and saw another sign – a black silhouette of a dog not unlike a Labrador, crouching, with a shit coming out of its arse. There was a large red diagonal line struck through it. I frowned. 'Wow. I really want to meet the Sign Man of Sausalito,' I said, pointing a finger in its direction. 'This guy either has an incredible sense of humour or he is clinically insane.'

I was dropped at an intersection in a quiet, leafy street and told to work four blocks. I had to get as many $25 Sponsors as possible or, failing that, take any financial donation I could. My pay would be 5 per cent of everything I brought back so the more donations I received, the more I'd take home. As the car drove off, with Dee gazing at me plaintively over her shoulder through the back window, I took in my surroundings. Large, affluent-looking houses were perched on plump, sprinkled lawns. Palm trees stood on each corner of the intersection and before me, in front of a large, low Spanish style bungalow, sat a row of espaliered trees in terracotta pots. The place screamed money.

I stood, rooted to the spot. I'd never done door-to-door canvassing before and, despite my brief attempt at begging back in New York, I was unused to asking strangers for money. Dee was no longer at my shoulder and suddenly, on my own, I felt anxious and nervy. I sighed and lifted my face upwards, hoping that the warm, late afternoon sun would be something of a panacea. Somehow, I had to muster some courage.

I flicked through the papers on my clipboard. How difficult could this be? I had the bare facts in front of me. But what if I was quizzed on the finer legal points of Proposition 103? I wouldn't be able to answer. It would be like when you're in a foreign country and you've learned one phrase, '*Un sac, s'il vous plaît*,' and then have to stand there, staring like a lemon, as all replies flow gently over your head.

I decided to be methodical. I was going to start with the first house on the left of the street, work my way down then cross over and come up the other side. I drew a small map on the back of the statement of support as an aide memoire, adding a big arrow and writing, 'You Are Here' by way of encouragement. As I walked up towards the first door, my heart was thumping in my chest, my mouth devoid of spit. I mumbled the Canvass Rap quietly under my breath and hoped, beyond hope, that I wasn't asked a question. We had $3.75 to live on. I *had* to get a sponsor.

The door was set behind a fly screen. I creaked it open in order to reach the bell and as I pressed down with the tip of my index finger a thin, airy sound tinkled forth. Footsteps gathered pace and as they came closer I ran a hand quickly through my hair. A woman opened the door, small, thin and bright-eyed. She had short white hair in a pixie cut and wore a faded tie-dyed T-shirt over cream knee-length shorts. She was barefoot. 'Hi,' she said, smiling.

'Hello,' I said, smiling back. 'I'm here today from Voter Revolt.' I held up my clipboard and tapped it with my finger. 'And I'm supporting Prop 103, the one about the car insurance where the Supreme Court passed the Prop. And the lady commissioner is holding back on implementing it. So we'd love you to get your twenty per cent roll back. But you're not getting it yet. Because of her. So we're looking for donations to help us keep up the pressure and make sure that the Prop is propped up! Ah ha!'

The woman let her head drift down to one side and fixing me with a quizzical air said, 'Are you Australian?'

'No, I'm English,' I replied, holding up the clipboard again. 'And so we're looking for sponsors. To be a sponsor you need to give me twenty-five dollars. For that twenty-five dollars you'll get a letter. Like this one. On the clipboard. Can you see that? I can hold it closer. Which will keep you updated as to what is going on. So. Is that something you'd be interested in? Being a sponsor?'

The woman raised her eyebrows. It wasn't the good eyebrow raise, it was the bad one, the one that told me that something I wasn't going to particularly care for was heading my way. 'Well, the thing is,' she began, rubbing her earlobe with one hand, 'I don't actually have a car.'

'Oh,' I said. 'So you're not that interested in car insurance?'

'No, I'm afraid not.'

'Huh,' I mumbled, letting my head nod a little. 'Okay. Well. Nice to meet you.'

'Goodbye,' she said, shutting the door.

I turned and walked back down the path to the street. Who didn't have a car in California? No matter, I thought to myself, it was a warm-up. I'd got across the main points, been relatively pithy and held up the clipboard twice. Onwards to the next door.

The next house didn't look quite as affluent as its neighbour. Whereas the first had been immaculately manicured, this had an air of weary neglect. The fence needed a lick of paint, a few rusting machinery parts cluttered up the rear of the front yard and the porch was scattered with small heaps of dried leaves, spiders' webs and a set of long-neglected swinging chairs. As I climbed the small flight of wooden stairs, the front door opened suddenly and an elderly man in a light brown cardigan and glasses peered out. 'What do you want?' he said, in a gruff tone.

'I'm with Voter Revolt,' I said, holding up the clipboard. 'I've come to talk to you about Prop 103, the car insurance thing.'

'You Australian?' he asked, frowning.

I blinked. 'No, English.'

'I've got a double-decker bus. Want to see it?'

I thought momentarily. Was 'double-decker bus' a folksy euphemism for his penis? I looked the man up and down. He was pretty old and clearly had a problem with his hip. If push came to shove, I could have him in a fight. 'All right then, yeah,' I said, with a light shrug and in I went.

The interior was gloomy. Autumnal tones that may have worked perfectly well in other parts of the world seemed consciously out of place in bright California and the endless shades of brown gave the place a deadened air. The man was walking towards a small occasional table set against the wall further up the hallway and as he reached it, he turned and held out his arm as if to present it proudly. 'There you go,' he said, his face breaking out into a wide smile. 'That's my double-decker bus.'

I looked down. The table, round and dainty and covered with a weathered lace cloth, had three ornaments on its top: a porcelain beer pot with a picture of a fat German in lederhosen on the side, a ceramic bunch of garlic and in the centre, in pride of place, a small metal bright-red double-decker bus. I picked it up. It was clearly decades old. 'How sweet,' I said. 'When did you get this?'

'End of the war,' he replied. 'I was posted to Europe in 1944. Want a game of darts?'

'Darts?' I asked, with some surprise. 'I'm not very good. But all right.'

One hour, two beers and five games later I left with a three-dollar donation in my hand. I'd actually won it playing darts so although it wasn't technically a donation, I was happy to throw it into the family pot. By my reckoning, with the 5 per cent commission I was on, I'd earned 15 cents in just over an hour. If I divided it by the number of doors I'd worked, that averaged out at 7.5 cents per house. But the statistics got worse. The next three doors had no one home, the fourth had a look of *Psycho* about it so I left it well alone and at the fifth a woman leaned out from an upstairs window and shooed me from her front yard while shouting 'If you've come looking for money I'll set my dog on you.' All of which meant my earning stats dived to 2.1 cents per house. This was not going to be enough to live on. Crossing over to the other side of the street, I fared a little better and by nine o' clock, when the car returned to pick me up I had managed to coax from the inhabitants of Sausalito the grand total of $28.

'What did you get?' I asked Dee, as I scooted into the seat next to her.

'Sixteen dollars,' she replied, shaking her head. 'I don't really want to talk about it. Every time a man answered the door he gave me his phone number. And I got two invitations to dinner. It was unbelievable.'

'Well, you are very pretty, Dee,' I said, leaning forward and giving Stacey my donations.

'You're going to have to try and get into triple figures by the end of the week,' said Stacey, looking at us in the rear-view mirror. 'What wasn't working? Was it the rap? Were they hostile?'

I shrugged. 'I'm not sure. They didn't really seem that interested. It's sort of hard to get passions inflamed about insurance.'

The car pulled up at the corner of another intersection and Arnem got in. 'I got fifteen sponsors,' he said, handing a lump of cheques to Stacey. 'And a bundle of cash. Think its just over four hundred dollars.'

Dee and I looked at each other, our mouths gaping open in astonishment. 'This is why he got the pizza,' whispered Dee. 'Sit closer to him. You might absorb his skills via osmosis.'

The sum total of our combined earnings, for our first night of employment in America, a collective ten hours of work, was…$2.20. 'Tell you what,' I said, staring down at our wages, 'Let's have a blowout. We could buy a small plastic spoon. Or some sachets of salt.'

'Emma,' said Dee, with a heavy sigh, 'I don't think Voter Revolting is going to be the answer to our problems. We don't have to be here until the afternoon so we can spend the mornings looking for other jobs. But let's not lose heart. There's always the chance that one of us might win that slice of pizza tomorrow.'

'You're right about the pizza,' I nodded. 'It's good to have goals.'

*

We had slept in a little later than we had hoped and as I wandered into the kitchen to put the kettle on to make coffee, I saw that Palmer had left us a note folded against the bread bin. I picked it up and read it, yawning. 'Palmer wants us to meet him and Yogi at some club tonight. It's her birthday, apparently,' I called out.

'We haven't got enough money to go to a club,' mumbled Dee, who wasn't quite awake yet.

'He says his treat. Although I expect that's just the entry fee. We can just drink tap water. Be nice to have a dance though, wouldn't it?'

Dee grunted.

'I've been thinking,' I said, shuffling back into the room we were sharing. 'I wonder if applying for jobs at the same time has worked against us? It's easier to give one person a job rather than two, isn't it? So how's about today, we go into places on our own? And see if it makes a difference?'

Dee sat up and ran a hand over her face. 'Yes, okay,' she said, reaching for a tissue and blowing her nose. 'Let's try that. What time have we got to be at Voter Revolting?'

'Three,' I said, picking a jumper up from the end of the bed and pulling it on.

'And what time is it now?'

'Just past ten. We should have put the alarm on. Ha!' I added, picking Dee's shorts from the floor, pockets stuffed with small scraps of paper. 'Are these all the phone numbers you got last night?'

Dee nodded. 'It was ridiculous. Pass them here, let's have a look at them.'

I tossed her the shorts and sat down next to her. 'Anyone decent?'

'No. Not really. But to be honest, I was so desperate for sponsors, the minute they started up with the flim-flam I just felt irritated. Haven't actually read these. Oh God. Look at that one.' She passed me an unfolded square of yellow paper. I read it.

'"I'm new in town too. Can you give me directions to your apartment? CALL ME!"'

'Oh wow. Listen to this. "You can give me a BJ any time!"' That is so inappropriate as a first port of call isn't it? Can you even believe someone wrote that?'

'Not to you I can't, no. I didn't know what a BJ was until I was seventeen. I can distinctly remember walking round the top hockey pitch at school with Joanne Forster discussing it because we'd heard Miranda Maitland had done one. And we came to the conclusion, after a vociferous debate, that you had to blow down a penis, like a trumpet. Blow quite hard. Straight into it.'

Dee laughed. 'Oh that's nothing. I was at a party once, in the fifth form. And our School Racey Girl was Monica North and we were aflame with gossip because she'd been seen going into the garden shed with Thomas Harwood. But the thing was, she had a brace. The one you can pull out. Not the fixed tram ones.'

'I had a brace,' I said, flicking through the rest of the scraps, 'used to spend the first lesson after lunch pulling it out and licking all the food off it. Disgusting.'

'Revolting. So she's at that stage of brace-wearing where they snip the front central bar.'

'Oh, I remember that. And you're forever catching your top lip in it. Hurts likes hell.'

'So she's in the garden shed with Thomas Harwood. And suddenly this blood-curdling scream rings out. Utterly blood-curdling. And out they come. Next thing we know, an ambulance has arrived and he's being carried away on a stretcher with Monica North bent over, head under the red blanket, scuttling along next to him.'

I looked up and frowned.

'Because, what had happened was that as Monica North was giving Thomas Harwood a blow job, her brace had become impaled in his penis.'

'Oh God, no!'

Dee nodded. 'And what was worse, Monica couldn't get her brace out so she had to go to hospital with Thomas still attached to his penis. True story.'

'You'd never live that down would you? Just never.'

'No. Her family emigrated to Australia.'

'Don't blame them,' I said, shaking my head. 'They probably wanted to get her as far away as possible.'

'Oh they didn't take her with them,' said Dee, eyes widening. 'Left her where she lay, Emma.'

I laughed then, giving Dee a quick pat on the arm said, 'Come on. Up and at 'em. Let's get ourselves a proper job.'

By the time we found ourselves sitting back in the Voter Revolt car that afternoon, we had, between us, walked into fifty-seven shops, restaurants, bars and businesses. Despite a relentless tide of knock-backs, Dee had found herself in an ice-cream parlour called Go Nutz that may be hiring, was asked to fill in an application form and told she'd hear from them within the week. And I had managed to bag an interview at a business run by a Frenchmen called Antoine whose job it was to introduce aromatherapy soaps and bath preparations to the good people of California. He was going to be away for a few days but when he was back, I was to go in and meet him. Neither of us wanted to get our hopes up. Our hearts, once impervious to calamity, were now a little more sensitive and raw. It was best to look forward to nothing. We both fared a little better that night: Dee made $59 and I had brought in $47, all of which gave us an in the-hand wage of $5.35. 'We've had a salary increase of over one hundred per cent,' Dee pointed out, beaming. Yes we had.

The club we were to meet Palmer and Yogi at was called The Holy Cow, a hot new singles' bar that had been open for just over a year. Above its doorway hung a large plastic cow adorned with a dainty pink halo. 'What in the name of HELL are you wearing?' laughed Palmer, as we joined them in the queue. He was sucking on a cigarette. 'You're going to a singles' club and you're dressed like boy scouts.'

I looked down at my and Dee's matching Converse trainers, our cotton shorts and T-shirts. We'd come straight from work. It hadn't even crossed our minds to dress up. I laughed. 'Fear us,' I said, leaning in to give Palmer a kiss on the cheek. 'How are you?'

'God!' he declared, raising a hand of faux despair to his cheek, 'I am *hating* this weather. My skin is like a crusty prophylactic.'

'How did you do with the revolutionaries?' groaned Yogi.

'We broke the five-dollar barrier,' said Dee, grinning. 'I like to think of that as an improvement.'

'Fuck me,' said Yogi, letting her head rock back. 'Five bucks? How long did you work for?'

'Together, just over fourteen hours,' replied Dee, smiling.

'Shiiiiiiit,' declared Yogi, shaking her head. 'I'll give you five lousy bucks *not* to go work.'

'Hey, Happy Birthday, Yogi!' I said, remembering. 'Sorry we haven't got you anything.'

Yogi waved her hand dismissively. 'No worries. I don't need a present. I love my birthday enough as it is.'

'I *hate* my birthday. It sucks to high heaven,' chipped in Palmer, stubbing out his cigarette with his shoe.

Yogi left out a small guffaw. 'Tell them the story, P. Jeeeezus I could listen to this *for ever*.'

Palmer raised one eyebrow. 'Okay. So I'm Jewish. But somehow, don't ask me why, I get to go to a Catholic School. I have not the first fucking clue what is going on. So its about three weeks before Christmas and I'm sitting in class. And the teacher goes "So who can tell me whose birthday we celebrate on December the twenty-fifth?" Up shoots my hand. And the teacher calls on me. And I say, "Mine." And the teacher says, 'No Palmer, whose birthday do we celebrate on the December the twenty-fifth?" And to me this is very simple. Because I know the answer so I shout out, "Mine. It's me!" Because that's true. It *is* my birthday on December the twenty-fifth. But the teacher thinks I'm horsing around and she's getting real mad at me so now she's shouting, "*No*, Palmer. *Whose* birthday do we celebrate on December the twenty-fifth?" So I'm confused and I'm thinking real hard and then I get it! And I go, "Oh! My *mom*!" Because *her* birthday is *also* on December the twenty-fifth. And now the teacher is purple! She is going crazy! So she hauls me up in front of the class and says, "One last time Palmer, WHO'S BIRTHDAY DO WE CELEBRATE ON DECEMBER THE TWENTY-FIFTH?" And I'm embarrassed and I'm crying and I don't understand because December the twenty-fifth *is* my birthday and it *is* my mom's birthday so I'm thinking and thinking and then something small and tiny rattles in the back of my memory. There *is* someone else who has the same birthday as me and my Mom. And I look up at my teacher, tears on my cheeks, and I go, "On December twenty-fifth we celebrate the birthday of me, my Mom and the little baby Gina."'

'Baby GINA!' cried Yogi, howling with laughter. 'Baby GINA!'

'I didn't know,' said Palmer, with a shrug. 'Ask me questions about bagels, I'll talk for a week. Men dying on crosses – no fucking clue.'

There were two burly doormen underneath the plastic cow, both sporting ponytails and wearing long black coats and sunglasses. We'd been waiting in line for over half an hour, Palmer keeping us amused with his chirpy banter while Yogi rolled with laughter. Other people had arrived and been allowed straight in quickly, which established to us that we were in the 'ugly line' and would have to wait our turn. Finally, finding ourselves flush up against the red velvet rope at the head of the queue, I looked up at the doormen and smiled. One of them, the larger of the two, reached for the rope's golden clip-hook and released it. I stepped forward. 'Nuh-uh,' he said, shaking his head. 'No way.'

'But I've been waiting for ages,' I said, frowning.

'No kids allowed,' said the man, pushing me gently away.

'No, wait,' I said, protesting. 'I'm twenty-two'

'Yeah!' said the doorman, laughing, '*Right.*'

'No, she is,' said Dee, chipping in. 'I know she looks like a twelve-year-old boy. But she really is twenty-two.'

'You got ID?' asked the other doorman, folding his arms and spreading his legs a little.

Dee and I looked at each other. Of course I didn't. My

passport, the only way of proving my age, was stuffed into my rucksack back at Palmer's flat. 'No,' I said, 'I was born in 1967. Will that do?'

'No ID, no entry,' said the doorman with a slow shake of his head.

'Oh man,' said Yogi, with a sigh. 'We should have told you. They are the ID *nazis* in America. We can try and go somewhere else but I guess we're going to have the same trouble all over.'

'It's okay,' I said, crestfallen. 'It's my fault. You go into the club and I'll head back to the flat.'

'I'll come with you,' said Dee, pushing her way out from the line. 'If I let you walk home alone, you might get picked up by a paedophile.'

A low-lying fog had rolled in from the bay as we made our way homewards and, with the moon high and bright in the sky, the city had an ethereal feel. 'I really hope we get those jobs,' Dee said, as we walked. 'And I know I shouldn't say it out loud but I can't help it. I've got a good feeling about it.'

I cast another look down at what we were wearing and remembered the picture of female executive perfection we'd seen in *Cosmopolitan*. 'Do you remember when we were on the plane to San Francisco?'

'God, that feels like a lifetime ago.'

'And there was that article in *Cosmo*, about extra sparkle?'

Dee nodded. 'Purpose and resolve, how can I forget?'

'Do you remember the picture of the executive woman, what she looked like? She was wearing a pencil skirt, smart blouse, belt, and pearls. We have got to scrub up, Dee. We mustn't muck this up.'

'You're right. Actually, I know it's cheeky, but Palmer's

flatmate has left a wardrobe of clothes. Do you think it's too naughty if we borrow some?'

'No,' I replied, shaking my head. 'I don't. Needs must. And we can always get everything dry-cleaned.'

'Once we've earned some money.'

'Exactly.'

We struggled on at Voter Revolt for the rest of that week, earning nothing more than scraps, our morale on life support. So when I got the call to go in and meet Antoine, the boss of L'Aroma, I was chomping at the bit. Dee had also been asked back to the ice-cream parlour and, determined to present ourselves properly, we flicked through the hangers of Palmer's flatmate's wardrobe pulling things out. Dee held dresses and skirts up against me until finally we found something that might look as if I owned it. 'I look like a fridge,' I whined, trying to readjust the breeze-block shoulder pads.

'To be honest, you look like a man in drag,' said Dee, cocking her head sideways. 'But this is San Francisco so I don't think that's necessarily going to be a problem.'

I was to meet Antoine in a small boutique on Union where the company had its retail outlet and offices. Aromotherapy, I'd been told on the phone, was a brand-new concept in complementary therapies that took plant essences and harnessed their smell to improve mood and health. They were, they told me 'at the cutting edge of soap'.

Antoine was very French. Tall and thin with a mop of dark floppy hair, he smoked Gauloises and wore very tight trousers. He had large, lazy brown eyes and, despite it only being ten in the morning, poured me a glass of chilled white wine within five minutes of meeting me. He brought out a tray of products for me to smell and touch: large almond-shaped soaps that smelled of sandalwood, ginger body scrubs and heart-shaped capsules that when heated burst open with a rush of lavender. He told me of the volatile nature of essential oils, of how intense aromatic compounds could affect a person's mood and improve their well-being. He explained how his soaps were not only a relaxation aid but could also provide clarity of mind and a balance of the energies.

'What do you think?' he asked, pouting his lips and pushing his fringe out of his eyes.

I kept my gaze firm and steady. I nodded slightly and picked up one of the large, almond-shaped soaps. This was the moment to declare my purpose and resolve. 'Yeah,' I said, sniffing. 'Smells nice.'

Ladies and gentlemen: I got the job.

(And so did Dee.)

Chapter Six

Working Nine to Five

$45.40

Jasmine. The fragrance of love. In a large lump of soap.
Not pithy enough
Jasmine. The fragrance of love.
Better.
Ylang-ylang. Fends off the smell of depression.
No, wait. I've got that wrong.
Ylang-ylang. Go to sleep happy.
Far more relaxing
Peppermint. Stops you farting.

I had started my job. It was goodbye to Voter Revolt and hello to essential oils. I had my own desk, my own pot of pens, my own pads and a computer. There were drawers filled with small red stickers marked URGENT and SEE ME FOR MORE INFO, a tray of stamps and a box whose sole purpose in life was to contain long thin strips of company logo ribbon. On the first day I had turned up scrubbed and spruced at nine thirty only to discover that I didn't need to turn up until eleven. L'Aroma, it would seem, was on Mediterranean hours. Instead of morning coffee, Antoine poured everyone a glass of wine. By twelve I was pissed, by lunchtime I had a hangover.

Lavender. Can help pounding head. Sniff it.
It's nice but there's something missing
Combine sniffing lavender with powerful painkillers
Wow! This stuff really works!

My job was to write copy introducing the phenomena of aromatherapy to the Californian masses. I was to keep it 'pithy, light yet informative' but at the same time, 'make the soap seem mystical, like a life-enhancing choice'. This was quite a challenge. It was only soap. So I would sit, sometimes for hours, thinking of life-enhancing soap-based scenarios. A woman, who has just found out her husband is cheating on her with her own sister is devastated and depressed. But after a patchouli and ylang-ylang shower scrub, she realises that life is worth living and chucks out all his clothes and burns them. A teenager, plagued with spots is taunted by school bullies. But after using a tea tree and lemongrass face soap, he earns the respect of all and scores the winning goal in a brooding grudge match. Grapefruit, eucalyptus, chamomile, aloe vera – they didn't just smell nice, they did shit. And it was my job to inform people of the shit they did.

I was also in charge of 'general office stuff', although when pressed on what, exactly, that might entail Antoine simply shrugged and smoked another Gauloise. Giddy with possibilities I set about designing a brand-new wholesale price list so that anyone who cared could now quote retail figures in a nano-second, using nothing more technical than two eyes and an index finger. I was so overwhelmed with achievement that, five hours later, after I'd finished it, I printed off loads and posted them to everyone I knew back in Britain. I even took one home to show Dee. She pinned it on the fridge under a magnet as I stood behind her, beaming.

Let loose with a rubber stamp I set about branding the word APPROVED on everything I could get my hands on: a notebook, the undercarriage of my swivel chair, the second drawer down of my desk, a box of paperclips, the tip of my shoe, the inside of my wrist. I would open a filing cabinet and stand, sniffing boxes of brand-new paper like a stationery junkie. I arranged elastic bands into coloured piles, stacked Post-it notes in size order and alphabetised bath bombs. Where once there was chaos, I now ruled a land of order. I was employed and in control.

It was amazing. After an interminable two months of misery, here we both were, leaping up in the mornings and taking buses to bona fide places of employment where we did things for actual money. I came up with concise summaries of soap-based remedies, while over at Go Nutz, Dee cut sandwiches in half and squeezed orange juice. We were the very essence of purpose and resolve. We had wrestled San Francisco like a large angry bull and finally, in a battle worthy of *Lord of the Rings*, brought it to its knees.

I was sharing an office with Mary-Beth, a vision of milky-fresh beauty, all porcelain skin and tumbledown blonde curls who was so filled with blue-eyed joy that instead of walking anywhere, she skipped. She skipped from the door to her desk, she skipped from her desk to the filing cabinet and she skipped from the filing cabinet to the stationery cupboard where Antoine would invariably join her, telling me he needed to have an urgent discussion with her about the finer points of the merits of foolscap and magenta ink cartridges. I'm not quite sure what went on in the stationery cupboard but something told me Mary-Beth was probably having some holes punched. No matter – I had a chair I could swivel, a small bowl for paperclips and a Rolodex card file for phone numbers that I could riffle at will. This was living.

My parents had left a long squawking message on Palmer's answer-phone giving me a list of numbers of where they were going to be over the next month. Keen to fill my Rolodex, I had written them all down and transferred them onto neat white cards with headers such as MUM AND DAD FRANCE and MUM AND DAD ITALY. I could flick through them whenever I was in the mood. It felt glorious. Given L'Aroma was an international company, a phone call, especially to France, was nothing out of the ordinary, so with Mary-Beth and Antoine firmly ensconced in an intense meeting about paperweights that involved a bottle of wine, a Billy Joel CD and a locked door, I felt free to enjoy my first perk of office life. I picked up the phone and dialled.

'Bonjour!' shouted my father, as he answered.

'You'll never guess where I am?' I said.

My mother bundled the receiver from my father's hand. 'Are you in San Francisco?' she said, in a high-pitched squeal.

'Yes, I am,' I replied. 'But can you guess where?'

'Alcatraz?' shouted Dad.

'I am sitting,' I began, giving my chair a little spin, 'at my desk that is in the office where I work. And,' I continued, 'I am working for a Frenchman. I am writing about soaps with medicinal benefits,' I continued. 'It's called aromotherapy. It's about essences and oils. It's about smells that make you feel better about yourself.'

'She's got a job in smells, Tony,' relayed my mother.

'I've got a computer. I made a spreadsheet. I've posted one to you. Anyway. How are you?'

'Well,' began my mother, with a conspiratorial tone, 'we've been having some *experiences...*'

'Creepy!' shouted Dad.

'First one – we were on our way to Switzerland and we'd stopped en route in this small village, completely non-descript hotel. Signed in. No bother whatsoever. The woman showed us up to our room and that was that. Next morning we go down to breakfast and there's no one there. No hotel staff, no guests, nothing. I go back upstairs and there's light coming from underneath all the bedroom doors. I open a few of them and they're all empty. Every single one of them. So we pack our bags, go down to pay so we can leave. Nobody there. Tony puts some money on the reception desk and we try to get out.'

'I tried to open the front door,' chipped in Dad.

'But it was locked! We were in an empty hotel and we couldn't get out! I opened a window, started shouting for help. Nobody came. Tony wandered into the kitchen. All he found was a really large knife.'

'It was massive!'

'At this point, I've had enough. I'm not staying in an empty hotel with an enormous cleaver so we threw our suit-case out of the window and *climbed* out. Can you imagine?'

'That's hilarious,' I laughed. 'Dee will love that. Can't wait to tell her.'

'So on we go,' my mother continued, 'and we found this lovely seventeenth-century chateau.'

'Oh, it was gorgeous,' added Dad, coming closer to the phone. 'The entrance was down a long lane, fields of sunflow-ers either side. It had three towers. Fifteen acres of woodland.'

'Really grand,' continued my mother, 'very dramatic entrance with two stone dragons either side of high wooden gates. And there was a paddock with some beautiful Arabian white horses, quietly cropping away, and three old-style pigeonaires…'

'What's a pigeonaire?' I asked.

'You know, a roost for pigeons. Like a dovecote but bigger. The place is an idyll and I'm thinking, oh yes, I can spend a leisurely week here. Your father can do some sketches; I'll drink some wine, wander about through the tall pines and ancient oaks. Bliss. So we've driven through the gates and from nowhere comes this hound from hell.'

'Massive bloody thing,' shouted Dad.

'Enormous mastiff-type dog, not quite a Rottweiler but bigger, rushes at us, barking ferociously. We couldn't get out of the car!'

'It had its paws on my window!'

'Spewing large globules of spit all down it,' wailed my mother, 'we were trapped. Again! Anyway, I kept my finger on the car horn, because it was an emergency and out came the owner. Lovely man, looked like he walked straight out of an Agatha Christie. Thick-set and small, wore expensive-looking clothes, smelled delicious. So he calls off the dog, apologises and takes us into the chateau. We're taken into a heavily panelled room, long oak trestle table, high backed chairs, various tapestries, stone walls…'

'Very too-ra-loo.'

'And all the while he's chatting amiably. He takes us through the house and out into a courtyard and there's a small table with a bottle of wine for us. How lovely, I think! He opens it, pours us all a glass and then another dog appears, a leggy thing, and Emma, it would not leave me alone.'

'Wouldn't stop nuzzling her!'

'And you know what I'm like with dogs. I can't stand them. And then the owner goes, "It's because you look like my wife. Sacha was my wife's dog." And then it all comes out. His wife died from a rare blood disease, very suddenly, everyone was devastated. Very sad business. And then he says, "Let me show you the chapel." So off we go and on the altar he'd put the last bottle of champagne they drank together with a pair of her shoes and her hat. And not only that, but all the statues had their faces covered with blue veils.'

'Gave me the willies!' yelled Dad.

'Well. At this point I'm thinking, how soon can we leave? But of course we can't, because he's given us some wine and has been charming so we're forced to see it through. So up we go to our rooms. Normally, I would have been all Wow and Whoopee. We were in a tower with two floors. Very grand. The bedroom was up a steep winding staircase hung all the way with spooky Russian icons. There were gilded mirrors everywhere and a host of faded paintings. A woman had recently died and all I'm thinking is when is her ghost arriving? At this point, Tony, who was downstairs calls for me to come and look.'

'I was rooted to the spot, Emma. Rooted.'

'And I go down and I see it. Massive picture, placed centrally, hanging on the wall. Emma – the portrait on the wall was OF ME.'

'Oooh hoo!' I said, grimacing.

'And then Tony opened the wardrobe and it was full of her clothes and not only that, but a strange perfume suddenly wafted through the air. It was HER. She was THERE. Anyway, you can *imagine* the state we're in. So we've been out and tried to drink as much wine as we can possibly consume without keeling over. We come back, Tony goes to the bathroom, lets out a small scream.'

'I did. I actually screamed.'

'And I go in and there's Tony, hand clutched to face, pointing towards a strange smear on the wall. And I go and look at it and blow me, but there was blood splattered across the wall. BLOOD! So we don't know how that's got there, let alone whose blood it is, and then I notice the connecting door.'

'There was a CONNECTING DOOR!' yelled Dad.

'Locked from the other side,' whispered my mother, in a dread hush. 'At this point, we're in bits so we get into bed, make a pact not to look in any of the mirrors and cling on to each other for dear life.'

'Then the noises started,' said Dad.

'Oh! The noises! Something was stamping on the ceiling. Actually stamping. And then there was a terrible panting noise. And then, within seconds of the stamping and the panting, the screaming started. Dulled but screams nonetheless. So Tony got out of bed and opened the shutters and all of a sudden, these huge white forms were diving and screaming. Emma,' proclaimed my mother, pausing for dramatic effect, 'they were barn owls. We were nervous wrecks.'

'I would have been in bits,' I said, nodding.

'Now then,' continued my mother. 'Shut your eyes and tell me ten things you can think of about Switzerland.'

'Umm, cuckoo clocks, chocolate...'

'Well that's all there is,' rattled on my mother. 'You have got it in two. Unless you count mountains.'

'Swiss Army knives!' shouted my father.

'We went over the border to Basel. It's got three thousand jewellery shops. It's Southend-on-Sea meets

Monaco. All it is, is old ladies staring at fifty-thousand-pound watches and clutching each other in excitement. And the Swiss have *such* tiny eyes! Is it any wonder nobody trusts them?'

'We're going to Germany tomorrow!' shouted Dad.

'Yes,' continued my mother, 'we are. I've been learning German words. *Nicht habe Kopfschmerzen!* – I don't have a headache. We'll send you a letter. I'm very glad you've got such a good job. I bet you're being paid a fortune. Are you being paid a fortune?'

'No, not a fortune,' I said, 'about a hundred dollars a week. But we've got Dee's wages too. She's been working in an ice-cream parlour. Although she says she's been cutting sandwiches mostly.'

'Well, she'll be good at that. Because she did anatomy. Are you both all right? You're managing?'

I paused before answering. If we'd had this conversation a week ago I would have broken down at this point and confessed all. I would have told her we'd been living on carrots, that we couldn't afford to take the bus, that we had sat on a kerb, Dee crying, and that I'd given serious thought to mutilating myself just so we could come home without feeling humiliated. But now, I didn't have to. I had a job that was paying me a decent wage and by my reckoning, Dee and I would make enough between us to get back to New York in comfort. We were going to be fine.

'Yeah,' I said, softly and surely, 'we're doing really well.' And for the first time since arriving in America, I genuinely believed it.

From the other side of the office, I heard Antoine's door unlocking. 'I better go, Mum,' I said. 'The boss is coming. Don't forget to send me the letter!'

'We won't! Thrilled you've got a good job! Love you, love you!'

The phone call had done me a power of good. I felt at ease, positive and as if, finally, I was letting go of my child-like ineptitude. I had blundered my way to the United States and rattled pointlessly around it like a headless chicken. But here I was, with my job in smells and my rubber stamp. I had a purpose and I was quietly banking our travel fund. There was only one slight problem with all of this. Because we absolutely, no question about it, had to be in New York on the first of October, we were only going to be able to work for a maximum of four weeks. We had come to America hoping that our pockets would be stuffed with three months of wages but as it was, we were going to be facing a cross-country odyssey on a much-reduced budget. We had originally intended to hire a car and drive, staying in motels along the way, but that was now well beyond our financial capabilities. What we needed to do was work out the cheapest way to cross the continent with no credit card and just the cash in our hands.

'There's a bus called the Green Tortoise that can take us to the Grand Canyon,' said Dee, consulting her travel bible. 'And then from there, we can take the Greyhound. I think that's going to be the least expensive option. It's still going to take a big chunk out of our travel funds. I don't think we're going to be able to afford motels all the way. Mind you, if we get overnight buses then we won't need to stay in motels.'

'Well, what about that idea I had,' I said, lifting a finger into the air, 'that we get a tent and camp? That way we can put it up anywhere. And it won't cost us a penny.'

'I think you're right,' said Dee, with a nod. 'Why don't you find a tent shop tomorrow in your lunch hour and pick up a small one?'

'Will do,' I replied and then I sat back, hands behind head, basking in the glory of my utterly genius suggestion.

The tent shop was a small, family-run business on Market Street. Filled with all manner of hunting flotsam and jetsam, my now professionally attuned nose was awash with the smell of canvas and rubber. Neither were suitable aromas for soap of course, but in terms of our impending escapade, they were as comforting as any bath salt. The sales assistant was a young man in a red checked shirt and khaki trousers with more pockets than sense. He had a chiselled, weather-beaten demeanour and looked as if he could tie any knot in a crisis. I was clearly in safe hands. 'Hello,' I began. 'I need to get a tent.'

'What kind?'

'The cheapest one you've got, please.'

'Okay. We've got a small single skin. How many people do you need to fit in it? We've got singles or doubles.' I followed him as he led me towards the back of the shop to a small spread of tents. Five were erected and on display. All of them were relatively compact. I stared at them.

'Is the single cheaper?'

He nodded. 'Yeah. The single is twenty-five dollars. The double's forty. So are you in a trailer or are you backpacking?'

'We haven't got a car so we'll be carrying it.'

'Okay,' nodded the salesman. 'Well, this one's quite light,' he added, gesturing towards a small blue tent to his left. 'Do you want aluminium or fibreglass poles?'

'Don't really know.'

'Okay. Well fibreglass is lighter but they can break easier so I'd recommend aluminium unless you're going to be trekking long distances, in which case you may prefer the fibreglass. How big do you want your rainfly?'

'Rainfly?' I asked, scrunching my nose up.

'The tent's umbrella. It's the waterproof bit.'

'One that covers the tent. That big.'

'Right. Well, this one here has a larger rainfly to that one. It's got a one-piece tub floor and comes with noseuum meshing and a roof vent.'

I stared.

'So what do you think?'

'I'll take the cheapest, thanks.'

'So that's the single here. It hasn't got much in terms of extras. You'll need to waterproof the seams. No meshing or roof vent. And it's for one person, right?'

'No, two, but we're quite small.'

He looked at me and frowned a little. 'How long's your trip? It's real compact. Are you sure you don't want the two-person tent? Frankly, we always recommend you get a tent that's for two more people than are staying in it. So you might want to think about a four-person tent. You'll be awful cramped otherwise.'

'We're camping for about four weeks. Don't worry. We'll be fine. I'll just take the single, thank you.'

'Okay,' he said, with a small concerned raise of his eyebrows. 'And do you need any equipment? Sleeping bags? Ground sheet? Stove? Mallet? Spare rope? Roll mats? Anything like that?'

'No, just the tent, thanks. That'll be great.'

He fixed me with a penetrating gaze. 'Are you sure you just want the one-person tent? And no equipment whatsoever?'

'Yes, thank you,' I said, smiling. 'Oh wait, how much are the sleeping bags?'

'They go from fifteen dollars to ninety-five.'

'No, we'll be fine. It's hot so I'm sure we won't be needing them.'

'Where are you going?'

'First stop Grand Canyon, then on to New York.'

'You know temperatures can fall to below freezing at the Grand Canyon?'

'I'm sure we'll be fine. Just the tent please.'

As I walked from the shop, tent tucked under my arm, I looked back briefly and gave the sales assistant a small wave of thanks. He was slowly shaking his head. Some might take that as a matter for concern. But not me. I had bagged us a bargain.

'The thing is Dee,' I explained later that evening, 'if I'd bought sleeping bags then we'd be down another thirty dollars. And inside the tent we'll be fine. We can lie on our towels and use jumpers for pillows. But if you think I should go back and get more stuff then I can.'

'No,' said Dee, shaking her head. 'We'll manage without. Anyway, I've got some good news and some bad news. What do you want first?'

'Bad news. What's the matter?' I asked.

'I have left Go Nutz.'

'What?' I said, eyes widening. 'You've only been there a week! But what about the money?'

'I broke the orange juice machine,' Dee began.

'Oh no,' I said, tossing the tent into the corner of the room and sitting down. 'Did they sack you? We haven't got to pay for it have we?'

Dee shook her head. 'I broke the orange juice squeezer and Mr Ho came over to look at it. And he turned to me and said, "You have strong hands for a girl." And I said, "My hands can do an octave in one, actually. They span nine keys."' Dee held up her hand to demonstrate.

'That's impressive.'

Dee nodded. 'And Mr Ho looked at my hands and then came up quite close to me and whispered, "You give me massage for thirty minute. I give you forty dollar." But I didn't quite understand what he was asking me to do so I didn't really say anything. I just stared at him. And so he went "All right! You drive hard bargain! Fifty dollar! And don't tell my wife!" So I left. And there it is. I am no longer working at Go Nutz.'

I raised my eyebrows and blew through my lips. 'Fifty dollars though, Dee…that would pay for sleeping bags…'

'I shall pretend I didn't hear that. I mean, yes, I do have a remarkably wide reach for a girl. But does that give men the green light to sexually harass pianists? No. It does not. Anyway, it's fine; I've got another job at the card shop round the corner. They had a sign up asking for staff. So I went in. You know what they say – you wait for a job for ages. Then two come at once.'

The next three weeks were spent in frugal circumstances as we had to save as much money as possible. We got up, went to work, had a packed lunch and came home again, where we would have as cheap a supper as we could muster and watch TV. Every cent we could squirrel away now meant a slightly more pleasant time on the road because whatever money we left San Francisco with had to last until we were sitting on the plane in New York, strapped in and ready to be returned home.

We had been in America for three months. And between us we had earned the following:

DEE:	Voter Revolt	$62.64
Card Shop		$356.80
Go Nutz		$80
EMMA:	Voter Revolt	$64.32
L'Aroma		$404.55
GRAND TOTAL:		$968. 31

After deducting sundries like bus tickets to work and food, we had a travel fund of $842.35. I sat, writing and re-writing our totted-up incomes and worked out that if we thought it was going to take 28 days to get back to New York (we had always planned to travel around and see the sights on our way back) then I should divide our total by that, thereby giving us a daily allowance.

'We've got thirty dollars and eight cents each to live on every day,' I pronounced, after about an hour. 'That's a lot better than I thought.'

'Gosh,' said Dee, who was packing, 'I didn't think it would be anywhere near that. Well that's good. We shall live like queens!'

This was all going incredibly well.

We had gone to bed relatively late after staying up with Palmer to watch the horror film *Child's Play*, after which we had taken it in turns to chase each other on our knees around the apartment while brandishing carving knives and screaming. We had laughed till our sides hurt and had gone to bed happy and glowing. 'What a time we've had,' said Dee, as we lay in bed. 'I never thought we'd leave San Francisco alive.'

'I know what you mean. It's been a struggle.'

'All those weeks trudging the streets. Relentless. I don't ever want to job hunt again as long as I live.'

'You won't have to, will you, what with you going to be a doctor? Imagine that, Dee. You're going to be a doctor. And save people's lives. And make people feel better. And scrape bunions. And lance boils.'

'You'd love that,' replied Dee, turning off the bedside light. 'You're obsessed with spots.'

'I am a bit. I can't deny it. The best one I ever had was when I accidentally stabbed myself in the chin with a fountain pen and it went septic. I looked like I had a tangerine stuffed into my lower lip. I went to bed, absolutely fine, and was woken up by my own chin, throbbing like an alarm clock. Our GP physically winced when he saw it. Actually recoiled. And the best thing was, I never had to squeeze it, or touch it because all I had to do to get pencil-thick green pus to ooze out of it was to grin. Ever so slightly.'

'That's disgusting.'

'And the thing was, I couldn't leave the house with it uncovered because every time I moved my mouth, out the pus would come, so my mum made me put an industrial-strength plaster over it.'

'Why did you leave the house at all? I'd have locked myself in a cupboard and not come out till it was gone.'

'I had to. I was taking my O Levels. And when we finished our last paper, we all went for a picnic and we spent the afternoon howling with laughter and when I got home, the plaster was straining at the seams.'

'Stop now,' yelled Dee, putting her fingers in her ears. 'I don't want to know.'

'And I got home, and it was literally bulging with pus. Bulging with it. And I took it off and I was staring at the gaping cavity whence the evil came and there was this strange rumbling from deep within my chin. A sort of pre-volcanic burble and suddenly, my chin just spurted pus. It was like my chin was being sick. Projectile pus.'

'Shut up!' screamed Dee. 'It's revolting!'

'And that,' I concluded, giving my pillow a quick punch, 'was my best spot.'

'I hate you for telling me that story,' muttered Dee, turning over. 'That's going to give me nightmares.'

'And then there was the time,' I began, 'when the tapeworm started coming out—'

'NO!' declared Dee, firmly. 'No more. That's it. We're done.'

I had fallen into an easy and deep sleep. It had been an extraordinary few months. We had begun with high hopes and expectations, but inexperience and naivety had left us with the knocking stuffed out of us. It had been a wake-up call to real life. Somehow, by sticking together and never giving up, we had pulled ourselves back from the brink and here we were, with a reasonable plan and a sense of purpose. San Francisco, however, had one more trick to pull.

Michael was a soppy black cat that lived in the flat downstairs. He had taken to padding in through our bedroom window in the late evening and would curl up with us, lying on his back like a baby, begging to be fussed. Sometimes, Michael would creep softly in when we were asleep and I would wake to find him lying half across my face and purring. But this time, he was mewing anxiously and pawing at the top sheet. I opened one eye and looked at him. He was fretting, backwards and forwards, crying, the hair on the back of his neck bristling. I looked around. Perhaps he'd seen something that had agitated him? Dawn had broken and a soft, dappled light filled the room.

'What's the matter?' I asked, sleepily, half sitting up. I looked to my right. Dee wasn't there. I sniffed. Michael was still pacing, his tail twitching. He stared at me and cried, urgently. 'What's that? Dee's trapped down the old well? I don't think she is. I think she's probably in the toilet.'

I looked around the room. It appeared quite normal. Everything was as it always was: the wardrobe, the dressing table, the pile of abandoned clothes down on the floor by my side of the bed, the neatly draped clothes over the back of a chair on Dee's side. As far as I could see, there was nothing out of the ordinary.

'If you're hungry, you'll have to go home, Michael,' I said, rubbing at one eye with my knuckles. The cat, still agitated, crouched low and hissed into the middle distance. I frowned and followed his gaze but I could still see nothing.

'Mice in the walls. Go to sleep, Michael,' I groaned, and let my head fall back on to the pillow.

There was no warning. Suddenly, a deep, unfathomable rumbling, not unlike the roar of a plane's engines, filled the room. The bed, pressed flush against the back wall of the bedroom, began to shake violently, its top edge rattling forwards so that my pillow fell downwards into the gap that had appeared behind my head. I sat up. The room was in chaos. Pictures were falling from the walls, lamps were crashing to the floor. I gripped into the sheets with my fingers to hold on but it was like sitting on the back of a galloping horse and I was being jerked, violently back and forth. To my right, the wardrobe's doors fell open and the clothes on hangers swung forwards, causing the whole thing to teeter and crash to the floor. I let out a small, startled scream.

I glanced up to see the windows bowing in and out as if they were no more substantial than cling film. Something to my left smashed. I turned and looked. It was the glass of water that had been standing on a cabinet. The broken pieces of glass jumped around in the small pool of water, rippling with every shock. I turned back to look at the windows. Through them, outside I could see transformer boxes exploding, phone lines bending. The door to the bedroom had fallen open and I could see into the kitchen just as the refrigerator was inching its way across the floor. Its door flung open and eggs, juice and vegetables tumbled out, spewing across the linoleum. Car alarms filled the air but under all of it grumbled the deep, unnerving noise of the seismic shifting of the earth.

I heard voices shouting: Dee, somewhere out of sight, and suddenly, through the doorway, a flash of Palmer's red hair as he dived under the dining table, yelling, 'EARTH-QUAAAAAAKE! DUCK AND COVER! DUCK AND COVER!'

Thankfully, we'd been given a lesson in how to survive an earthquake. They're a necessary evil for Californians and in San Francisco, the city that had been dealt such a cruel blow in 1906, earthquake preparedness was a way of life. It's a common mistake that the safest place to stand under if you're trapped inside a building during an earthquake is a doorframe. It isn't. In fact, it's one of the worst things you can do. Instead, you should get under or next to a heavy piece of furniture and protect your head and neck. If the walls around you collapse, it'll create a space where you can stay protected until you're found.

Dust seemed to be exploding from every nook and cranny and small cracks were starting to appear in the plaster-work. I didn't know much about earthquakes but one thing was for certain: I didn't feel safe. Coughing, I swung my legs from the bed and, avoiding the broken glass on the floor and clinging to the edge of the bed for stability, I stumbled out towards the dining-room table where Palmer was crouched, arms over his head.

I crawled across the floor and under the table where I curled into a ball, head down, the floor all the while rolling and pitching. Palmer give out a soft moan, 'Please don't let this be the Big One. Please don't be the Big One.'

Dee slid into view. 'I was on the toilet!' she yelled, crashing into the wall. Everything was in violent motion; the walls were shuddering, side tables were bumping across the floor, the overhead lampshades swaying like boughs of trees in a storm. Dee got onto all fours and scuttled towards us in a stilted, crab-like motion. I reached out for her as she neared the table and pulled her under. We were both breathing quickly, adrenalin shooting through us, and as I caught her eye, I sensed we shared an emotion that was a blend of fear and exhilaration.

San Francisco was long overdue a devastating earthquake. Predictions of an imminent and catastrophic tectonic shift were commonplace. 'Bad luck and misfortune will haunt you for all eternity.' The words rattled between my ears. The earthquake growled on. Was this it? Was this the Big One?

It was over as quickly as it had started. From start to finish it had been no more than twenty seconds. A few car alarms bleated in the distance but as the ground settled, they fell silent. We sat under the table, ears pricked, but there was nothing. No bird song, no traffic, no voices wafting up from the street. A strange and sudden quiet filled the room. It felt eerie and disconcerting. 'Jesus,' murmured Palmer, stirring to my right, 'that was massive.'

I went to get up but Palmer put his hand out to stop me. 'No, don't move yet,' he warned. 'There might be after-shocks. Wait a couple of minutes.'

'I think I peed on my foot,' said Dee, twisting her head to look at me through a gap between the floor and her arm. 'I fell off the toilet when it started. Grazed my elbow.'

We all crouched, none of us saying anything, muscles tensed, ears cocked. Another low rumble followed, this time a lot quieter, the shaking less intense. I pictured the earth-quake as a giant from a child's fairy tale, one that stomps into a village and stamps at everything in a blind rage, swip-ing a few half-hearted after-blows as its vehemence slowly diminishes. San Francisco was holding its breath, waiting for the giant to stumble off into the distance. 'Okay,' said Palmer, a few minutes later. 'I think that's it. Watch out for the broken glass on the floor. Actually don't move. I'll go get a pan and brush.'

We crept out slowly and surveyed the carnage. The earth-quake's destructive force had left everything in a tipsy-turvy state. Books were off shelves, food was on the floor, and furniture was skewed and up-ended. We stood in shock, punch-drunk from the suddenness of it. Palmer was sweeping the broken glass into a dustpan, Dee was taking a look at her elbow and I stood and glanced back into the bedroom.

Michael was sitting staring at me. He held my gaze then, with a twitch of his tail, he cocked his leg and licked his anus. And on the world turns, I thought. On the world turns.

We had been very lucky. The big earthquake to hit San Francisco that year was still silently brewing. Six weeks later the Loma Prieta earthquake, measuring 6.9 on the Richter scale, struck the San Francisco bay area. Sixty-three people were killed, 3,757 people were injured and almost 12,000 were left homeless. Palmer, Yogi and Joplin were all fine. We had missed it by a whisker.

San Francisco was telling us to get going.

Chapter Seven

Oops, I Did it Again $842.35

The trek from coast to coast is a classic, steeped in tradition, swathed in romance and here we were, rucksacks on back, about to embark on that grand adventure for ourselves. With four weeks to get to New York, we had time a-plenty to meander our way across the continent, taking in all the wonders America had to offer. We had no itinerary other than a first stop at the Grand Canyon. Dee had declared a determination to see the Edward Hopper paintings in Washington but other than that, it was a case of staring at a map and sticking a pin in it.

While our pockets were far from bursting with gold, we had somehow managed to scrape together a sufficient travelling fund. It would be a journey on a shoestring but one that would be more than adequate with a little prudence and self-restraint, qualities neither of us possessed. All the same, we were ready to have a crack at it.

The cheapest way of getting to the Grand Canyon was by Green Tortoise bus and we'd been told to go to the second lamp post on the left of the corner of First and Natoma, instructions that gave the escapade a touch of the Neverland from the off.

'Oh look,' I said, as we approached a motley crowd of people juggling and singing, 'it's a craft fair.'

'No,' said Dee, slumping her rucksack to the ground. 'I think that's the queue for the bus.'

I had never seen so much tie-dye in my life. Bare-chested, long-haired men in baggy pantaloons and sandals were banging bongos, one woman, eyes closed and arms aloft was singing something about a Sun Goddess, there were a couple of people juggling and a disproportionate amount of people indulging in random swaying.

'Excuse me,' said Dee, bending down to speak to a skinny fellow in a floppy hat sitting cross-legged on the pavement, 'is this the queue for the Green Tortoise bus?'

He looked up and grinned. 'Yeah! Join the party dudes! Wanna puff?' He held out a fat, smoking joint.

Dee glanced at it, smiled politely and said, 'No, thank you, I've had breakfast.'

The boy nodded, then, undeterred, held it up in my direction. 'Take a toke?' he said.

As unlikely as it may seem, at that point I had never managed to have an illegal drug in my life. I had no moral objection to drugs, but until then, I just hadn't come across them. I was stimulated enough as it was and it had been pointed out to me on several occasions that if I ever had drugs it would be verging on reckless. Having said that, as I stared down at the gently smouldering cigarette, one thought wafted through my mind, 'When in Rome...' And so I smiled, picked the joint from the boy's fingers and took two quite deep puffs. 'Thanks,' I said, and handed it back. 'Goodness,' I added, with a small cough, 'that's got quite a strong taste.'

'It's been dipped,' said the boy, head bobbing.

'Dipped?' I asked, frowning slightly. 'Dipped in what?'

Before the boy could answer, a cheer went up from the crowd. The bus had arrived. I turned round. A large, green hulk of a thing had pulled up. It was the sort of vehicle you'd see at a Sunday Fayre surrounded by Steam Engines and overweight men in caps and gingham neckerchiefs. It had a large pregnant bonnet across which was painted a lazy looking tortoise. The driver appeared in the doorway. He was wearing hessian trousers, a cheesecloth top, had hair to his shoulders and a spirit of laissez-faire. He was barefoot.

'Hi,' he said with a small wave and a nod. 'Wanna go somewhere?' Everyone cheered. 'Cool. Just take off your shoes and come on board!'

'It's a Schpang van,' whispered Dee, giving me a nudge. 'How thrilling.'

'Schpang?' I asked, staring up eyes agog.

'Hippy concentrate. The essence of the New Age. Au naturel. Milk straight from the cow. To cry at a butterfly. To trust your life to the moon. Schpang.'

'Oh,' I answered, bending down to untie my Converse. 'Sorry,' I said, looking over my shoulder at the boy who'd given me the joint. 'What did you say it was dipped in again?'

'Acid,' he answered, grinning. 'Good shit.'

I froze. 'Dee,' I whispered, tugging at her sleeve. 'Did you hear that? I may have done some acid. When I say, "may", I mean, "I have". But I only had two puffs, Dee. Two puffs.'

'I know,' said Dee, picking her shoes up and turning to look at me. 'I heard. It might be quite mild acid. And you only have to sit on a bus. How do you feel?'

I blinked. There was a distant fuzziness gathering momentum somewhere behind my left ear. 'I'm not sure. I think I need to be very still,' I said.

The bus's interior was a maelstrom of chaotic comfort. Instead of seats, there was one large mattress with comfy cushions scattered hither and thither. Our bags were placed in a rickety overhead luggage rack and we were invited to find a spot and stick to it, thus engaging the Tortoise Buddy-Up system whereby you looked out for the people either side of you so that no one was left behind at pit stops. I turned and found myself staring at a woman with a predilection for grinning, which was unfortunate given her teeth resembled wooden gravestones. 'Hi, buddy,' she beamed. I smiled back but something wasn't quite right. I could see her mouth moving but no sound was coming out of it.

I looked past the woman to take in the rest of the bus. We were sitting towards the front, just behind the driver and suddenly, without warning, the far end of the bus rushed up towards me and receded back again like a large, unexpected wave. I shook my head. 'What the hell...' I muttered. 'Did you just see that?'

The woman's mouth moved again but I could hear nothing. A dry, itchy sensation filled my mouth, and a creeping wooziness crawled up the back of my neck. Somewhere I could hear a loud, terrible thumping and my breath was catching in my throat. I looked around to see Dee staring at me, her eyebrows lightly frowning. Again, her mouth was moving but I couldn't hear a word she was saying. A surge, not unlike the sensation of going over the top of a roller coaster, shuddered through me. The thumping was intensifying and I realised, with some alarm, that it was my own heart, slamming against my chest. I didn't know where I was or what I was doing and as Dee's face loomed towards me, my eyes rolled upwards and I passed out.

'Here,' I heard a voice mumbling through a sea of treacle. 'It's coffee with some sugar in it. Give her that.'

I was vaguely aware that someone was holding me up and I could feel a warm plastic cup being lifted to my lips. The hot, bittersweet liquid filled my mouth and as I swallowed the world around me slowly came back into focus. To my surprise, I was sitting on some garden furniture. Dee was holding a cup of coffee to my lips and the woman with the gravestone teeth had her arm behind my back. I blinked.

'Where the hell am I?' I asked.

'We're in Safeway,' explained Dee. 'Drink that coffee.'

'What are we doing here?'

'Do you have any recollection of the last four hours?' asked Dee, a vaguely amused expression fleeting across her face.

'Four hours? What?' I said, taking another gulp of the coffee.

'So you don't remember getting into the foetal position and shouting, "No, no, I'm having a bad trip, man!"'

I stared and swallowed. 'No,' I replied, shaking my head.

'Do you remember crawling on your hands and knees around the bus asking people to tell your mum you're sorry you got permanently brain damaged?'

'Shut up, I did not.'

'Yes,' nodded the gravestone-teeth woman, 'you did. When we brought you in here you told us the fish on the fish counter were giving you the fear. My name's Harmony, by the way. Glad to have you back.'

'You told me they were singing songs from Eurovision. Do you remember the bit where you were trying to explain for half an hour how you no longer had a corporeal body and were now just eyeballs on a network of nerves? And that you were worried there was a man at the back of a bus who was actually a giant with no head?'

I couldn't believe what I was hearing. 'I've been out of it for FOUR hours? You are shitting me?'

'I think you went a bit sugar low,' said Harmony. 'I've seen it happen before.'

'How embarrassing,' I said, biting my bottom lip. 'I feel fine now. Bit hungry.'

'You told me you'd met the devil,' continued Harmony.

'Did I?'

She nodded. 'You ran round a church anti-clockwise three times at midnight on Halloween.'

'Oh yes,' I recalled. 'That's true. I did do that. When I was at school. But it wasn't the devil. It was Mr Warwick, the churchwarden. Although he does have suspiciously pointy ears.'

'Emma,' said Dee, taking the now empty coffee cup from me. 'No more drugs for you, I think.'

'Two puffs, Dee. I only had two puffs.'

'The thing is, there are some people who are built for recreational drugs and then there are some people who aren't. I think we have now firmly established, once and for all, that you are a person who has no tolerance for drugs whatsoever. You had two puffs of marijuana and you lost your tiny mind.'

'Dipped in acid, Dee! Marijuana dipped in acid!'

'Hey, everyone's getting back on the bus,' said Harmony, gesturing over to the parking lot. 'We better buddy up.'

I kept my head down for the rest of the journey, reading a book and playing the odd game of Hangman. People on the bus would occasionally catch my eye, mime a toke and laugh and I would smile back and nod my head. It was all faintly embarrassing. I had done drugs and drugs had done in me. Never again.

*

We had crossed into Arizona and the landscape was so extraordinary that most people were on their knees staring out at the strange red promontories rising haphazardly up from an otherwise flat dustbowl. There was no rhyme nor reason to it, isolated pillars standing sentry like meerkats, and then the occasional gasoline station, the odd diner, small pimples of mankind that popped up in an otherwise uninhabited landscape, sporadic reminders that we still had some part to play in this alien terrain.

From Flagstaff we had driven through dense woodland, ashen aspens soaring skywards. It was an unexpected twist, given the barren surrounds, and served as a curtain to the wonders beyond. It is a startling truth that nothing can prepare you for the Grand Canyon. As we came out from the forest, the land settled into a flat void and beyond it, the greatest hole on earth. One mile down, 18 miles across and 277 miles from tip to toe. It was spectacular.

We'd been dropped off at the South Rim and had left our rucksacks at the visitor centre so that we could hike free of encumbrances. Dee had picked up a leaflet on the front of which was a sepia-coloured illustration of old-time explorers carrying walking sticks en route to conquering a small peak. They all had bags tossed across their chests and were wearing hats to protect them from the desert sun. I blinked upwards towards an already scorching sky. 'Do you think we should buy caps?' I said, gesturing back towards the visitor centre?

'They were twenty dollars each,' Dee replied. 'I checked So no – no hats. But I think we'll be okay. We're not going down into the canyon. All the day passes have already gone. We'll just do a hike.' She opened up the leaflet and pursed her lips. 'Okay. "Day Hikes and walks on the South Rim of the Grand Canyon. Day hiking in Grand Canyon can be an opportunity to experience the canyon's rich natural beauty and immense size. There is only one Grand Canyon. Please respect it and the rights of others. No collecting or damaging of rocks, fossils, plants or animals is allowed. Throwing or rolling rocks is prohibited."'

'But I love rolling rocks.'

'"Always carry plenty of water, at least two litres per person,"' Dee read on, '"Mules have right of way. If you meet a mule string, stand quietly by the side of the trail and observe all instructions by the wrangler. Wear a hat."'

'Oh.'

'"Be sure to wear hiking boots or adequate footwear."' We both looked down at our battered black-and-white Converse baseball boots. 'That's it.' She flipped the leaflet over to the map on the back. 'Shall we do the Rim Trail?' she asked, pointing to a snaking line that followed the lip of the canyon to the west. I nodded. 'Good. Right. Well let's get water and then we're sorted.'

It was quite disconcerting, given that the average spin on the planet is 70 years, to walk through a geological roadmap that stretches back for millions. Like the tiny particles of rock bludgeoned along by the river below us, we were as nothing, a blink of an eye in the canyon's existence. The geography was breathtaking: pink ziggurats dotted the horizon, strange peaks that shifted colour, deep ruts and buttresses that sat atop floating plateaus and, scouring down the centre, the livid white-water peaks of the Colorado River, cutting new gorges with every whipping pass.

As we walked, Dee provided a running commentary on the flora and fauna while I tagged behind, long blade of grass in hand, staring out at the magnificent abyss. With

Dee chatting about 3 million years here and 6 million years there, I had tried to comprehend the timescale of the thing but the enormity of it was making my brain bend. If ever you wanted a physical reminder of the insignificance of man, this was it.

We had been hiking through the heat of the midday sun and, sweating and red-faced, we stopped at a russet crest of stone to take on water and, more pressingly, so I could deal with a large blister throbbing away on the ball of my foot. 'Have you got a plaster, Dee?' I asked, squinting upwards.

Dee looked into her bumbag. 'No,' she replied. 'I've got a tissue. But I have used it.'

I grimaced. 'It's quite bad. Look at the size of it.'

Dee bent over to take a look at the angry sore patch of skin on the bottom of my foot. 'Hmm,' she nodded. 'Don't pop it. It could get infected.' She turned away and stood, hands on hips staring out into the canyon. 'There are seven climactic belts here. In one place. That's incredible. Desert at the bottom. Ice-capped peaks at the top. That's two. Don't ask me what the other five are. Because I can't remember. It's the whole world in a hole.'

'It's amazing one river made it all isn't it?' I said, poking at my foot.

'And the wind. And rain. And ice. And the sun,' added Dee.

'Even so. It's still impressive. I can't even make a lasagna. Oh. I've accidentally popped my blister. Can I have that tissue, please?'

The popping of my blister seemed nothing more than a slightly painful inconvenience that afternoon, but as is often the way with small moments on which fate turn, its significance would not be played out till later that evening. The fact was, with a sharp stabbing pain in my foot, our pace was slowed considerably. So by the time we had returned to our starting point in order to secure a spot in the campsite, the Ranger's Office was shut. 'Oh that's annoying,' said Dee, with a small tut. 'We've only missed them by about ten minutes.'

I had wandered back over to the canyon's rim to enjoy the spectacular sunset that was in full swing. 'This is better than watching a film,' I said, as the rocks changed colour before my eyes. 'And don't worry about the ranger. We can just find a spot and sort it out in the morning.'

'Yes,' shrugged Dee, 'I suppose. Oh look. Deer.' Three deer were clambering up the canyon side and were no more than five feet away from us. 'How lovely. That leaflet I picked up about the canyon wildlife said there were deer. Didn't think we'd see any though.' Human and deer stood watching each other. Dee and I froze, not wanting to scare them. The lead deer, a female, came to the top of the rim but our presence was clearly off-putting and with a long, lingering stare she thought better of it and spun round to return to the canyon. We turned and smiled to each other. 'I love a close encounter with nature, don't you?' grinned Dee. I nodded.

'Look at this place,' I said, gesturing out towards the canyon. 'It's mind-blowing. It's inspiring. We have such a short time on earth. This is why people invent things and build cathedrals. To leave a mark. It makes me want to try and do something great.'

Dee frowned. 'Are you having a Schpang moment, Emma?'

I laughed. 'I suppose I am a bit.' I cupped my hands around my mouth. 'Mind the Gap!' I yelled. 'There you go. Normal service resumed.'

Having retrieved our rucksacks we wandered into the canyon's campsite and found an empty spot at Pine Number 269. The ground was flat, a little stony, with patchy scrubs of rough grass poking up at intervals and with the sun down and no lighting we were illuminated by nothing more than a full moon and a blanket of bright stars. A German couple were in a tent to our left and a hatchet-faced woman in military precision shorts was to our right. There was a small campfire quietly smouldering in the midst of the clearing and it was giving off a sweet, woody aroma. I dumped my rucksack to the ground. 'Okay,' I said. 'Pass me the tent and I'll stick it up.'

Dee stopped, blinked and, frowned. 'I haven't got the tent,' she said. 'You've got the tent.'

I looked down at the base of my rucksack. A creeping ice-cold sensation hooked its way up my spine. 'What?' I began, in a barely audible whisper, 'but I...'

Neither of us spoke for five minutes. We stared at each other, our mouths occasionally dropping open as if to say something but we were both so shocked at our own ineptitude that we were literally rendered dumb. *We had left the tent in San Francisco*. It was a clusterfuck of the highest order.

'Well,' I began. 'It could be worse.'

'How?' asked Dee, shaking her head in disbelief. 'How could it be worse?'

'One of us could be dead,' I proffered.

'Okay,' said Dee, sitting down on her rucksack. 'Let's think about this. We need to work out how we're going to sleep in a forest with no tent. A forest, I might add, that is rammed to the brim with wild animals.'

'How many wild animals?' I asked.

'It's a lot of wild animals,' said Dee, folding her arms. 'According to that leaflet there are bobcats, skunks, raccoons, coyotes, scorpions and mountain lions.'

'Bears?' I asked. 'Has it got bears?'

'I hope not,' answered Dee, 'because if there are bears they'll stand behind that pine, see us, and think "Mmmmm, sandwiches."'

'Okay. So we can spread our towels out to lie on. And then we can wear a jumper on our legs. And we can use our rucksacks as pillows. Or we can lie on our rucksacks,' I said, giving that suggestion a quick test. 'Maybe not,' I added, sitting up again.

'Or,' said Dee, glancing over towards the Germans, 'we could ask them if they've got any spare kit? I can't believe we missed the rangers by ten minutes. We could have rented a tent from them.'

'That was my fault,' I said, pointing down towards my foot. 'Blister. I'll go and ask.'

Miraculously, the Germans, who were clearly in the flush of love's first bloom, were more than happy to lend us a sleeping bag. They had two but were confident that they could get by with one. Leaving them happily giggling, I carried it back over and unzipped it so it could be used as a double blanket while Dee arranged our towels so that, against all the odds, we managed to create a rough but ready sleeping area. 'This isn't half bad,' I said, with an encouraging nod. 'As long as there aren't any bears.'

'Or scorpions,' added Dee. 'Or snakes. Or spiders. Right then,' she continued, with a firm nod. 'Let's have supper.'

The one thing we *had* managed to bring was a pre-packed meal made the day before in San Francisco. We had two peanut butter sandwiches, a carrot each, a corn on the cob, a packet of choc chip cookies and a pair of beers. I had also gone crazy and bought a Pepperoni stick, arguing that after a long day of hiking we'd be crazy not to have some protein. Dee had stared at me, raised her eyebrows and heaved a heavy sigh. But she'd let me get one anyway, because it was only a dollar. I had offered Dee a bite but she had declined arguing that any 'protein' it might have in it was almost certainly 'genital-based'.

Given our circumstances it was as grand a supper as you could imagine. We had a canopy of stars above us, a moon glistening behind the pine tops and a pleasant campfire crackling before us. I finished off my salami stick and ran my fingers through my hair. 'That was all right. We've done well here, Dee. Bringing those sachets of salt was a master stroke.'

'What are we going to do without a tent?' Dee asked, placing our spent corncobs into a thin plastic bag. 'We can't sleep on towels all the way to New York. Can we buy another one?'

'Where from? We're in the middle of nowhere.'

'I suppose it's going to depend on whether we can afford another one as well,' said Dee, attempting to plump her rucksack into a decent head pillow. 'I'll assess the team finances in the morning. And we can have a rethink.'

Even though we now faced the prospect of having to cross a continent with nothing to sleep in, I was strangely untroubled. I was tuckered out from a day of hiking, my belly was full and a night in a forest felt exotic and adventurous. This wasn't so bad. In fact, I couldn't think of a single thing wrong with it. I lay back, having removed a small stubborn stone that had been niggling at my lower spine, and stared up at the cloudless night sky. I had never seen stars like it. I was only used to city skies, the odd brighter star poking through the light pollution, but here, with no streetlights for miles around, the stars were unopposed. Their depth was endless;

milky layers of constellations, satellites gliding back and forth while the occasional shooting star flamed sideways, blazing up the sky. This was living. As I drifted gently off to sleep, I had not a care in the world.

I woke to a strange, inexplicable tugging sensation. Something was gently pulling at my hair. Because I had been in a deep sleep, it was hard to tell whether I was still dreaming or whether something genuinely mysterious was afoot. I was lying on my side and as one sticky, sleepy eye creaked open I could see Dee, staring at me with a rigid yet alarmed expression. 'Do not,' she mouthed, 'move ONE muscle.'

I frowned. What was she talking about? Suddenly, my head jerked back. The gentle tug had turned into a painful yank. My eyes sprang open. Instinctively, I brushed my hand to the back of my head and sat up. 'No!' yelled Dee, face filled with panic. 'Don't move!'

I turned and stared at a small black mammal with a slightly elongated body, long front claws, bushy tail and, running down its back, two distinctive white stripes. Attracted by the smell of the Pepperoni, my hair was being eaten by a *skunk*.

I let out a small, anxious yelp and, without thinking, jumped up and rushed at the creature in an attempt to shoo it away. It was a terrible error. The skunk, startled at the unexpected movement, did what came naturally. It stamped its front feet, arched its back and then, turning round, raised its tail. 'Oh NO!' yelled Dee, leaping out of the way. But it was too late. A thick scorching stink of liquid hit me full in the face. The smell was excoriating, an unbearable, sulphurous stench that caused me to gag instantly. Coughing and spluttering, I flailed backwards. Scraping at my face and chest with my T-shirt I tried to rid myself of the pungent juices of the skunk's anal glands, but to no avail. I'd been hit front and centre and there was nothing I could do about it. I stank.

'Oh my God,' choked Dee, backing away from me. 'That is AWFUL.'

I stood, clutching my nose and retching. 'What am I going to do?' I wailed. 'What am I going to *do*? Dee! I smell all wrong!'

'Go and have a shower, right now,' Dee gagged, wafting a hand in front of her nose. 'Oh, Emma. You smell like a cesspit.'

Eyes weeping from the stench, I stumbled through the forest towards the wash block. If I could have scraped my skin off there and then, I would have. Using soap to rid myself of skunk spray was about as effective as sending a small kitten to stop a charging rhino. The smell was neither neutralised nor eradicated. It was ingrained, like a dark immoveable stain. Without access to hydrogen peroxide, baking soda or a vat of tomato juice, there was nothing to be done. I would reek for days.

I had actually been very lucky. If it hits the eyes skunk spray can cause temporary blindness, so the fact I stank like a sewer was a bag of beans compared to what could have happened.

'I could smell you coming,' said Dee, as I wandered back into camp, desolate and despairing. 'This is a bad business. Here,' she said, proffering up a toilet roll, 'do what I've done and pack your nostrils with loo paper.'

So we lay, toilet roll hanging from our noses, as the odd, sudden retch punctuated the silence. Damn close encounters with nature. Damn them to HELL.

I still stank in the morning. I was a vase of rotting flower water, a rubber tyre quietly burning. Dee, who had retreated to a safer distance, tried to rally my mood. 'Let's think of the positives,' she said, chewing her lip and staring skywards. 'It'll be like pigs. They can't smell their own shit.'

'Or farts,' I mustered weakly, 'everyone likes the smell of their own farts.'

'Exactly!'

Our team finances meeting was held in a clearing covered in pinecones because, as Dee suggested, it would act as a 'convenient air freshener'. I sat on one side, Dee sat on the other. She had spent a few moments totting up the cash in our bumbags and had been frowning a lot and jotting down a few numbers in the back of her diary. She looked up at me.

'How much did you work out we had to live on a day?' she said, flicking the pen between her fingers.

'It was about thirty dollars each, I think,' I replied, picking up a pinecone and holding it against my nose.

Dee pursed her lips and sighed a little. 'I think you were a bit off, Ems,' she replied, tapping at her diary with her pen. 'Between now and when we have to get back to New York, we've got twelve dollars a day. That's it.'

'What?' I said, startled.

'Twelve dollars a day between us – that's six dollars each. You forgot to take off the bus fares. And divide by two. This is much worse than I thought.'

There was a moment's silence as the enormity of our predicament sunk in. We stared at each other.

'How are we going to afford a tent now?' I asked.

'Well, we can't,' said Dee, with a small shake of her head. 'We're going to have to think of something else.'

'Sorry I got the maths all wrong,' I said, with considerable regret.

'That's all right,' said Dee. 'It's my fault for trusting you to do it in the first place. Okay. Let's think. We have three options. We can travel by night so we're always sleeping on the bus. Although we won't be able to do that on days we're not travelling. We can sleep rough. Though we both know that would be a terrible error. Or we can try and work out if there are any people we can stay with who'll put us up for free. Who do we know?'

'Joplin,' I replied. 'We could always go back to San Francisco. And get the tent.'

'No, we can't do that, but let's call Joplin and see if she can help.'

And so we did. Joplin had a friend in Los Angeles who could put us up for a few nights. In the meantime, Joplin was going to scour her contacts list and see if she could set up a trail of house hops that would get us back to New York.

We had nothing to sleep in and I stank.

Reader, we were fucked.

Chapter Eight

Wherever I Lay My Hat

$342.29

Like thieves, we arrived in the dead of night. We had followed Joplin's instructions to the letter and found ourselves standing outside a house in Pasadena belonging to a lesbian rabbi called Shirley. It was a bungalow, painted white. A cricket was chirruping somewhere behind us and a weather vane that looked for all the world like the Grim Reaper was gently swaying. A note was pinned to the door.

'Gone to bed. Key under pot on porch. You'll need to turn off the intruder alarm. Just press the button. Your bedroom is the third room on the left of the corridor off to the right of the front room. Shirley.'

I looked around. To my right there were two cushioned armchairs, a small, low wooden table and, hanging from the eaves, a few flypapers encrusted with glue-bound insects. Dee, resting her rucksack against the front door, bent down to lift up a cactus that was to her left. 'Got it,' she said, holding up a small, silver key.

It was disconcerting letting ourselves into a stranger's house, as if we were indulging in a pre-arranged heist with a pinch of insider help. Dee slipped the key into the lock and turned to me. 'When I open the door, start looking for the intruder alarm. It'll be on the wall I expect,' she whispered.

'Shall I bring the rucksacks?' I whispered back.

'No, leave the rucksacks. Look for the intruder alarm. Then come back for the rucksacks.'

As Dee opened the door, I peered over her shoulder. A small, dim night lamp was weeping a trickle of gloomy light but other than that, the house was in darkness. The lamp was so ineffective that beyond its tight radius of illumination, there was nothing to be seen. I blinked to try and adjust my eyes to the pitch black. 'Can't see a thing,' I mumbled.

'Put your arms out and have a feel around,' said Dee, moving away from me. 'Oh hang on…what's this?' There was a small crash to the floor. 'Shit. Picture. Keep looking.'

I took a sideways step towards the wall and felt around with my fingertips. 'Do intruder alarms count down like bombs?' I muttered over my shoulder.

'I think so, yes,' said Dee. There was another crash to the floor. 'Shit.'

It was difficult not to feel anxious. I wasn't used to creeping about in a stranger's house, trying to disarm the security system. My hand hit something metallic. It had a handle on it. I squinted and pulled down. Suddenly, my face was bathed in a red, flashing light. 'Got it, Dee. Got it.' I said, in a small, triumphant whisper. 'Oh no. It *is* counting down. We've got twenty-three seconds.'

'Press the button,' urged Dee, coming over.

'Which one?' I asked, pointing hopelessly at the number pad in front of me. 'There's at least ten buttons. At least.'

Dee pondered, and then said, very quickly, 'Press all of them.'

I stabbed at the number pad with my forefinger but the red, accusing countdown still ticked onwards. 'But the note said there was one button,' said Dee, shaking her head. 'ONE button.'

'This is like the end of James Bond films but actually a lot more tense.'

Dee, nudging me to one side, took over on the button pushing. Still, the clock ticked downwards. Five, four, three… 'Dee!' I squealed, suddenly. 'Do something!' Two. One.

A loud, moaning alarm rang out. Dee, still poking at the buttons, took the jumper tied round her waist, and tried stuffing it into the box to muffle the sound. 'Oh God,' she said.

I spun round. There was a vase sitting on a table against the wall. Without thinking, I pulled out the flowers and grabbed it. 'Take your jumper out!' I hissed. 'Take it out!'

Dee pulled back and with some ferocity, I tossed the water from the vase into the intruder alarm. There was a fizzing crackle, a sharp pop and then silence. Behind us the night-light went off. 'Oh no,' said Dee, ominously. 'We've broken the house.' Our next problem was working out where, exactly, the third room off the corridor to the right of the front room was. We stood, rucksacks on back, and tried to get our bearings. Ahead of us there was a dark cavern of space. I shrugged. 'I've got nothing for you, Dee. Geronimo I am not.'

Dee edged forward in the darkness. 'I think that's a corridor ahead of us. But this isn't the front room. This is the hall.'

'Something going off that way too,' I noted, pointing off to my right.

Together we crept forwards, gingerly, like a pair of heavily laden cats. There was no noise in the house other than a thickly ticking clock and the sound of our own footfalls. As we skulked onwards, I pointed a finger towards a set of large glass doors in the distance. Moonlight was streaming in and we could see a large room with two sets of sofas and a fireplace. Above us, an overhead fan was slowly turning. 'There's a corridor over there and another one over there,' I whispered. 'They're both to the right.'

'One's a bit more to the right though,' mouthed Dee.

With Dee taking the lead, I held onto the back of her rucksack. 'This is like that bit in *The Sound of Music* when Maria first wanders round the baron's mansion,' I whispered. 'And every time I see it I think "Ooooh. Don't touch anything."'

'I know,' answered Dee, glancing back at me. 'I have extreme breakage anxiety. Especially now we've destroyed the security system.'

'I probably shouldn't have thrown water directly into an electrical device. I panicked.'

'There's a large stained-glass Star of David on the wall to your right, Emma. Don't go anywhere near it. In fact, don't even look at it.'

'Do you think Shirley will make us pay for everything we've broken?'

'She might. We'll tell her in the morning. Third door on the left. Here it is.'

Unable to turn on a light, we entered the room and stood very still to let our eyes adjust to the dark. Through the gloom I could just make out that the room seemed to be filled with umbrellas. Opened decorative umbrellas were everywhere: hanging from the ceiling, fanned on the walls, sticking up from pots. On every other surface, there were ornamental geisha dolls, staring down in sinister supplication. 'Bit eerie, isn't it?' said Dee, dropping her rucksack to the floor. 'If there's a ventriloquist dummy in here as well, we're leaving.'

Our night-time raid was over. Mission accomplished. Now all we had to worry about was confessing everything in the morning.

I was transfixed. Our hostess was not what I had expected. Shirley, the lesbian rabbi, had a black beehive, coiffured to within an inch of its life, and the oddest face I'd ever seen. Her top lip, bloodied with red lipstick, was yanked into a half grin while her eyes looked startled as if they'd been hoisted unexpectedly, like flags flapping in the wind. It was all incredibly *tight*.

'Wow,' she said, in a deep nasal monotone, 'what's that smell? I'll close the window.'

Dee and I exchanged a furtive glance. I shuffled awkwardly and stared at my shoes.

'I'm very sorry,' said Dee, taking the bull by the horns, 'but when we came in last night, I'm afraid we ran into difficulties with the intruder alarm.'

'I know,' said Shirley, still sniffing the air. 'It's fine though. I had Belinda come over and look at it on her way to work. She's my electrician. She's a lesbian. Funny. Seems worse with the window shut.'

'Can we pay for the damage?' Dee asked, unzipping the top of her bumbag.

'Thanks, but really it's fine. Wanda owed me a favour. Her girlfriend is a plumber and I got her a job. With another lesbian. So it didn't cost me a dime. Wow. That smell is *really* clinging.' She reached into a cupboard next to the sink and pulled out a can of air freshener. 'Someone must have run over a skunk.'

'Thanks so much for putting us up,' I said, proffering a small grin.

'Oh, no worries,' said Shirley, wafting the can through the air. 'I know Joplin's mom. And you know, I'm always happy to lend a hand to lesbians.'

Dee and I exchanged another glance.

'So you had breakfast?'

'No. We were going to go round the corner. When we arrived last night I saw there were some coffee shops. We can go there. Get a bagel.'

'You should go to Millicent's. They're lesbians. In fact, don't go to any of the others. They're not lesbians. So look, stay a few days. Go to Disneyland, see LA, I'll see if I can hook you up with another house stopover. I can try my sister in San Diego. But she's away this weekend. I can call her Monday. And take my car. I don't need it.'

'Thank you,' we both said.

'Oh and I'm really sorry,' Shirley added, with a sigh, 'but my sister in San Diego...she's not a lesbian. Is that okay?'

'Right,' I said, moments later as we paced off down the street, 'Shirley thinks we're girlfriends. This is awkward.'

'We might have to pretend we are, Emma,' said Dee, eyebrows knitted. 'She seems obsessed. Did you see the telephone directory?'

'No.'

'It was a lesbian and gay telephone directory. Only lesbians and gays. Imagine that. She's got a lesbian electrician. A lesbian plumber. And she only eats lesbian bagels. *And* you're only allowed to phone gay people.'

'I don't know if I can pretend we're girlfriends.'

'We don't have to go overboard. But, just to warn you, I might call you darling.'

Contrary to instructions, we had not gone to Millicent's but instead had treated ourselves to a pair of jalapeño bagels stuffed with cream cheese and crispy bacon from a totally heterosexual coffee shop that was doing two for one for only three dollars. Terrified that Shirley would find out, we stood on the corner of the street to polish them off and down our coffees. 'If we live on carrots for three days,' Dee suggested, 'then we *can* go to Disneyland. It's twenty-five dollars to get in. But we can pretend you're a child to make it cheaper.'

'I definitely want to go to Disneyland,' I said, licking cream cheese from my upper lip. 'I don't care if we have to look for food in bins to do it.'

'Disneyland it is, then. Before we head back, we should go and nick a napkin from the lesbian bagel shop. And then leave it, nonchalantly, in a prominent position so Shirley can see it. This is the sort of brilliant thinking I'm known for.'

As a child, Disneyland was somewhere I thought I would only ever go to if I were dying. In 1989, it was still a place that carried with it an air of the exotic and I didn't know anyone who had been. The closest I had come to a theme park was the odd evening at the local visiting fair where skanky blokes with spider webs tattooed on their foreheads held on to you for 'safety' on the waltzers. Fairgrounds, every teenage girl knew, were just an excuse for minor sexual abuse.

This, however, was something else entirely. I stared up at the sign that adorned the entrance: WELCOME TO THE HAPPIEST PLACE ON EARTH, it yelled. I grinned. Off to my left

I could see Disney characters wandering about and waving. Children were flinging themselves at them, arms out, wanting to be hugged. It was near impossible to be cynical. It would have been easy, given the curled-lip attitude that prevailed through the late '80s, to have treated Disneyland with the cool reticence it deserved. But there was no point. It was what it was.

It did feel amazing to be there. Here we were where Nikita Khruschev, then Soviet Premier, had been famously denied entry in 1959. He'd come to Los Angeles declaring that he only wanted two things: to meet John Wayne and to go to Disneyland. The authorities, terrified that the crowds would present a threat to the Soviet leader's life, refused to let him go. He was furious. 'Then what must I do?' he railed. 'Commit suicide? What is it? Is there an epidemic of cholera there? Have gangsters taken hold of the place?'

As I wandered up Main Street, the slice of Victorian-era America with its horse-drawn streetcar and homely stores, it amused me to think of Khruschev, the irascible and petulant commander of the second-largest nuclear arsenal in the world, stopping for a silhouette portrait or getting a Mickey Mouse hat with his name embroidered on it. How odd that the most powerful Communist on the planet had wanted to spend a day indulging in an unfettered celebration of capitalism?

The park was great fun: jungle cruises through the exotic forests of Africa and Asia, rides that took you back to the great pioneering days of the old West, futuristic visions of travel through space and time and the greatest Haunted Mansion I had ever been in. At fairs in England, there was always a Haunted House ride, a slightly damp-smelling pitch-black affair where cardboard skeletons with reflective strips that looked as if they'd been torn off the safety armbands you were given to wear home from school, would jump out at you as you turned corners. Sometimes the blokes with the spider tattoos would get involved and you'd feel a hand inching its way towards your tits. It was another pretext for mild molestation.

The Disneyland Haunted Mansion, however, was fantastic. Wandering through a mausoleum with a white hearse drawn by an invisible horse, we were led into a grim parlour where a gloomy butler awaited. We were ushered through to an octagonal room where we were encouraged to stand in the centre, away from the walls. 'Welcome FOOLISH mortals,' boomed a voice. 'I am your ghost host! Your cadaverous pallor betrays an aura of foreboding, almost as though you sense a disquieting metamorphosis. Is this room actually stretching? Or is it your imagination?' The walls around us were covered in portraits and as the floor began to move downwards, so the pictures elongated to reveal their true nature. A picture of a prim young lady with a parasol extended to reveal she was on a tightrope balanced precariously above an open-mouthed crocodile while the portrait of a gentleman lengthened to show that he was sitting on top of a fat fellow who was on top on the shoulders of a thin man who was up to his chest in quicksand. Everyone laughed. It was great.

Pitched into blackness and with the sound of thunder clapping about us, a hologram of a hanging man appeared overhead but, with no time to linger, we were moved on down a dimly lit corridor, pictures mutating as we went, into a fog-filled room. Doom Buggies awaited us. How apt, I thought, as we climbed aboard. Perhaps we could take one and travel the rest of the way in it to New York? Restless ghosts and devilish demons filled the dioramas. Ravens cawed, corpses tried to break free and at one point, passing a mirror, it seemed as if a ghoul was in the Doom Buggy with us. Everyone screamed. It was perfection. 'Hurry back...' growled a small spectre as we exited. '...and be sure to bring your death certificate.'

As we headed back to Shirley's that evening, I realised that in just over two months, Disneyland had been our one and only day of unbridled fun. It was difficult, given our predicament, to remember that we were technically on *holiday.*

'Oh no,' said Dee, as we sat down on the large sofa bed we were sharing. 'Look what Shirley's left out for us.' She passed me a book.

'Lesbian short stories,' I read. 'This is getting ridiculous. We'll have to tell her.'

'I don't think we should. It might break her. She'd probably have to call in Lesbian Pest Control and fumigate the house. Mind you,' Dee added, with a sniff, 'she'll probably have to fumigate it anyway. You still smell.'

'I know,' I said. 'If anything, it's worse.'

Dee put her feet up and reached for *Crossing America.* 'I'm slightly worried about having to go to San Diego next. It's entirely in the wrong direction.' She tapped a finger at the small map inside. 'Although it is very near Mexico. We could go to Tijuana for the day. Visit two countries and drink very cheap tequila. Though we'll have to be careful. We overspent today.' Dee reached down for her bumbag and pulled it on to the top-sheet where she counted out our remaining funds. 'Wow. We spent fifty-three dollars today.'

'Which leaves us with what?'

'Two hundred and eighty-nine dollars and twenty-one cents.'

'Which is how much a day between now and the first of October?'

'Just over five dollars each a day. God. We really are at the mercy of strangers.'

'If it gets really bad, you can always sell me into the slave trade.'

'Nobody would have you,' retorted Dee, with a grin, 'you smell like a rancid hole.'

Our situation, while not quite dire, was certainly critical. Living frugally was nothing new. I'd just been a student. I'd spent a previous summer in Edinburgh sleeping under a coffin in a Masonic Lodge with 40 other people and nothing more than one small sink to wash in. We had two large plastic bins. One was full of pasta, the other was full of cornflakes. I had survived. Five dollars a day was luxury compared to that. All the same, our predicament was far from ideal. Small acts of random kindness were now our only hope. Like human batons, we were to be passed across America into as yet unknown hands. It was a lottery. And we were the bouncing balls.

'Thank you very much, Shirley,' we said, grinning, as she packed us off onto the Greyhound to her sister in San Diego.

'Oh, don't mention it! I'm just sorry there was that dreadful smell all weekend. Can't think where it was coming from. I'll get Hannah over to check it's not the drains.'

'Is she a lesbian?' asked Dee, hauling her rucksack into the bus storage compartment.

'Oh yes,' Shirley replied, with an emphatic nod.

'Well, thank you again,' Dee added, turning to shake Shirley by the hand. 'And thanks for arranging for us to stay with your sister.'

'No problem. Hope you make it back to New York.'

Dee smiled and then turning to me, said, 'Come on, darling. Best be off.' And then, quite firmly, slapped me on the arse.

Rhoda was an altogether different kettle of fish from her sister. Petite and neat, she had the aura of Miss Ellie, a straight-up, straight-down Apple-Pie American Mom. Warm and friendly from the off, she had driven us to her small ranch just north of San Diego. It was an oasis of water-sprinkled green in otherwise dusty surroundings, a large white timbered house standing tall and alone in the middle of nowhere. A few flowering cactuses livened up the perimeter while nectar feeders drew hummingbirds to the porch. The smell of a just-baked pie hung in the air. This was going to be lovely.

Having been shown to our rooms, Rhoda took us on a small tour. The house was decorated in tasteful, muted tones while the occasional startling family portrait blared down from the walls: Rhoda and her husband, flanked down the years by two boys – hairstyles, collars and a notable decrease in enthusiasm being the only things to mark the changes. We saw three toilets, two bathrooms, a kitchen and a dayroom before being led into the main living area where a football game was being shown on an enormous television in the far corner. Perched in front of it there was a large chair, shaped like a football helmet, from which I could see one hand, clutching a beer, and a pair of impossibly long legs finished off with a pair of battered cowboy boots.

'Dale!' called out Rhoda. 'The girls are here!' She turned to us and added, with a whisper, 'He's football crazy. We'll get no sense out of him till the game's over.'

A face appeared from behind the arm of the chair. Dale, square-jawed, grisly and sun-beaten, waved a hand, shouted 'Hi' and disappeared again. Rhoda raised her eyebrows.

In honour of our arrival, Rhoda had ordered both her children home for a welcoming barbecue. Larry, a thin weedy-looking fellow with skin the colour of water, was the eldest. He stood in a lime-green Aertex top tucked into brown shorts and stared at us suspiciously. The younger was Garth, a goth, who had brought his girlfriend, Tuesday, with him and had, so far, managed nothing more than a string of random grunts. The two of them, both dressed in black, huddled themselves into a shaded corner on the back veranda away from the direct sunlight while Larry stood, beer in hand, his face screwed into a ball of inconvenience.

'So do you have goths in England?' asked Tuesday, her face paler than someone from Finland with gastric flu.

I nodded. 'Yes. They hang out at most of our major shopping centres.'

'Cool. Cool.'

'So Mom said you're sort of in trouble,' asked Larry, twisting his mouth sideways. 'Lost your tent or something?'

'We didn't lose it,' Dee explained, pouring herself a soda. 'We forgot it.'

'I don't think we're very good at travelling,' I added, with a smile.

'No,' answered Larry. 'Don't sound like it.'

'Can you get the barbecue started please, Larry,' asked Rhoda, carrying out a large bowl of crisps that were shaped like goldfish. 'Your father's still watching the football. And Garth can't be trusted round charcoal.'

'Can I do anything to help?' I asked, feeling a need to be useful.

'Oh!' replied Rhoda, putting a hand up to her forehead to think. 'Well, you could bring out the steaks for me. They're in a tub in the sink. If they're not defrosted just stick them in the microwave.'

'Okay,' I said and skipped off to the kitchen.

There was every cause for alarm. I had little if no knowledge of frozen foods other than how to put a Vesta curry in an oven or stick fish fingers under a grill. As I stared down into a sizeable plastic tub and prodded at the huge T-bone steaks stacked inside it, I wondered what to do. They were still covered in a slight crystallised frost and were solid to the touch. I looked up at the clock on the wall. It was 1 p.m. Outside, Larry was sparking the barbecue into life. The steaks needed to be defrosted in the next half-hour but as I gave them another poke and felt the hard, textural crunch of frozen meat I realised this would require technological assistance.

I took the plastic tub out from the sink and carried the steaks to the microwave. I gazed up at it. We didn't have a microwave at home, mostly because my mother insisted they gave you cancer in your sleep and caused radiation sickness. I had a vague recollection of a friend from school having one and possessed a hazy memory of seeing her put a totally frozen cheese and tomato pizza into it. The pizza had gone in on an ordinary *plate*, which felt astonishingly space age. It came out completely cooked five minutes later. I'd been agog with wonder. And the plate was perfectly fine.

I peered at the front of the microwave and poked at the corner of the large glass panel. It popped open. Remembering the plate incident, I placed the tub, with steaks still inside, on the round disc and shut the door. I stared at the digital display panel. There was a symbol that looked like a snowflake. So I pressed it. A light began flashing for the timer. I looked back up at the clock on the wall. They were quite thick steaks; twenty-five minutes should do it. I tapped the timer and pressed start. The thick hum of radiated heat began to weave its magic. My work was done.

Back out in the garden Larry was poking at the flaming charcoals with a stick. Garth and Tuesday looked as if they were in grave danger of dissolving into small, blackened puddles and Dee was watching the hummingbirds on the feeders. The early afternoon heat was scorching, there was not a cloud in the sky and all there was to be seen was one gently circling buzzard off in the distance. 'I don't eat meat,' said Tuesday, as she watched Larry poking nonchalantly at the barbecue.

'Neither do I,' added Garth, wiping his forehead with the thin black sleeve of his hole-riddled jumper.

'Since when?' asked Rhoda, who was slicing tomatoes on a chopping board?

'Since two days ago,' replied Garth, scratching the side of his neck.

'Meat's really bad for you,' chipped in Tuesday. 'It gives you cancer. And it makes you aggressive. It's all the steroids in it. It's why women are more hairy. It's probably a conspiracy by hair-removal cream companies. They've got it sewn up with meat farmers.'

Larry shook his head in disbelief. 'You're joking, right?'

Tuesday shrugged and started picking at a long thread that was hanging from her long-sleeved T-shirt. A serpent's tail weaved down the arm; the front was emblazoned with a very depressed-looking vampire.

Larry stared at her. 'Like, you do know vampires eat meat right?'

'Actually, they drink blood.'

'Blood's meat.'

'No it isn't.'

'You should ask Dee,' I said, foolishly chiming in. 'She'll know if blood is meat or not. She's going to be a doctor.' All eyes turned to Dee, who was standing with her hands behind her back, minding her own business. She shot me a short glare.

'Okay, then,' said Larry, thrusting his stick into the burning charcoal. 'Let's get a definitive answer. Is blood a sort of meat? It's liquid meat. Am I right?'

Dee opened her mouth, knitted her eyebrows together, and looked off into the middle distance. She looked as if she was about to answer but didn't. Her face screwed into a ball of concentration. Finally she said, 'To be honest, we didn't really cover this sort of thing at university.'

'It's totally not meat,' insisted Tuesday.

They both stared at Dee, waiting for a definitive answer.

'Well,' said Dee, 'Let's consider it logically. Meat is the muscle on a life form. It's solid matter. So in that instance, no, blood is not meat.'

'In your face, Larry!' yelled Tuesday, triumphantly.

Dee blinked and cleared her throat. 'But blood is an integral part of meat. And in some cultures, they bleed animals, wait for the blood to coagulate and then eat it. It's very high in protein. And I don't know many vegetarians who would touch anything if it had blood in it. So it's definitely a meat product.'

'There! It's a MEAT!' yelled Larry.

'She just said it wasn't a meat!' yelled Tuesday, in return.

'We didn't cover vampires when we did anatomy. Sorry,' said Dee, pursing her lips together.

Rhoda, wanting to change the subject, interrupted, 'So, Emma. You live near London?'

'Yes,' I nodded. 'About thirty miles away.'

'I really want to go to London,' mumbled Garth, tossing his heavy fringe out from his eyes. 'Trafalgar Square. I want to see that.'

'See the lions,' I smiled, reaching forward to take a handful of crisp goldfish.

'They have lions in Trafalgar Square?' asked Tuesday. 'Like, in cages?'

'No,' I replied, crunching, 'stone lions. Big, stone lions. People sit on them. It's a traditional thing to do.'

'And the changing of the guard,' added Rhoda. 'That must be wonderful to see.'

We had entered into safe territory. A gentle round of questioning that ran the gamut of the waxy sensations of Madame Tussaud's, the near-baffling revelation that Big Ben was the bell not the clock tower, and the shocking news that the Queen of England lives bang in front of a roundabout. All of it served to soothe the atmosphere and plaster over any embarrassing cracks that were threatening to fracture the afternoon.

Conversation drifted onwards: Rhoda was intrigued to know all about Margaret Thatcher and Garth wanted to know whether the Sex Pistols were still hanging round the King's Road. I was leaning back in my chair, listening to Dee explain that we came from Great Britain, not England, and that Wales and Scotland were not, as Tuesday believed, islands off the coast of Cornwall but were countries in their own right that made up the United Kingdom. A faintly synthetic aroma wafted gently towards me. I lifted my nose and sniffed and looked at my watch.

'I'll go get the steaks,' I said, quietly, and slipped away to the kitchen.

As I peered into the microwave I was surprised to see that it seemed to have filled with a mysterious fog. I opened the door and a damp, acrid smell gushed out. As the thick smoke dispersed, things got worse. The plastic tub had collapsed in on itself and it and the steaks had fused into a single life form. I gingerly lifted out the whole thing. It looked like something that had crawled weeping out of the transporter pod in *The Fly*. I was staring at a beef-efficient storage system hybrid. And it was wrong.

'And then,' Dee was saying as I stepped quietly back onto the veranda, 'there was the rioting...'

'Rhoda,' I mumbled, looking very sheepish. 'I've had an accident with the steaks.'

Everyone turned and looked at me.

'An accident?' she asked, looking up. 'Don't worry if you dropped them on the floor. We can stick them on the barbecue.'

'No. It's a bit worse than that. I've killed lunch.'

Rhoda, after reassuring me that it really wasn't a problem, picked up her car keys and headed out to pick up a bucket of chicken. We'd waved her off from the garage and as we watched the dusty trail kicked up by the wheels fade into the distance I turned round and noticed an incredibly flash motorbike.

'It's Dad's,' said Garth, puffing his fringe upwards. 'We're not allowed to ride it. In fact, we're not allowed to touch it. In fact, we probably not even allowed to look at it.'

'Hell,' said Larry, 'you might not be. But I can.'

I looked at the pair of them. I didn't know much about brothers but with the atmosphere in the garage starting to bristle, I could sense the brewing of a fraternal face off. With a defiant stare, Larry paced over to the motorbike and slung one scrawny white leg across it.

'I wouldn't do that if I were you,' warned Garth, watching his elder brother straddle the gleaming motorbike. 'If Dad sees you he'll go crazy. You're just showing off. Quit being so stupid.'

Being an only child, I had grown up blissfully unaware of the complexities of sibling rivalries but it was quite clear, as Larry and Garth glared at each other, that in the swirling physics of brotherly love there is one eternal truth: for every rebuke there is a completely opposite response. Larry, eyes ablaze, stared at his brother. 'I can do what I like,' he spat. 'And I certainly don't need permission from you. I know what I'm doing. Quit being such a kiss-ass.'

I looked over at Dee who had her hand to her mouth. Tuesday, who was standing next to her, was rolling her eyes. Still glaring at his younger brother, Larry tightened his jaw and flicked the key in the ignition. The garage filled with the deep throb of the motor. He pulled a face of smug satisfaction, as if in his own mind he was Steve McQueen, about to jump the barbed wire in *The Great Escape*. In reality, it was a bit like looking at a pipe-cleaner man astride a Harley. Never before was one man's body so violently unsuited to a mode of transport.

'Quit it, Larry!' yelled Garth.

A flash of defiance shot from the elder brother's eyes and, still glaring, he twisted the accelerator with his right hand. But he didn't have his other hand on the brake and rather than just revving loudly, the bike, highly tuned and powerful, shot forward, the force catching Larry by surprise.

'Jesus!' yelled Garth. 'Pull the brake! Pull the brake!'

Larry, momentarily startled, accidentally twisted the accelerator again. The bike rose up on its rear wheel like a stallion. Dee let out a small squeal of alarm. Garth's hands shot to his forehead. Larry, face set in a grimace, managed to squeeze out a small, regretful 'Shit,' but as quickly as it was up, it was down and we watched, incredulous, as the bike skidded left, then right, hitting a pile of cans, then shot forward, onto the driveway, veered left again and then toppled sideways, before coming to a sliding stop. Larry, trapped under the bike, was scrabbling on the ground like a just-landed shrimp.

'What in the name of HELL?' came a booming voice from the front door. It was Dale. He looked *livid*.

'I told him not to do it,' pleaded Garth, gesturing towards his brother.

'It was an accident,' groaned Larry, pulling his leg free from under the bike. He stood, clutching at his left arm. 'I just sat on it and it sort of took off...I think I've broken my wrist.'

Dee and I, sensing an almighty row, edged backwards, and as the wrath of Dale came showering down upon his vastly disappointing sons, we slipped through the back door of the garage and took up sanctuary on the veranda.

'It's always like this,' explained Tuesday, with a shrug. 'Last time it was over a bowl of spaghetti.'

*

Given that the day ended in a torment of resentments, it was something of a relief when Rhoda offered to drive us into Tijuana the following morning. Not only that, but she'd made some calls and had found us someone who could put us up in Santa Fe which, while not quite on track, was at least moving us eastwards. The drive to Mexico was no more than an hour and as we approached the vast fenced border, Rhoda pulled into a large car park on the American side. 'So it doesn't get stolen,' she explained, wrapping her handbag about her.

We walked the short distance to the border station and I was shocked to see how many Mexicans were standing, noses pressed through the wire, staring forlornly towards America. There was something pitiful about it, not least because they all seemed to be staring at the one icon of capitalism visible from the Mexican side of the border: a large McDonalds restaurant that sat accusingly about 100 feet away. 'A couple of years back,' Rhoda explained, nodding towards it, 'a man went crazy in that restaurant. Shot a heap of people.'

Actually, Rhoda was mistaken. The McDonalds massacre had taken place in a restaurant two miles from the border in San Ysidro but the misconception had stuck after law-enforcement officers on the day of the shooting had made the same incorrect assumption. They had surrounded the McDonalds that overlooked the border and remained there for fifteen minutes before realising their error. In 1984, James Huberty, a disgruntled 42-year-old survivalist, killed 21 people and injured 19 others in a shooting spree that was to last 77 minutes. He was finally shot dead by a sniper lying on the roof of the post office opposite. In a bizarre twist, Huberty's widow, two years after the massacre, tried to sue McDonald's, claiming that her husband's meltdown had been caused, amongst other things, by eating too many chicken nuggets. The case was dismissed.

As we passed through border control we had crossed an invisible line in the desert but it felt as if we had moved worlds away. The effortless affluence of San Diego was starkly replaced by streets strewn with beggars and dirty-faced children swarming round tourists, hands outstretched and tugging for any scrap of kindness. It was the first time I had experienced mass poverty and it was impossible not to be shocked by it.

We decided to take a taxi to the Avenida Revolución and had been ushered swiftly into the back of an ancient-looking sedan by a rotund fellow with a heavy moustache. The car had pulled off almost as soon as our door was closed and it was only after we were underway that we realised our driver was a child of no more than 12. He was so tiny he could barely see over the steering wheel and our journey was a series of neck-jerking kangaroo hops as he alternated between seeing where he was going and pressing the accelerator. He dropped us off outside the Hotel Caesar, which, he told us, in broken English, was where the Caesar salad had been invented.

'They tell you that every time,' said Rhoda, with a small shake of her head.

Tijuana was not what I'd been expecting. Years of watching *Zorro* as a child had left me with a romantic notion of Mexico: all adobe houses and jet-haired girls in voluminous petticoats dancing barefoot in the dust. Instead, this raucous border town was gaudy and loud, an out-of-town theme park for day-tripping Americans. Men in sombreros and brightly coloured ponchos peddled every idiosyncratic nick-

nack you could think of – maracas, striped blankets, cheap
silver-plated bracelets guaranteed to turn your skin green in
hours, stuffed donkeys heaped in plastic sacks, burritos,
straw hats – yet none of it felt authentic, everything seemed
to be a parody of itself. Begging children with weepy brown
eyes and mucky fingers carried little cardboard trays and
followed us everywhere, pulling at our sleeves and offering
up bracelets of sweets, sparkly buttons and tattered postcards
of Jesus with roving eyes. Every inch of pavement was
covered with souvenirs to be bought, garish and kitsch, the
most baffling being the two-foot-tall plaster-of-Paris icons
that stood to attention: Jesus next to the Virgin Mary, the
Virgin Mary next to Buddha and Buddha next to that other
great religious idol, Porky the Pig. It was cheap and disposable commercialism.

'Have picture taken with my zeeebra!' yelled a man in an
overly large sombrero. He took hold of me by the elbow and
was trying to guide me towards the kerb. 'You! Now!' he
grinned. 'Picture with my zeeeebra!'

The man was directing me to a rather sorry-looking
white donkey, its head hung low. It was covered in black
painted stripes.

'Ten dollar!' yelled the man, smiling. 'Ten dollar
for picture!'

Given that Dee and I had only a little more than ten
dollars to live on a day, a picture with the fake zebra was quite
out of the question. 'Sorry,' I said, shaking my head. 'No
thank you.' I looked a little closer at the man pulling me
towards his painted mule. His moustache was coming off, the
glue melting in the heat. Even his facial hair was a sham.

It was impossible not to feel depressed. Mexico was, no
doubt, a vibrant and wonderful place, but choosing to spend

one day amidst the worst it had to offer left me feeling hollow and unsatisfied. The cheap trinkets, the poor-quality deceptions were only there to cater for the daily influx of gawping tourists who came for nothing more than the cheap tequila. And the most dismal thing of all was that we were no different.

'Rack 'em and stack 'em!' I cried as three shot glasses were placed in front of us.

We had retired out of the scorching heat into a semi-squalid bar. It had no windows and the only light inside blazed in through the open doorway. There was no air conditioning and the only relief from the boxed-up sweat of the room was from one high overhead fan. Flies were everywhere, and around us small groups of people sat slumped at tables, browbeaten by the heat into lethargic submission.

The waiter was standing by a stool at the bar. He wore dirty beige cotton trousers and a white shirt that was undone and crumpled. He had flip-flops on his feet and was smoking a fat, pungent cigarette, the smoke of which swirled provocatively in the haze of light streaming in through the doorway. He was unshaven and had a look of permanent exhaustion about him.

We had chosen a table that was quite near the entrance where the little breeze there was could be best enjoyed. It was a flimsy, metal-legged thing with a garishly decorated Formica top, the sort you'd see in a catalogue from the 1950s. It was wobbling a little, so Rhoda folded a napkin and placed it under one leg.

We had ordered tequila, of course, and the waiter, having placed three glasses in front of us, had wandered back to his stool to finish his cigarette. He pulled a tray out from the counter in front of him and, reaching for a bottle filled with a thick golden liquid, placed it there together with a glass dish of limes and a tarnished silver salt pot. He pulled his cigarette from his bottom lip and balanced it on the edge of the bar.

'Mescal,' he mumbled, bringing the tray over. 'Bottle's nearly done. You want the worm?'

He held the bottle up and shook it a little so that we could see the thick dead grub bouncing around.

Rhoda's face lit up. 'Oh, you've got to do the worm when you're in Tijuana!' she said, beaming.

'Isn't it supposed to make you hallucinate?' I said, frowning. 'Because I'm not so great on stuff that makes you see shit. That's already been well established.'

'No,' laughed Rhoda. 'The only reason the worm's there is to show it's good tequila. The worm they put in it is the grub of the moth that lives on the plant they make the stuff from. It enhances the flavour.'

'*Para todo mal, mezcal y para todo bien tambien,*' said the waiter, pouring out the tequila. 'For everything bad, Mescal, for everything good too. Come, drink. *Parr'iba, pa'bajo, al centro y pa'dentro!*'

'Up, down, centre and in!' translated Rhoda, lifting her glass and saluting the waiter before slamming it back and sucking furiously on a lime segment.

'You do the worm,' said Dee, pushing the offending glass towards me. 'Just chuck it down. And don't chew.'

I stared at the short, stout glass in front of me. Bobbing gently inside it was a fat, corrugated grub, stained yellow with a dark brown snub at its tip. I blew my lips outwards and took hold of the glass. 'Here goes nothing,' I said, with a small look of uncertainty and then, lifting the glass to my lips, tipped the whole lot into my mouth.

The mescal was thick and bitter and instantly, I wanted to cough, which I did, but as my cheeks blew out, I slapped a hand to my mouth and managed to keep everything inside. The worm was bouncing around, skimming off my tongue and teeth and I looked up, grimaced a little and swallowed. The mescal burned down my throat causing my eyes to water but then, with some horror, I realised that the worm had not been dispatched. I stuck my tongue out. It was still there, lodged squarely in the centre. Dee let out a small, alarmed scream. I flapped my hands. 'More tequila, quick!' I wailed.

But there wasn't any. The bottle was empty. So I grabbed a quarter of lime and sucked frantically on that. But there wasn't enough liquid. I couldn't swallow the worm. I was going to have to *chew it*. I grabbed Dee's forearm and bit down. The texture of the worm was rubbery and hard, a bit like eating a stubborn piece of gristle. Dee, realising I was trying to grind it, raised her hands to her face and screamed a bit more. Heaving and on the verge of tears, I battled on, gnawing desperately to try and break the thing up but still, it would not go down. Rhoda, laughing like a drain, went over to the bar and came back holding a glass of water. I grabbed it and took a deep, desperate glug. I swallowed. I opened my mouth. The worm was *still* there. Dee screamed again. I gulped more water, threw my head back and swallowed again. *Still* it would not go down. I was *frantic*.

'Don't lean back!' yelled Rhoda. 'You need the worm to float to the back of your mouth! Not the front!'

I took more water. I was making small, involuntary whining noises and, standing up, I bent my head into my chest, waited until I felt the worm bouncing round my epiglottis and swallowed. It was gone. 'Oh God,' I said, clamping my eyes shut. 'Oh GOD.'

'That was disgustingly compelling,' said Dee, leaning forward. 'Is there any chance you can do it again?'

'No,' I said, taking another glug of water. 'That was actually *shocking*.'

But it wasn't the biggest shock I was going to have. Not by a long chalk. That delight was yet to come...

Chapter Nine

Hello!
I Must Be Going $279.21

Before we left for Santa Fe, Rhoda, who had been a glorious hostess, insisted I call my mother. Should I, I wondered, confess all, admit to the tent fiasco and explain our precarious financial position?

'Don't be ridiculous,' advised Dee. 'She'd phone the British Council and then appear on the front page of every major newspaper in tears. She'd start some sort of ghastly ribbon-based campaign. No. Tell her nothing.'

According to my flimsy fax sheet, they were now in a hotel in Venice, somewhere I'd never been but had always assumed was a city of halcyon beauty and refinement. In my mind, Venice was a hazy wafting of gentlemen in fedora hats accompanying ladies with parasols, the streets would be filled with heavenly children while rotund fellows in black tie stood on balconies singing arias. It was, by reputation, the very essence of cultured.

'It's a shit hole!' wailed my mother. 'An absolute shit hole!'

'It's nice to look at, mind,' chipped in Dad.

'Oh yes,' continued my mother, 'it's nice to look at. But that's how they suck you in. You arrive at sunset, you journey by boat from the airport and you think, well! Isn't this LOVELY! You pass all the tiny islands, the weather is glorious, what a start! And then you realise that you have to carry your luggage up five flights of stairs and there's no water to flush the toilet.'

'I tried twelve times to flush the toilet this morning,' added Dad, ruefully.

'TWELVE times! And did it shift? No. The stench is UNBEARABLE. We may as well be in a third-world country. So I go and complain to the owner. Short, fat thing, mono-brow. And all she does is give me two buckets and tell me a water tank is on its way and we need to queue and fill up. It's like something out of the Second World War! So I watch from the window as Tony queues up to get our two buckets of water.'

'I told them I was Welsh.'

'Which was sharp thinking. Because no one's got anything against the Welsh. So he gets his two buckets and then I stand at the top of the stairs and shout down instruc-tions. REST NOW! PUT THE BUCKETS DOWN! TAKE A BREATH! I mean, it could have killed him. I couldn't allow it. So we throw the water down the toilet. And then I sent him down to get two more buckets.'

'What were you doing while Dad was getting the buckets?'

'Overseeing events, Emma. I think it's important to stick to your skill set. The room we're in is the size of a matchbox. Utterly suffocating, seventy pounds a night and no breakfast!'

'I've been bitten alive!' shouted Dad, in the background.

'Oh! The mosquitoes!' wailed my mother. 'A battalion of mosquitoes descended. It's been a bloody massacre. Tony looks disfigured; I look like a pockmarked leper. He's got two enormous red lumps on either side of his nose. I've got one on my cheek, one in the middle of my forehead and one the size of a grape on the end of my chin!'

'She looks like the Wicked Witch of the West!'

'So we've slunk round Venice looking like the people who come for the dead. Having said that, one very stylish Italian woman did ask me where my bag came from. Although I did notice she was staring fixedly at my spots.'

I was longing to tell them the mess I'd got myself into but something stopped me. Perhaps it was time to stop expecting my parents to get me out of every scrape and tumble. I had spent my adult life clattering about like a newborn foal but when I returned to England, I had vast and important decisions to make. I had to prove to myself that I could cope. And so I said nothing, but instead told them that the Grand Canyon was amazing and raved about Disneyland. This was all they needed to know. I wasn't entirely sure when I'd get to speak to them again, so we said our goodbyes and made jolly remarks about Heathrow. Going home had become a reality.

Rhoda drove us to the Greyhound station later that morning and waved us off. I think she'd genuinely enjoyed having us, in that way that women who are surrounded by slightly useless men do when they suddenly find themselves with a chance for female company. It had been a funny old start to our journey – the debacle in the forest, the odd foibles of the lesbian rabbi, the burglar alarm, the microwave – and I wondered if this is just what happens when you don't know where you're going next? We had one certainty: we had to be in New York on the first of October. What happened between here and there was anyone's guess.

We had accidentally got on the slow bus to Santa Fe, a meandering route that stopped off at every point between San Diego and our destination so that, rather than arriving in the early evening, we got in at about two in the morning, far too late to call Nathan, the artist friend of Rhoda's who had kindly agreed to put us up. The Greyhound station, which apparently is the smallest in America, was closed and we peered in through the glass windows into a tiny building that wasn't much bigger than a small village post office.

There was a 24-hour convenience store opposite and so, dragging our rucksacks behind us, we decided to sit out the night and wait until the office reopened in the morning. I hadn't slept on the coach and was heavy with tiredness and as we pushed our way through the heavy glass doors, there was a belch of illumination, coruscating strip lighting that left me feeling slightly nauseous.

The store was empty apart from a pasty-looking fellow manning the till. He was in his early twenties, had buckteeth and was wearing a red paper hat that veered sideways. The name-tag embroidered in yellow on his maroon shirt told us he was called Kirk. He had a greasy complexion, his skin thin and grey while his hair, long and brown, was tied into a pony-tail. He looked as if he hadn't seen daylight in months. He looked up and put down the magazine he'd been reading. 'What can I do for ya?'

'We just got off the Greyhound,' explained Dee, hoisting a thumb back in the direction we'd come from. 'But the station is closed. Do you mind if we wait in here? It feels a bit safer than just sitting out in the dark.'

'I don't mind,' shrugged Kirk. 'But I guess you'll have to buy something.'

Dee turned and looked at me. 'See if there's anything you want. Try and stick to no more than a dollar.'

I slung my rucksack to the floor and wandered over to a stand. Cans of bug spray and disposable lighters were stacked next to thin strips of cured beef that were only a dollar if you bought three. Bargain. That was supper for three nights right there. I picked them off the shelf. Dee took the packets and looked at them. 'They look like off-cuts from our anatomy cadaver. Still. They are protein. We'll take these please.'

I lent onto the counter, head in hand and stared at Kirk as he ran it through the till. On his right arm there was a large, white rectangular dressing, which he kept scratching at. 'Dang, this itches! Shouldn't touch it though. That's the worse part.'

'What did you do?' I asked, blinking heavily.

'Got me a tattoo,' grinned Kirk, proudly. 'Had it done a couple of days ago. But hell, it is driving me *crazy*!'

'What's it of?'

'*Starship Enterprise*,' he said, with a nod. 'And it says Captain Kirk underneath. Cos that's me. Kirk. Captain Kirk.'

'To boldly go where no man has gone before,' I said, yawning.

Kirk's face lit up. 'Hey! You a Trekkie too? Whaddya think of *TNG*?'

I shook my head.

'*The Next Generation*?' explained Kirk. 'Cos even though everything about it is way better than TOS – the acting, the effects, the plots – it's still not as good, right?'

'TOS?' I asked.

'The Original Series.'

'Umm, to be honest, I don't think I've seen the new one. But yeah, I liked the old one.'

'Cool, cool,' nodded Kirk, grinning. 'So, do you guys want a hot doughnut or a corn dog? They're real good. I cook them myself,' he added, gesturing towards a microwave.

We settled ourselves towards the back of the store where it was marginally less blinding. Dee had found a can of lemon air freshener and had quietly squirted some in my vicinity before saying loudly, 'Whoops. I didn't think that would go off! Sorry!'

'Wow,' I said, sniffing my grubby top. 'That really is lemony. That's nuclear lemony.'

'I just thought it might help with the smell. You're still a bit skunky.'

In the dark, the brightly illuminated 24-hour store was the irresistible beacon for all who wandered the night – the sleaze with his drunk date looking for booze so they could carry on the party; the flame-eyed crazy in need of a sugar rush; the tousled, half-dressed insomniac who came in just for the company; the bleary-eyed husband dispatched to get pickles for his pregnant wife – one after another, they pulled up in their cars and crawled into the store. We sat, head in hands, and watched the strange ebb and flow of the night-time trade. 'We're like the nighthawks,' said Dee, head in hand. 'In the Hopper painting, you know. The one looking into the diner at night. Nighthawks. That's us.'

Despite feeling exhausted, I was unable to nod off and instead had entered a strange plasma-like state of consciousness, like a lava lamp made flesh. Dee, on the other hand, had managed to fall into a deep sleep. She was sitting bolt upright. It wasn't natural or right. She was like a horse. Kirk kept himself to himself, flicking through magazines and listening to his Walkman, switching it off only when a new customer came in. Occasionally, he tossed another frozen foreign body into the microwave and the air would be filled with the warm smell of processed food. 'I love cooking,' he told me, as he placed something unidentifiable into a cardboard carton.

It was close to seven when I saw the flash of something large and silver pulling past the store. I nudged Dee, who was still asleep. 'I think the Greyhound is here. Let's go see if the office is open. God, I'm *so* tired,' I mumbled, letting out a gaping yawn.

'Don't worry,' said Dee, who seemed alarmingly refreshed, 'Once we get to Nathan's you can have a bath and a snooze.' We left the 24-hour store, thanking Kirk as we went, and scuffed our way towards the Greyhound. A young couple were outside looking at a map while a group of lads were standing over a pile of suitcases. We walked past them towards the station. 'Once we've phoned Nathan,' Dee began, her hand pushing on the door, 'we can see if they've got any local info pamphlets. And then we can—'

Dee came to an abrupt halt and stood, stock still in the doorway. Her rucksack slipped from her shoulder and she turned to me, eyes wide, mouth agape. As is often the way when you are looking at someone in the grip of a cold panic, it takes a while to digest and process the situation but there was no time for digesting and processing. Dee had clearly seen something and I wanted to know what. I walked towards her and peered past her into the Greyhound station. There were a few people inside. One was picking a map of Santa Fe from a dispenser, another was putting a dime into the telephone box and another was sitting on a blue plastic chair and doing up his shoelace. I stared at him. I stared at him again. 'Oh my God,' I whispered.

He looked up. 'I don't BELIEVE it!' he screamed, leaping from his chair and bounding over towards us. 'Ha ha! This is AMAZING!'

It was Guy. The man who had pursued me relentlessly through my last term at Oxford. The one from the BUNAC meeting. The one I always avoided. The one who, if I was at anything and he turned up, I left. And here he was. In Santa Fe. In the smallest Greyhound station in America. Kill. Me. Now.

He clasped me to him, my arms hanging limply by my side. 'WOW!' he yelled. 'Total WOW! Can you believe this?'

'No,' I said, mustering a half-hearted smile from the depths of my bowels, 'No, I really can't.' I looked and smelled like an old kipper. And here I was, standing face-to-face with someone who had hunted me down with the tenacity of Pepe Le Pew. Which was ironic. 'I was sprayed by a skunk a few days ago,' I said, clearing my throat. 'Just to explain the smell.'

'Actually I can smell something really lemony. Like a toilet freshener.'

'I gave her a quick spray,' explained Dee, with a nod. 'Trust me, it's an improvement.'

'Sprayed by a skunk, though? Wow.'

'In the Grand Canyon. Long story. It is wearing off. But it has lingered, hasn't it, Emma?'

I nodded silently.

This was a ghastly turn of events. I was shattered beyond reason and somewhere, in the back of my tortured mind, dark thoughts of how I could kill a man and get away with it began swirling. Hang on though, I thought, perhaps he was here to catch a bus and LEAVE.

'Are you waiting for a bus?' I asked.

'No,' he replied, beaming. 'Just arrived.'

Shit.

'Where are you staying?' I asked.

'Don't know yet,' he answered, crossing his arms and rocking on his heels. 'But hey! Maybe I can hook up with you two?'

'We're staying with a friend of a friend,' chipped in Dee.

'Perfect!' he grinned.

Shit. Shit. Shit.

All I wanted to do was lie down on the floor and weep. This was, without a doubt, my worst living nightmare. Bad enough that he was staying in Santa Fe, even worse than that he now appeared to be hell-bent on staying with *us* and then an even more terrifying thought gripped my soul. Perhaps we were *stuck with him till New York!* I blinked and shook my head. No. He was still there. I wasn't hallucinating.

Shit. Shit. Shittity. Shit. Shit. Shit.

Dee had peeled off to use the phone to call Rhoda's friend Nathan to tell him we'd arrived and warn him that our party was now increased by the sum of one. Guy stood, hands in shorts' pockets, and talked at me while I nodded and chipped in the odd interested sound. I didn't hear a single thing he said to me. The only thoughts screaming between my ears were *how do we get rid of him* and would it be possible to just *run away?*

I had often wondered if I was the sort of person who would cope well with a sudden shock. I fantasised that I might be one of those people with epic jaws who could face adversity head on and allow any impediment to ping care-lessly off my chest. Turns out I wasn't. I was a wreck, a shat-tered hull. Half an hour later as we climbed into Nathan's cream-coloured Mercedes I stared at Dee, lifelessly. Her eyes widened and she grimaced. Guy had tossed his bag into the middle of the back seat between us. Dee silently pointed towards a bulging pocket. I followed her finger and saw a large, unopened packet of condoms. I retched and swiftly wound down my window. I had entered a newly discovered ring of HELL.

Nathan, at least, was as affable a fellow as you could hope to meet. In his mid-thirties, he was a tanned and attractive artist with a shock of blond hair. If I hadn't been in such a maelstrom of despair I might have cheered up there and then, but it was hopeless. I was wearing a scowl deeper than the seven seas. I was bothered beyond belief.

We were taken to Nathan's house, a small adobe bunga-low just north of the city centre. It was comfortable, deco-rated throughout with Mexican influences, cosy window seats scattered with cushions and bookcases everywhere. I would be sharing a room with Dee while Guy would have the study towards the back of the house. 'I think,' said Dee, as we all stood in the kitchen, 'that before we go out, we should have a couple of hours' sleep. Just to recharge the batteries.'

'Good call,' boomed Guy, nodding. 'I didn't catch much kip on the overnight. So I'll get a few hours' zeds in too. Then let's go into Santa Fe, yeah? Check out the sights! We can go stand on the steps of that church that's in *Twins*. Ha ha!'

'I must have done something infinitely evil in a previous life,' I wailed, moments later, flinging myself down onto the bed. 'Please tell me it's not happening. "Bad luck and misfortune will haunt you for all eternity!" So far, it's been true!'

'Emma,' said Dee, sitting down on the edge of the bed next to me, 'we are not going to be beaten by a biscuit. It's mumbo jumbo.'

'But what are we going to do now? We're stuck with him.'

Dee sat and pondered. These were the moments I loved her for, her calm contemplation while the world about her raged. 'He said something in the car about having come from

Washington,' Dee began. 'And that he was heading to California. He's moving in the opposite direction. We'll be fine. It'll be here and that's it. We've just been incredibly unlucky.'

'Think how big America is, Dee. What are the chances? I mean, really? I am CURSED!' As I spoke, a terrible, stabbing cramp gripped my lower abdomen. 'And talking of curses,' I groaned, 'I think my period's started. Even my womb is repulsed by him.'

I was in agony. I had managed to sleep on and off for a few hours but the cramps had kept me awake and I had lain, scrunched into the foetal position, in mental and physical anguish. Despite my better judgement, I had agreed to get a bus into Santa Fe centre, thinking that a gentle stroll might walk off the worse of the pain but I was pale and bent over and the scorching heat was doing nothing to improve my mood.

We had decided to go to the Palace of the Governors, the oldest continually occupied public building in the United States. Built in 1610, it was a low, adobe structure with a long balustrade across its front. It had once been the seat of government for the Spanish colony of Nuevo Mexico but was now a museum, paying host to all manner of historical state artefacts. I trailed round after Dee and Guy, staring at gramophones and pistols, and reading about Frontiersman Kit Carson and his battles with the Navajo, but with every passing minute I was feeling increasingly unwell.

'Huh!' exclaimed Guy, tapping at a leaflet he'd picked up. 'You know *Ben-Hur*, the film, well the guy who wrote the book was the governor here and he finished writing it in this building. Like, *here*. He wrote the crucifixion bits after he'd come back from seeing Billy the Kid.'

'Interesting,' nodded Dee, who was peering at a clock with a large bullet hole in its face.

'I don't feel very well,' I said, with a small groan. 'I think I need to sit down.'

Dee turned to look at me. 'Yes,' she said, 'you have gone a bit green. Can you bear to stay out, though? We've spent half our daily allowance on these tickets. And they include the History Museum as well. Do you think you can manage it?'

'Not sure,' I said. 'Perhaps I'll just go and sit in the toilet for a bit.'

'Here,' said Dee, reaching into her bumbag for some painkillers. 'Take these. We'll wait for you outside. Take as long as you need.'

Guy sniffed and said nothing. Sensible.

I was in a pretty bad way. Cramps that normally lasted an hour were lingering and getting worse. To add to my woes I was drenched in sweat and felt disorientated and confused. It was hard to tell whether my hormones were running riot or whether the sudden presence of Guy had sent me into a tailspin, but either way I was in an advanced state of befuddlement.

I had sat in the toilet for about twenty minutes, waiting for the worst to pass and for the painkillers to kick in. The cramps had eased but I still felt groggy and as I walked out from the toilet and staggered my way back to the palace's balustrade, I was stumbling and tripping over my own feet. Dee and Guy were standing on the corner, chatting in the sunshine. A coach of tourists had pulled up and elderly Americans in sun visors were disembarking, all reaching for their cameras and snapping away. I staggered onwards.

Seeing me approach, Dee turned to me and smiled. I came closer but her smile suddenly fell and her face mutated into a look of abject horror. Guy, also looking at me, grimaced and turned his back. I was confused. I looked behind me. Nothing there. What were they looking at? Dee, wild-eyed, rushed forwards and grabbed me by the arm.

'Emma,' she hissed, urgently, 'go back to the toilet. Now!'

'What?' I mumbled, dizzy with pain and the heat. 'What's the matter?'

'Look!' Dee urged, pointing downwards with her finger.

I cast my eyes down. Hanging from the button of my shorts was the used tampon that was meant for the toilet, dangling in all its bloodied glory, bouncing gently between my thighs. How it had got there, I had not the first clue.

I was standing in a public place with a used tampon swaying from my shorts' button, like some sort of ghoulish key chain. I shook my head. 'No.' I said. 'No. Dee. No.' As is often the way in emergency situations, it's a toss up as to what to do first. In this instance, I had two clear choices: get rid of it and then kill myself. The question for me was – in what order?

Dee ran back to Guy, who'd bought a few postcards, and came back with the paper bag he'd been given. 'Put it in this,' she urged. 'Quickly.'

By now I was half weeping, half laughing. The elderly tourists were still snapping away. I'd be in their holiday pictures. Let's hope they don't get out a magnifying glass to have a closer look, I thought. This was the single most embarrassing event of my life and here I was, rooted to the spot, unable to do anything. Dee, firm yet calm and realising I was in a state, flicked opened the paper bag and slipped it under the offending appendage. 'There,' she said, 'now unhook the string and I'll put it in a bin.' I watched as she quietly disposed of the package of ghastliness. My face was burning with embarrassment. I was an abject failure. I couldn't even put a tampon down a toilet. I was a fucking idiot.

Guy, equally mortified, was at a loss as to what to say. Dee put her arm round me and tried to stop me crying. 'It could happen to anyone,' she soothed, lying through her teeth. 'And it doesn't matter. Not many people saw.'

'Only that coach full of tourists,' Guy proffered, trying to make light of the matter. 'Some holiday snaps they'll be. Ha ha!'

We both glared at him.

'Right,' said Dee. 'I think we all need to sit down and have some lunch. And we're not getting up again till Emma feels better. And you,' she added, shooting Guy a solid stare, 'can keep quiet.'

We found ourselves in The Green Onion, a bar that served cheap food, had an electronic dartboard and a basketball machine where, for one dollar, you could throw five baskets. It had bare, wooden floors, large oak tables with trestle seating and one very loud jukebox. We had six dollars to spend to keep ourselves within our daily allowance but Dee, thinking I needed some red meat for sustenance, insisted I order a steak, which instantly took us over our limit. 'It's all right,' she said, with a sigh. 'It's sort of an emergency. And we can be more frugal tomorrow. I expect it'll be massive. So we can share it.'

Guy, who had worked for a firm of lawyers in New York, a job he'd arranged before he'd left Oxford, was flush with cash and gallantly went to the bar and bought a round of beers. 'Thanks,' I said, acknowledging the gesture. 'Sorry about that. I expect I'll laugh about it one day. In twenty years.'

'It's times like this when I think I'm lucky to be a bloke,' replied Guy, sucking on his beer bottle. 'It makes you realise how debilitating all that business is. It's really crippling, isn't it? I suppose that's why some jobs don't have women.'

Dee looked up and frowned. This was dangerous ground for a young man. 'Like what?' she asked, fixing him with a hard stare.

'Well, umm...' thought Guy, shifting in his chair, 'like astronauts. No woman's ever gone to the moon.'

'That's not because of periods,' quipped Dee. 'That's because there aren't any *shops*.'

After lunch, I began to feel much better and we headed back to the central plaza. The Cathedral Basilica of Saint Francis of Assisi stood at its far end, small in terms of European cathedrals I'd been used to, but next to the low-roofed adobe structures that surrounded it it had a grand and towering air. Around the cathedral and in every shady nook, native Pueblo Indians and artists were selling their craftwork: turquoise and silver jewellery, paintings, small, carved wooden animals and decorated pots. We couldn't afford anything, of course, so Dee and I decided to just smile a lot and nod.

We couldn't spend another dime that day, so we'd had a quick consult of Guy's guidebook to find everything that was free and had headed to the Loretto Chapel, which, by all accounts, had a 'miraculous staircase'. The staircase in question was a wooden spiral structure that connected the floor of the chapel to the choir loft above it. According to legend, the builders of the chapel had forgotten to build any sort of stairway up to the choir loft, leaving the nuns who lived there in a quandary. But then a mysterious man had turned up, locked himself in the chapel for three months and then disappeared, leaving behind him an intricate spiral staircase, with 33 steps, no central support and all held together by nothing more substantial than small wooden dowels. We all stared up at it.

'If all he had was a set-square, one saw and some warm water, then that,' I said, nodding upwards, 'is impressive.'

'And they don't know where he got the wood from,' said Guy, reading his book. 'The timber's not native to this area.'

'Perhaps it is a miracle,' said Dee. 'You should run up and down it a few times, Emma, see if it turns your terrible luck around. Actually, don't. It doesn't look very safe. You'd probably bring it down.'

'And the chapel with it,' I nodded, ruefully.

We'd arranged to meet up with Nathan, our host, at six. He had offered to drive us to a sculpture park in the village of Tesuque, five miles outside the city, and he was keen for us to see it at dusk so we could enjoy the sunset. The park, he told us, normally closed at five but he was friends with the owner and so had arranged for us to see the place after hours. It was, he told us, a prominent bronze art foundry where, during the day, visitors could watch molten bronze being poured into moulds. 'Do you use the facility?' asked Dee, who was sitting in the front passenger seat while I was in the back with Guy.

'Yes, I've made a couple of pieces here. Some of my more complex works, actually.'

'I don't know how I feel about modern sculpture,' answered Dee, confidently. 'I'm never sure what I'm supposed to think.'

Goodness, I thought, as I sat back and watched Dee and Nathan argue the merits or otherwise of modern art, it must be amazing to be so good-looking. There was Dee, bathed in the sort of light reserved for Hollywood starlets and there was Nathan, all tanned muscles, hands flecked with paint and brilliant at parking. Beautiful people, I mused, have different lives to the rest of us. Clothes fit them perfectly and they never get spots. They are never excessively hairy or lumpy. They never have thick ankles, their teeth are gorgeous and they don't smell. I turned and looked at Guy. His pale white legs were covered in thick, dark hairs and he was wearing socks with espadrilles. The flies on his shorts were undone and I could see his pants peeping through the gaping slit. They had Minnie Mouse on them. I leant my head back and contemplated the day's events. Ghastly didn't begin to cover it but through it all, Dee had been a steady trooper. It was amazing that she was friends with me. Forget the staircase, *that* was the miracle.

The park was hidden away in the nook of a mountain, surrounded by livid red rock. The last sunlight of the day was bouncing between the sheer walls of jagged stone, refracted and reflected, a mellow pink that melted the rock's hard edges. There was a cabin to our left and through the window I could see a couple of people standing together and chatting. There was a veranda in front, covered in pots of paint, saws, power tools, lengths of fat, gnarled rope and a few random heaps of twisted metal. If anything, it looked like the entrance to a scrapyard. To the right of the porch there was a man in cut-off dungarees. He had on a large mask and was cutting the metal casing from a large washing machine.

'Hi, Tom,' waved Nathan, as we wandered past. The guy stopped and waved back. 'He's making a tank entirely from domestic products,' Nathan explained. 'Fridges, cookers, that sort of thing. Real clever.'

The bulk of the sculptures on display were scattered about a small oasis of green and veered between aggressive, mathematical shapes and softer nudes, one of which was set in a fountain, legs daintily pointed downwards while it held in its hands a long rod that dangled stars over a grinning moon. If truth be told, I preferred the more naturalistic pieces to the random slabs and slates yet, at the same time, the strange chaos of the more twisted pieces seemed a fitting metaphor of our time in America. 'In the disorder,' Nathan explained, 'there is still order. Amidst confusion, there is always clarity.'

If I was the chaos, I thought, then Dee was the clarity. The steady point to which I could always return. I think there is nothing greater in life than a best friend on whom you can always rely. Dee was my North Star and I would be lost without her.

Guy got back on the Greyhound the next morning. I would never see him again.

Chapter Ten

And All That Jazz

$243.21

We had a slight problem. Nathan knew lots of people who were happy to put us up but they all lived west of Santa Fe, which was going to be of no use. With a quick tot-up of the family fund and a plan that meant we would sleep on the Greyhound two nights in a row, Dee deduced that if we lived off the beef jerky we still had from the 24-hour convenience store then we could not only go to New Orleans but we could spend one night in a youth hostel there. 'It's really cheap,' she explained.

'And what will we do then?' I asked.

'I don't know,' replied Dee. 'But we've got three days to come up with something.'

We had three changes to negotiate, the first at Albuquerque, in the shadow of the deep pink Sandia mountains, the second at Amarillo, 'It's the helium capital of the world,' Dee told me, and the last at Houston, where I quietly hoped I'd see a rocket. From there, it was plain sailing to the Mississippi and New Orleans. All we had to do was stay awake for the relevant changeovers. Given our terrible run of bad luck, we decided that it would probably be for the best if one of us was awake at all times. 'We can sleep on shifts,' explained Dee. 'That way we won't fuck up.'

I nodded. This was an excellent plan.

*

We watched while the driver tossed our rucksacks into the hold and then, happy in the knowledge that our every worldly possession was stowed safely, we boarded the Greyhound. The first stretch to Albuquerque was the warm-up, a mere 63 miles and before we knew it, we were crossing the Rio Grande and disembarking, standing on the tarmac and watching our rucksacks being off-loaded. I had attempted to take my rucksack off myself as my mother's words about never losing sight of luggage rattled somewhere round the back of my brain, but had been told, quite vociferously by the driver, that he knew what he was doing, thank you very much, and I was to back off. Back right off.

'I think he put a tag on our stuff that said it's going all the way to New Orleans,' said Dee, nudging me. 'They must have a system.'

'Have we got enough for a coffee?' I asked, opening up our first packet of beef jerky.

'Not really,' said Dee. 'Maybe tomorrow we can think about sharing one. If we're desperate.'

The journey from Albuquerque to Amarillo was considerably enlivened by the fact we were travelling on the legendary Route 66. Decommissioned only three years earlier, the stretch we found ourselves on was technically the new interstate 40 but was also signposted as 'Historic Route 66', a scrap of the once mighty Mother Road that straddled the continent. There was something impossibly romantic about being on a trail steeped in tradition and as we journeyed east from Albuquerque, we passed ghost towns, old neon signs and small Indian settlements. The road rose from the Great Plains to meet the Rockies and then dipped into Santa Rosa, an oasis of green amidst the flat red mesas. We passed through Austin, the midpoint of America, and then down through the panhandle plains towards the yellow wild-flowers of Amarillo. It was a shame that we had neither the time nor the money to have journeyed this once great road with more care and attention. One day, I thought to myself, I shall come back and do this properly. One day.

We had a long three-hour wait at Amarillo and I had stood, staring into the opened hold of our Greyhound until Dee pulled me away telling me to 'stop worrying about the rucksacks'. We were on packet number two of the beef jerky and we sat on a small wall in front of a diner chewing on it as the smell of cheeseburgers wafted over us.

'Try shutting your eyes,' I suggested, 'and pretending you're eating some delicious roast beef.'

Dee closed her eyes and bit down hard on her strip of jerky. 'No,' she said, chewing hard, 'not working. Although I may be in grave danger of breaking a tooth and possibly my own jaw.'

Our journey took up again at dawn and the road from Amarillo to Dallas was relentless and flat. Ranches and the odd oil drill punctuated the landscape but other than that, planes stretched as far as the eye could see. Every now and again the driver would stop to deliver a parcel and we would wander off into a lonely diner, use their toilet and meander back again. It was slow and it was dull. Dallas then, when we approached, was all the more startling as it rose from the edge of the horizon like Oz, a great sparkling city dropped onto a spot where it had no business being. There was no full-length stop here but a momentous chill went through the pair of us when we realised we were driving down Commerce Street, the road where that other Kennedy was killed with that infamously bendy bullet. At Dealy Plaza there was a man with a placard that read, KENNEDY WAS

KILLED BY THE CIA. He was being stared at by another man eating a sandwich. A small cluster of tourists were standing behind him, cameras all pointed towards the Texas School Book Depository.

'I wonder who did kill JFK,' I pondered, tapping Dee on the shoulder.

Dee had set up store immediately in front of me as, much to our astonishment, we were, bar a couple of people down near the front, the only people on the bus. She turned round and looked over the back of her seat.

'Don't know,' she shrugged. 'Definitely not just Lee Harvey Oswald. In fact, I'm not entirely sure he had anything to do with at all.'

'Do you think we'll ever find out?'

'Doubt it. It'll be one of those eternal mysteries. Conspiracy theories start here.'

I nodded. 'Do you think when we get to Houston we can share a cup of coffee?' I asked. 'I think I might be desperate now.'

'Me too,' Dee replied. 'And I think I'd rather die than eat another bit of beef jerky. It's like chewing nose gristle. Or a sunburned ear.'

We'd been on the bus for 36 hours. We hadn't washed, we hadn't been able to change our clothes and had survived on nothing but highly salted meat scraps and the odd glug of water. We had, at one point, sat and stared like Pavlovian dogs as a woman and her family tucked into a lovingly prepared picnic of spicy chicken, coleslaw, soft rolls and home-made lemonade. Somewhere during the night when I was on staying-awake duty, I had fallen into conversation with an unshaven man sitting on the back of the bus. He'd just got out of jail for Grievous Bodily Harm. Never mind that, I thought, I just wanted to talk about food. So we talked about 'grits', a thick, maize-based porridge, for half an hour. And nothing else. By the time we reached Houston I was at breaking point and after much lobbying from me, Dee had relented and released the family purse so that we could sit on plastic chairs and share one solitary cheese-burger and one solitary coffee. After two days of jerky, it was positively ambrosian.

We reached New Orleans just after lunch the next day and after the cool air conditioning of the Greyhound it was some-thing of a shock to walk out into the thick heat. I had never experienced humidity like it. The air was saturated, the atmosphere dense and stifling and within minutes I was drenched in a thin layer of sweat. I had wandered round to the hold of the bus where our driver, wiping his forehead with a handkerchief, was starting to unload the bags. 'Go wait over there,' he said, throwing me a look over his shoul-der. I followed his gaze and saw a sign that read PICK UP.

The room was a sparse affair, moss-green walls, a few chairs and a counter, behind which stood a uniformed black woman who was cooling herself with a hand-held fan. Everyone looked wilted and wound down as if the heat had sapped them of all energy. Next to the counter there was a low belted carousel and presuming that's where the bags would come, I stood next to the entrance flap, a curtain of slatted rubber, and waited. Given that our bus was the only one that had recently arrived and that no more than six people had got off I thought it was safe to assume that this would be as straightforward as it came so when, thirty minutes later, noth-ing had come out I was understandably baffled.

'Excuse me,' I said to the woman behind the counter. 'Is this where the luggage comes?'

'Nuh-huh, that's for packages. Yo' get yo' bags outside,' she replied.

I shot Dee a short, exasperated glance. 'He told us to come in here,' I muttered as we made our way to the door. Back outside and there was one man sitting on a wooden bench smoking. About five feet from him, on a raised kerb was Dee's rucksack. But of mine, there was no sign. I turned and went back into the pick-up room.

'Hi,' I said, quite urgently, 'is there any other place where the luggage might have been left from off that Greyhound?'

'Which one?' she asked, pursing her lips.

'The one that just came from Houston,' I replied, turning and pointing where the Greyhound had been but was now gone. 'The one that was just there. That Greyhound.'

'Well, it gone now,' said the woman, with a shrug.

'Right,' I said, a small surge of concern rippling through me. 'But my rucksack was on it. And it hasn't come off.'

'If it was on it, it would have come off it,' said the woman, pushing a piece of paper around the counter top. 'Yo' sure it was on it?'

'Well,' I replied, blinking. 'I saw it in Albuquerque.'

'Anything might a-happened to it since Albuquerque,' answered the woman.

I heard the door open behind me. 'Emma,' said Dee, in as grave as voice as I had ever heard. 'I've just been talking to that bloke on the bench. He thinks he saw a guy taking a blue rucksack. I think it's been nicked.'

Well, didn't this cap everything off nicely? I now had nothing except what I was standing up in and faced the prospect of three weeks on the road without a change of clothes or a toothbrush. I shook my head in disbelief, my hand raised to my forehead. My rucksack had been stolen. STOLEN.

'Look on the bright side,' said Dee, sighing heavily. 'Whoever took it is going to have to do an awful lot of washing.'

'Things can't get worse,' I said, shell-shocked. 'It's not possible that anything can get worse. What am I going to do?'

'You can share my stuff. It won't be so bad. I can lend you some T-shirts. And pants. And you've still got your bumbag. So you've got your passport. And your letters from your mum. So it could have been mega-terrible but as it is, it's only really terrible.'

'Really terrible,' I nodded, wiping at my eyes with the back of my hand.

'If anything,' added Dee, 'you've built up an immunity to calamity. Bring on the next one! That's what I say. Bring it on!'

Despite Dee's valiant attempts to rouse my spirits, having my rucksack stolen was a low blow. We took a bus to the Marquette Youth Hostel and I sat with my forehead slumped against the window, staring out at old men with high-waisted trousers and fat women fanning themselves on porches. The heat rose up from the sidewalks, intoxicating and woozy, swampy and solid. I was trying hard not to give in to waves of despair but I was as miserable as I could possibly be.

The Marquette was a white, two-storey building with a balcony and looked a little worn, as if it too was fed up of the heat. The interior was clean, if slightly shabby, and we were directed up to a six-bed dorm where we would be sharing a bunk bed in the corner of the room. We spoke very little. I was in a deep fug of self-pity and Dee was anxious to jump into a shower and slough off the film of sweat that had enveloped her since getting off the Greyhound. The room didn't have air conditioning but one overhead fan sliced lazily above us. It wasn't terribly effective, but it was still better than nothing.

'Here,' said Dee, handing me a fresh top and some shorts. 'Go have a shower and put these on. You'll feel better.'

I nodded and did as I was told. As I stood in the cold water of the shower, my face upturned into the spray, I realised that, in the scheme of things, losing my every possession didn't really matter. It was only stuff. Stuff that smelled quite bad. Nothing in my rucksack had any sentimental value and everything could, in the fullness of time, be replaced. I had to draw a line and move on. I have always believed that if there is nothing to be done then there is also no point in dwelling on the problem. Moody mulling never got anyone anywhere and as the water washed away the accumulative scum of the past three days, so it cleansed my mind of sorrow. Onwards and upwards.

'I have a plan,' Dee declared, as I returned, hair wet and dripping. 'I found this,' she added, waving a leaflet at me. It was pitch black and had a skull on the front. 'Voodoo cemeteries with real live voodoo people. Fancy it?'

'"The City of the Dead"?' I read, taking the leaflet. '"Meet the voodoo priestess, Marie Laveau, dead for a hundred years." It'll be an actress in a dress,' I added. 'Oh wait. It says here you can make requests. If you stand by her grave, turn round, mark it with three crosses, her ghostly spirit will grant you your wish. Let's do it.'

The City of the Dead was more soberly known as St Louis Cemetery Number 1. Mausoleums and stone vaults, bleached white by the sun, stood interlocked in a weird ghoulish grid system, like a housing estate for corpses. The dead of New Orleans, we discovered, could not be buried underground because the water table through the city was so high. The coffins were buried at such shallow depths that every time it rained, they used to pop back up out of the ground. 'Imagine that,' said Dee, in a chilled hush. Because of it, stone vaults were the only option and entire families were buried within, each previously deceased family member moved from their own coffin, placed in a body bag and shoved towards the back every time there was a new arrival. It didn't always go according to plan. During a Yellow Fever outbreak in the city, people were accidentally buried alive, so to ensure further unfortunate events didn't occur, bells were placed at the top of tombs so that anyone still living could ring it and be set free. 'That's where we get saved by the bell from,' said Dee. 'And graveyard shift. People were sent out at night to listen for any ringing bells.'

The majority of the tombs were in a terrible, tipsy state as if dilapidation had followed a night of excess. It was eerie, this place, bubbling on top of a swamp, and there was an unsettled air as if its inhabitants were itchy and restless, the leaning vaults, the broken tombstones all looked like attempts at a mass break-out.

'There it is,' whispered Dee, tapping my forearm. 'The tomb of Marie Laveau.'

It was a tall, thin rectangle, about ten foot deep. A small piece of red cracked brick lay at the base along with a heap of coins and other votive offerings: a plastic pumpkin, a doll with no head and a handful of coloured beads draped over one corner. The facia itself was covered in hundreds of red tiny triple crosses, each one a voodoo complaint, calling out to the dead priestess and the nether world of sorcery. I bent down and picked up the broken piece of brick. 'You're not going to actually do it, are you?' asked Dee, eyes widening.

'Why not? Someone took my rucksack. And before that there was the cookie. Don't forget that. Maybe it's time for me to start fighting fire with fire. Bring on the big guns. Unleash the Underworld.'

'Why don't you just ask whether we can get back to New York on time?' suggested Dee, holding back my hand as I poised, ready to make my marks. 'Whoever has got your rucksack has been punished enough already. Trust me.'

'Oh, all right then,' I agreed. Quickly I scribbled three crosses on the tomb and dropped the brick back to the floor. 'Dear Marie Laveau,' I began. 'Please can we get back to New York in time so we don't miss our flight home? Thank you.'

We both waited, staring at the criss-crossed facia. Nothing happened.

'Do you think we need to leave some money?' I said, gesturing towards the heap of coins at our feet.

'We can't afford it,' said Dee, shaking her head. She glanced down. 'I'm amazed people do leave money. That's about fifty dollars down there. I'm surprised no one's nicked it.'

I stared down and chewed my lip. Dee turned to walk away. 'Come on, then,' she said, 'let's go to the French Quarter.'

I watched as Dee strolled ahead of me. I looked back down at the heap of money at my feet. Some might argue that stealing from the grave of a voodoo priestess wasn't necessarily a good idea, especially with the terrible luck I'd already had, but we were *so* desperate for money. Surely

Marie Laveau wouldn't miss a bit? 'She doesn't need it,' I whispered to myself and, quickly checking that no one was looking, I bent down and scooped up a handful of coins. 'It's not like I can have any worse luck than I've had already is it?' I muttered to myself as I ran to catch up with Dee.

But I didn't say another word. Because deep down, I knew I could.

I had told Dee that I found some coins I didn't realise I had in a back pocket of my bumbag. She was ecstatic and it meant we could have a bowl of French onion soup each and one large sandwich, which we shared. Above our table and snaking down the wall, there hung a large stuffed alligator, its jaws bearing down towards us. I looked up and saw a bead of condensation trickling down one tooth. 'Huh,' I commented, nodding towards it. 'That's slightly unnerving. As if it's coming to get us.'

Dee was mopping up the last of her soup. I stared again at the alligator and a cold chill ran through me. I had stolen money. It made me no better than whoever had taken my rucksack.

I looked at Dee and blinked. 'I've done something terrible,' I began. Dee glanced upwards. 'You know the money I told you I'd found in a pocket?' She nodded, running her last crust around her bowl. 'I lied. I took it from Marie Laveau's grave.'

Dee stopped what she was doing and stared, incredulous. 'You did *what?*' she asked, in a quiet whisper.

'I stole money from a voodoo priestess. I'm freaking out about it. I don't know what to do.'

Dee blinked and shook her head. 'This is a terrible mistake,' she declared, pushing back her chair. 'You've stolen money from a grave. From a GRAVE, Emma. The heat has turned you mad. We have to give it back.'

'I know,' I answered, grimacing. 'I don't know what came over me. What shall I do? Shall we go back to the tomb and give back the same amount of money that I took?'

Dee sat back and thought. 'How's about,' she began, 'instead of putting it back on the tomb, we give the exact amount of money to someone who needs it more than us? How's that? That way it evens things out in the scheme of things.'

'Okay,' I nodded. 'We have to give nine dollars and thirty-five cents away. But we need to choose wisely. This is bad shit, Dee. I'm really sorry.'

Before we could put right what I had done wrong and fend off the threat of a voodoo curse, we needed to know where we were going. The man from the Greater New Orleans Tourist and Convention Commission was a short man in his forties with a polite beer belly and a clean-shaven face. His hair was dark, closely cropped, and he had a sprinkling of grey about the temples. To look at, he was the sort of man you could happily imagine making painstakingly accurate scale models of villages. He exuded patience and calm. We had gone in to see if we could find a guide to the city's famous French Quarter and had found ourselves alone, with him, in a large open room. There were a few posters on the walls and a couple of racks with some pamphlets. Overhead, a ubiquitous wooden fan chopped quietly through the air.

'I've got a walking tour brochure,' he said, in a soft lilt. 'I can give you that. Would you like me to recommend a route?'

'Yes, please,' said Dee.

It was very quiet in the Greater New Orleans Tourist and Convention Commission and very still. Behind us, a clock was thickly ticking, above us was the gentle thud of the fan's heavy blades. There was a counter at one end of the room and we followed the man over to it where he produced a narrow, rectangular pamphlet. Dee and I leant forward. The counter was made of marble and, as I rested my forearms on it, the smooth coolness was a relief from the relentless heat. The pamphlet was high quality, made from stiff, glossy paper. On its front there was a pen-and-ink drawing of a street in the French Quarter filled with bustle: a horse-drawn carriage packed with people, a couple laughing on a balcony, and, rather ominously, a man walking an alligator on a lead. It was black and white but the awnings were splashed with a turquoise blue. As he opened it, the paper crackled and creaked.

The pamphlet was arranged in a concertina so that as he opened it out, more secrets were revealed. There were two maps, one of the main parts of the city, which acted as a guide for drivers and the other, a section of the French Quarter for those on foot. On it, there were 37 numbered dots, coloured yellow, all of which referenced points of interest listed inside the pamphlet. 'Okay,' said the man, in a low drawl. He picked up a red biro and shook it a little. 'Ink clogs up in the heat,' he said, absent-mindedly.

'So we are here,' he began, gently, lowering the pen to the map. The point lingered and it let out a small, tacky tap. A tiny clot of red ink seeped onto the paper. 'You might want to start by heading along Moon Walk,' he said, the pen leaving a sticky trail as he spoke, 'if you want to walk by the river.' His voice, almost at a whisper, had a soporific quality, hypnotic. 'Sometimes, there are entertainers there. Jazz musicians, tap dancers. You can buy watermelon too. There's a nice restaurant on that corner. I'll draw it on.'

I watched as the wet ink from his red biro slowly formed shapes on the paper in front of us. Every touch, a gentle sticky tack.

'And here,' he went on, circling two squares, slowly and deliberately, 'is the marketplace. They sell local produce. Crab boil. That sort of thing. It's been there since the 1720s.' He drew round the area leisurely and deliberately. 'Up here,' he whispered, tapping slowly at the empty square above the market, 'that's the Ursuline Convent. It's one of our oldest buildings. First nunnery in Louisiana and the first school for blacks. It's a very fine building, currently having some restoration work. From there,' he continued, sliding the pen softly upwards, 'is the Beauregard House. General Pierre Beauregard. He was the confederate general who ordered the first shot of the Civil War. He lived there for a time. Rented it.'

As he spoke, he unconsciously made small clotted shapes: dots, arrows, and circles. Something strange was going on. I was mesmerised by the gentle hand movements, the soft, lilting voice and the gluey, syrupy noise of sticky ink on shiny paper. I couldn't move.

'If you want to see a house that's been fully restored,' he murmured, 'then you can go here. To thirty-three.' The pen slid right. 'The Gallier House. James Gallier Jnr. He was an architect. It's an opportunity to see how the wealthy would have lived in the mid-nineteenth century. If you carry on from there, you get to the Clay House. Henry Clay. He was a statesman. He built the house for his wife. And then, you get to the LaLaurie House. It's haunted.'

He stopped; the pen hovered over the paper. I swallowed.

I was feeling very odd. 'You want me to carry on?' he asked, rotating the pen slowly between his fingers.

I couldn't speak but Dee, who was leaning over the map with her head cupped in her hands managed to mumble something that sounded affirmative.

'Okay,' he continued, lowering the pen back down onto the paper. Another minuscule clot seeped out. 'This is the city's most famous residence. The home of Delphine LaLaurie. She was the hostess of wild social gatherings but gossip surrounded her. Talk of her servants. Why were they emaciated and afraid? A neighbour confessed to police that she had seen Delphine LaLaurie beat a Negro slave girl, the same girl who later fell from the rooftop to her death. But on the night of 10 April, 1834, a terrible fire broke out.' As he spoke, he drew small, red flames. 'Neighbours broke in and found seven starving servants all chained up. Rumour spread that Delphine LaLaurie herself had started the fire. A mob gathered. A carriage burst from the rear gates of the house. Delphine LaLaurie escaped, never to return to New Orleans. The house was torn down by the mob. It was later rebuilt but ever since, some say, the house has been haunted. You can hear screams, the sound of whips. If you linger for long enough.'

He was leaning on one arm now so that all our heads were no more than inches apart. The paper had risen up a touch and he paused to stroke it back into place. He cleared his throat a little. 'If you come down from there,' he glided the pen downwards and then left, 'you get to the Presbytere and St Louis Cathedral. The Presbytere was a monastery but now it's a museum. You can see a lot of art in there. Paintings, that sort of thing. The cathedral is right next door.' He stopped and absent-mindedly made the shape of a cross. 'It's the oldest cathedral in the city. It's Catholic. Oh. Something you might like. Up here.' He raised the pen to a yellow dot marked 7. 'The Hermann-Grima House. That's a wax works.'

As he spoke in that silky, mellow tone and with that elusive clock ticking somewhere behind me, he wrote the word 'WaX' methodically in an empty square on the map. He had written the X as a capital and was overwriting it, slowly, again and again. I could hardly bear it and as he drew a thick, gloopy line under it, I had a massive, freestanding, no hands anywhere orgasm.

I let out a small, shocked groan. Dee looked at me. She seemed a bit cross-eyed. Were we in the grip of black magic? Was Marie Laveau working her tricks already? 'Sorry,' I mumbled and shifted uncomfortably. This was an unexpected turn of events. I'd had glossy pamphlet red biro sex with a stranger. And he didn't even know it.

'Dee,' I said, moments later, as we stumbled out into the heavy heat. 'Did you find that a bit...you know..?'

'Let's never speak of this again, Emma,' she replied, letting out a deep sigh. 'I think the sooner we give away that money the better.'

We were in Jackson Square, an airy plaza with grass and trees. At its north end stood the white stoned St Louis Cathedral with its famed triple steeples, before it the triumphant figure of the bronzed General Andrew Jackson astride a rearing stallion, hat in hand. 'I think,' said Dee, looking up at the great Catholic structure, 'that we should go in and have a deep cleanse.'

'This was the cathedral Marie Laveau used to conduct voodoo rituals in,' I replied.

'Perfect,' said Dee. 'We'll give her money away and then shower ourselves in holy water. I don't care who knows it. I am heebie-jeebied beyond belief.'

As we walked across the plaza, we could hear the sound of a jazz band playing just beyond the trees. They were standing to the right of the cathedral, in front of the Presbytere, a six-piece band: two guys on drums, a tuba, a trombone, a cornet and a boy in a trilby, no more than eight years old, on trumpet. He was wearing a T-shirt with a picture of Bob Marley on it, tatty denim shorts and a pair of black Doc Marten shoes with no laces. The rest of the band was on a raised pavement that ran across the front of the Presbytere, but the boy was below them, in front, the star of the show. He was amazing: confident, accomplished, a real showman. Another boy of about the same age meandered over with a wooden board tucked under one arm. He placed it on the floor next to them, stuck out a blue plastic bottle that had the word TIP written on it in bold black letters, and then gently began a soft shoe shuffle that shifted gear into a high-octane tap routine. A crowd gathered. It was electric.

Dee and I looked each other. We didn't have to think twice. We took Marie Laveau's $9.35 and put it in the bottle. Dee heaved a sigh.

'God, that's a relief,' I said, shaking my head. 'I am never stealing from the dead again. It's bad juju.'

Having splashed ourselves with water from the font of the St Louis Cathedral and said ten Hail Marys each, Dee decided that we probably were free of the voodoo curse and it would be perfectly acceptable to continue our early evening stroll. Dusk was drawing in and the night sky had taken on a luminous, pumpkin-coloured quality, streaks of crimson slashing across the horizon. The city had been relatively quiet up till this point, the fire of the day keeping everyone in shadows but as the sun went down, a more playful New Orleans was rising from the ashes. It was getting dark and New Orleans was ready to party.

Sharp suits were popping up everywhere, men with slicked-back hair and impossibly shiny shoes. Music began bursting, like overripe tomatoes, from shaded doorways, filling the air with raggedy sounds that set toes tapping and hips swaying. Instead of night-time crickets, New Orleans had reedmen and buglers, impromptu performances everywhere you turned. As we strolled into Bourbon Street, a piano was being pushed up the pavement by two men while another followed behind playing it. It was glorious and unfettered, it was music gone feral.

Preservation Hall was an old jazz club on St Peter Street in the north of the French Quarter, which ran from the uptown side of Jackson Square, lakeside towards Rampart. An old coach-gate house, its bare anonymous exterior gave the place an abandoned demeanour that belied the vitality within. It looked like nothing: battered brown walls, one lonely looking wrought-iron balcony and a gated door from which hung one scruffy looking sign that said OPEN 8–11. A long queue snaked away from the entrance and realising that space inside was limited, we joined it.

A shrunken black woman who looked to be at least 80 years old stood in the doorway, holding out a battered brown hat. It looked as if it had once been a trilby but its edges had softened into a rounded pot. Her skin was crinkled and thin, like tissue paper, her hair a madness of white curls and her clothes as plain and tatty as the building around her, yet her eyes were a shock of bright blue, full of life and mischief. 'Two dollars each!' she called out, as people inched towards her.

We threw our four dollars into the pot and walked up a battered corridor. The walls were undecorated plaster, faded pink and beige, and hanging from the wall were a host of old memories: mounted records, old posters of the Preservation Hall Jazz Band, a promotional picture of Sweet Emma Barrett, all of it contributing to the mood. We were about to enjoy New Orleans jazz, old Dixie style.

The concert hall was relatively tiny, no bigger than a large sitting room. At one end there was a set of drums, a double bass, a piano and a few chairs on which rested a clarinet, a trombone and a trumpet that looked so old it was practically black. Cushions were on the floor in front of the band area while old wooden stall seats clung to the edge. The walls were grey and stained and covered in dark portraits of old-time jazzmen, staring down calmly at the audience. One large sign hung behind the drum kit: TRADITIONAL REQUEST $2, OTHER $5, THE SAINTS $10.

The lighting was low and gloomy and we sat, cross-legged on the floor, squashed into the heave of bodies around us. The place was packed. With no air conditioning and no windows, the room was assuming an intense fug. A solitary fan whirred in the corner but the heat was smouldering, the walls beginning to glisten with a collective sweat. The room had a swimming, steamy air and after half an hour of waiting, a door towards the back opened and out walked five men. All of them were in their early sixties, if not older, white-haired and round of belly. They were in short-sleeved shirts, belted trousers with high waistbands and all of them wore the cheekiest grins you'd ever care to see. A reverential hush descended as they settled themselves and took up their instruments.

There was no chat, no welcoming pre-amble but with one barely perceptible nod, the clarinet player kicked the room into action while the pianist, bent double, ran his fingers over the keyboard like a wayward child tumbling down a hill. The drummer caressed the drum skins with a soft wire brush, the banjo player plucked a boogie-woogie syncopation full of surprises and the trumpet player, blue silk handkerchief in hand, filled the space with soaring, wonderful complaints. Soulful anthems and bluesy renditions of old tunes that began slow and melancholy shifted into joyous, rattling expressions of carefree abandon. It was jazz alchemy, a slice of devilish heaven as the band freewheeled their way around the classics. This wasn't just a nostalgic salute to old-time Dixie, it was as alive and vital as anything I had ever heard.

Dare I say it, but despite the awful start to the day, we were actually enjoying ourselves.

Chapter Eleven

One Day at a Time, Sweet Jesus

$199.96

As errors go, it was fundamental. We had got on the wrong bus and instead of winging our merry way towards Washington, where Dee was desperate to see the Edward Hopper collection, we found ourselves on a fast track to Pensacola in Florida. It wasn't entirely our fault. We'd wandered onto an empty bus emblazoned with our rightful destination, but the driver had got on and changed it. We knew nothing until we pulled into Pensacola and were blithely informed it was the final stop. But things got worse. The next bus out was in three days. Not only that, but the extra journey wasn't covered by our Ameripass ticket and we were going to have to shell out another $120. It was a disaster. Dee did an immediate audit of our financial predicament. We now had $2.10 each a day to live on.

'How are we going to manage that?' I asked, shaking my head. 'That's a big bottle of water each and what? One apple?'

'Water will fill us up,' said Dee, thinking fast. She turned and scanned a rack of pamphlets.

'And where are we going to stay for the next three days? There's another twenty-four-hour convenience store over there,' I said, gesturing out of the Greyhound station towards a neon-lit shop. 'They seem to be quite accommodating. And the staff may take pity on us. They might give us corn dogs. Or food they were planning on throwing away or tossing to raccoons. Actually, maybe we could just hang out with a pack of raccoons? They're good at scavenging.'

'Just beyond Gulf Breeze,' said Dee, with a sense of determination, waving a pamphlet in my direction. 'There's a campsite called Fort Pickens. I think we should head there and hope for the best. It's ten miles away.'

'How are we going to get there?'

'We're going to have to walk.'

The noonday sun was ferocious. We were on a parched grass verge along a four-lane highway, above us a scorching sky. Cars sped past at an insistent rate. Some blew their horns, others yelled from their windows, some simply blared by, snatches of loud music that came and went in a heartbeat. Over it all, we lumbered onwards. The small bottle of water we had was gone within fifteen minutes and we took it in turns to carry Dee's rucksack, ten minutes on, ten minutes off, each time a little more uncomfortable as a dank, adhesive sweat saturated our T-shirts from the neck downwards. The road we were trudging beside was so straight and relentless, the surroundings so anonymous, it was as if we were walking on the spot, going nowhere: a Sisyphean task to which there was no end. There were no landmarks, nothing to focus on, just an infinite stretch of dusty scrub to scuff through. As walks go, it was bleak.

We had stopped talking to each other an hour in. My throat felt like a cactus and my lips had assumed the dried, cracked quality of an overbaked cod. I had no hat, my limbs felt like dead weights and I was so hot it would have been more pleasant to be sealed in a plastic bag and popped in a pan of boiling water. Desperate for a drink, I turned to Dee and mumbled, 'You know you can die of dehydration? Do you think we should, you know, do a Sarah Miles?'

Dee looked at me, red-faced and desiccated. 'I am not drinking my own urine, Emma,' she replied. 'Not yet, anyway. And besides, we've got nothing to pee into and I am so parched I'd be amazed if we had any pee. I am devoid of moisture. Devoid of it. I'm actually contemplating licking my own sweat.'

I nodded in despair. I was beginning to feel light-headed and disorientated. My steps, at first steady and methodical, had become erratic and weaving. Cars blended into lanes, colours smudged by, shapes flashed through my peripheral vision. I was near delirious so when I looked up and saw what I thought was a giant waffle in the sky on the horizon, I immediately assumed that I was hallucinating. I stared at it and blinked, salty sweat stinging my eyes, but it was still there, a giant waffle floating in the air. I gestured towards it with a finger. 'Can you see that?' I asked, holding Dee by the arm. 'Or am I going crazy?'

Dee stopped and looked up towards the horizon, hand on forehead to shield her eyes from the sun. She swallowed with some difficulty and nodded. 'It's some sort of massive pastry,' she said, lips clacking.

'There's a giant waffle in the sky, Dee,' I said. 'Are we both going mad or have we died without noticing? Is heaven filled with crenulated pancake batter?'

Dee shook her head and croaked, 'Can't speak. No spit.'

As we traipsed onwards, the waffle, floating above a heat haze, came into sharper relief. It wasn't a hallucination. There really was an enormous waffle in the sky, not exactly floating but attached to the roof of a restaurant, a dull brown-bricked building that in any other circumstance would be unworthy of mention but for us it was an oasis and as we burst into the air-conditioned restaurant, gasping and desperate, it was as if we'd reached Nirvana.

'Water,' I gasped, throwing myself towards a waitress. 'Two glasses of water, please.' I turned and looked sideways at Dee who had collapsed over the counter surface, head resting in the crook of her elbow. A strange salty froth had gathered about the edges of her lips. She looked like a rabid dog.

The waitress, who was standing on the other side of the counter polishing glasses, took a good look at us. 'You want ice?' she asked, reaching for a large tumbler. I nodded. She flicked a tap in front of me and stood, hand on hip as the glass filled with water, all the while fixing me with an interested gaze. 'Where you come from?' she asked.

'Pensacola,' I replied, panting.

'No, I mean, *where* you come from? Australia?' She took the second glass and stuck it under the tap.

'England,' I said, staring at the glass of water in her hand.

'Oh!' she declared, grinning suddenly. 'I'm second-generation English! My folks come from York-shire. They were in the cereal business. Breakfast cereals. Uh huh. You on vacation?'

'Water. Please,' murmured Dee, holding out both her hands.

'Oh!' laughed the waitress, shaking her head. 'Look at me. Rattling on. There you go.'

We took the ice-cold tumblers from her hands and glugged, desperately and violently. Water dripped down our chins and fell down the front of our T-shirts. 'If it's tap water,' asked Dee, gasping, 'is it free? And if it is, can we have some more please?'

'My!' said the waitress, eyes widening, 'you girls are *thirsty*.'

'We've walked here from Pensacola,' I explained, running the back of my hand across my mouth.

'You've done *what*?' squealed the waitress, astonished. 'Oh my. Well of course you can have more water. And don't worry about the money. My goodness. You've *walked* here from Pensacola! Why on earth?'

'We got the wrong bus from New Orleans. We were supposed to be going to Washington. And the next bus doesn't go for three days. So we're trying to get to Gulf Breeze. And the Fort Pickens Nature Reserve. It's a campsite. But we haven't got enough money to catch a bus or take a taxi. So we have to walk.'

The waitress, who was a petite woman in her early forties, folded her arms and pursed her lips. She was wearing a pink-checked uniform that was slightly too big for her. Her make-up was ineptly applied: brownish blusher that was smeared on like dirt, green eyeshadow that filled her sockets like pea soup and a bright red lipstick that made her face look as if it had been tied up with a small bow. A small, concerned frown had settled on her forehead as if she were deep in thought. 'You're trying to walk to the Fort Pickens Nature Reserve? Actually walk there? Do you have any idea how far away that is?'

'I thought about ten miles from Pensacola,' answered Dee, taking her second glass of water. 'But we've been walking for three hours. So maybe I got that wrong.'

'Too right it's more than ten miles. More like twenty! You girls can't walk there. Not in this heat.'

I gulped down some more water. 'We haven't got any choice,' I replied. 'We're financially embarrassed.'

'We've only got two dollars ten each a day to live on. It's a long story,' added Dee.

The waitress was still shaking her head in disbelief. 'Well, this won't do,' she replied. 'I tell you what. Seeing as you're from the old country and you seem like good people I'll give a holler out and see if we can't lend you a hand.' She turned and looked out over the restaurant. 'Hey, everybody!' she called out. 'Can anyone give these girls a lift to Fort Pickens? They're from England.'

We turned and looked over our shoulders. There were only four people in the restaurant. A teenage boy, lips covered in sugar, a stout woman in half-moon spectacles, a thick-necked man in a grey T-shirt and, over in the far corner, in a raised booth, a man with thick brown hair slicked back and a black open-neck shirt. He was wiping his mouth with a napkin. He looked at us and, screwing up his napkin, raised his chin and shouted, 'Yeah. I can take them.'

I shot a quick, incredulous grin in Dee's direction. What luck was this!

'There you go!' beamed the waitress. 'Now you won't have to walk. So, do you know Geoffrey Boycott?'

'Excuse me?' I asked.

'Geoffrey Boycott. The cricket player,' explained the waitress, smiling. 'I know everything about cricket. I looked it up. He's from York-shire too. It's a sport they play in York-shire. There are eleven batsmen and sticks called wickets. It's like baseball but nicer outfits.'

'Yes, we know who Geoffrey Boycott is,' Dee interjected, 'but we don't actually know him. We're not acquainted, I mean.'

'Oh,' said the waitress, looking genuinely disappointed. 'But you've been to York-shire, right?'

I turned and looked back over my shoulder in the direction of the fellow who'd offered to give us a lift. I raised a hand in his direction and smiled. He shuffled to the end of his booth and then, as he got out, he disappeared from view. I frowned. Where had he gone? And then, as he reappeared from behind a row of booths and walked towards us down the central aisle, I realised: our saviour was a midget. A midget with a clubfoot.

'Hello,' I said, bending down to shake his hand. 'I'm Emma. This is Dee. Thank you so much for helping us. We really appreciate it.'

'You have no idea how much we appreciate it,' added Dee, similarly bending down to shake the fellow's hand.

'We were about to drink our own urine!' I added, laughing slightly inappropriately.

'Samson,' said the man.

'Excuse me?' I asked, blinking.

'My name is Samson. It's the long hair,' he quipped.

'Oh yes!' I replied, pointing at his fulsome locks. 'Samson. Very good.'

'So you want a lift to Fort Pickens, right?'

'Yes please,' nodded Dee. 'We've just got this rucksack. Is that okay?'

'Sure. I've got a two plus two. You okay with the squeeze?'

We both nodded and grinned. I had no idea what he was talking about.

We thanked the waitress and moved out to Samson's car, towards the back of the parking lot. To be fair, it wasn't quite what I had been expecting. It was a low-to-the-ground red sports car with funky tail lights and a sleek squared-off front. My eyes popped out of their sockets. 'Is that a

Ferrari?' I gasped, pointing at the tell-tale yellow badge emblazoned with a rearing black stallion.

'Yeah,' nodded Samson, pulling the keys from his pocket. 'Ferrari Mondial T.'

'Wow,' I mouthed to Dee.

'I've had some work done so I can drive it,' explained Samson, gesturing to his specially designed seat.

'It's amazing,' said Dee. 'I've never been in a sports car before, let alone a Ferrari.'

The car was incredible. Tan leather interior, Ferrari foot mats, bucket seats in the front, and two smaller seats in the back. 'What's that?' I asked, pointing at what looked like a sound system in the dashboard.

'CD player.'

'What's a CD?' I asked.

'They're going to replace records. And cassettes,' replied Samson, settling himself in the driver's seat.

'What? Pffft. As if.'

'You okay in the back?' asked Samson, glancing over his shoulder at Dee. She was crouched on the back seat, knees up against her chest, her rucksack sitting in the space beside her.

'Absolutely fine,' she replied, thrusting a thumb upwards. 'Beats walking any day.'

Samson turned the key in the ignition. A deep throbbing purr growled through the car. I was grinning from ear to ear. Well, this was swanky: us in a Ferrari being driven about by a millionaire midget. Swit Swoo. 'Seeing how you've never been in a Ferrarri,' began Samson, pulling out of the parking lot, 'would you like me to drive you around for a bit?'

'YES!' we both yelled.

This was glorious: top down, sunglasses on, arm resting on the door I let my head fall back and gazed up as the exotic canopy of palm trees flitted by beneath a deep blue sky. Where once we had resented the heat of the day, we now basked in the breezy splendour of a hot Florida afternoon. It was all about how you got there, and we were travelling in style. As we drove, we brought Samson up to speed on our adventure thus far and, despite the relentless misfortune that had beset us from the off, we found ourselves laughing. It was quite therapeutic to assess our woebegone attempts to cross a continent. It was like reading a school report that, on the Wheel of Good and Bad, was SO bad, it was good again.

'And then, the skunk sprayed me. Actually sprayed me.' I was saying.

'She STANK!' yelled Dee, from the back.

'Never smelled anything like it,' I said, shaking my head. 'Took days to wear off.'

'So, Samson,' said Dee, tapping him lightly on the shoulder. 'What do you do?'

'I work in the adult entertainment industry,' he said, flicking the indicator, and shifting down a gear.

'What sort of thing?' I asked. 'Like you run bars? Clubs? That sort of thing?'

'No. I produce porn films.'

There was a light cough from the rear of the car.

'Hmmm,' I said, trying very hard not to catch Dee's eye. 'That's…um. Goodness. I've never seen a porn film. That's true. People find it hard to believe but I have never seen a porn film.'

'Do you want to see one?' asked Samson, adjusting his sunglasses.

'Well, I…'

'Because you can come to my condo. I can show you some of my films. We can hang out. Party. What do you say?'

'Umm...'

'I don't have to drop you off at the reserve right away, yeah? You can come back with me. We can do some partying. Take some stuff. Do some fucking.'

'Oooooh...'

'We can all fuck. I can fuck you. And then I can fuck you. Maybe I can fuck you both at the same time. If you want, you can fuck each other. I don't mind. I can watch. But what do you say? We can call it a thank you for the lift. You know, cos I'm going out of my way here.'

An awkward silence filled the car. I wasn't entirely sure what to say or do. Only one thing was rattling through my mind: how do I say no without hurting his feelings? If Samson had been an average, able-bodied man I've have given him what for then and there. But I'd never met a midget before and was consumed with the misconception that, because he'd been dealt a low blow in life, I should cut the man some slack. I stared at him. It looked like I was going to have to have sex with a millionaire midget porn baron.

My mouth fell open but no words came out. I was struggling with an internal moral monologue: how do you tell a disabled stranger who's just done you a massive favour that you do not want to engage in any sort of sexual shenanigans with him? I wondered if I could just give him a hand job. I imagined it. No. No, I couldn't.

'Thank you, Samson,' said Dee, resourcefully, from the back of the car. 'We'd love to but I'm very sorry to have to tell you we both have our periods.'

(We didn't.)

We travelled the rest of the way in near silence and 20 minutes later, after a somewhat majestic journey across the awesome Pensacola Bay Bridge we were dumped, rather unceremoniously, at the end of a long dirt road that wove into the Nature Reserve. I had barely shut the car door before the Ferrari was speeding away, one small middle finger sticking up in our direction. I was quite shocked. 'He gave us the finger, Dee,' I gasped.

'Ferrari or no Ferrari,' said Dee, hoisting her rucksack onto her shoulder. '*That* was a dirty little man.'

The road we had been dropped at was on the very edge of the Nature Reserve and the Fort Pickens campsite, according to a small road sign, was another four miles away. Our long walk was far from over. For an hour we sweated our way down a road framed either side by white sand, the landscape flat and barren until we passed a small house just past Langdon Beach. The surroundings then became wooded, tall pines with small scrubs of vegetation, long grasses and wild flowers. Nobody had passed us as we walked and so we found ourselves wandering down the middle of the road, blindly following the double yellow line that ran down its centre.

We had found a small Ranger's Station, no more than a wooden hut, but it was locked and no one was there. Instead, there was a large hand-drawn sign resting against the door. BEWARE: LYME TICKS IN AREA. AVOID LONG GRASS.

I looked at it and frowned. 'Lyme ticks?' I asked. 'Where have I heard of that before?'

'Do you remember back in Oxford, when we went to the BUNAC orientation?'

I nodded.

'Guy told us about Lyme disease. Remember that?'

'Oh! The flesh-eating thing. The one that paralysed his friend or something?'

'Necrotizing fasciitis,' replied Dee, with a sniff. 'Yes. Or is it? Actually, I'm not sure now if Lyme disease *is* the flesh-eating thing. No matter. Whatever it is, it's clearly awful.'

'Oh,' I said, wiping the sweat on my forehead with the bottom of my T-shirt. 'Well. That's good. We've wandered into a plague zone. Something to look forward to.'

'What do you think we should do?' asked Dee, gesturing towards the empty hut. 'There's no one here. Shall we just carry on? See if there's anyone around the campsite?'

'Yes. Let's see if we can find a shop or something. I'm parched.' I cast a look at the long grass that was on either side of us. 'Lyme ticks can't jump can they?'

'Not sure,' replied Dee, with a small shrug. 'But let's keep to the middle of the road just to be sure. And here,' she added, lifting up her rucksack, 'take a strap. We can carry it together.'

We wandered onwards. More signs about Lyme ticks lined the roadside. On one, there was a small photocopied picture of the deadly creature. It was oval in shape, almost like a guitar plectrum. The lower half of its abdomen was a reddish brown while its top half displayed a large black dot, as if someone had left an inky thumbprint. 'Actual size,' I said, peering at the poster. 'God. It's no bigger than a seed. That's hardly fair. I've always thought things that are really dangerous should be sized accordingly. So you can see them coming. They should be large and bulky. Mangled fur. Tusks. Cerise with an orange plume.'

Dee bent forward and read, '"Early symptoms include headaches, fatigue and depression."' We both looked at each other.

'Well, we've both got those. We've had those for weeks.'

'"And a circular skin rash,"' Dee read on. '"If untreated, can cause severe neurological problems and can lead to permanent paraplegia."'

'Wow,' I added, 'they're really selling this place.'

'Emma,' said Dee, with a sigh, 'we're not going to get Lyme disease.'

'"Bad luck and misfortune will haunt you for all eternity." That's all I'm saying.'

The track we were on had opened out into a large clearing. A few motor homes were parked here and there, tents were dotted about and we could see families sparking up barbecues and sitting around tables. We meandered through but, as far as we could make out, there was no shop, just a wash block in the centre of the site. Desperate for some water, we went in and drank straight from the taps. 'It could be worse,' said Dee, wiping some water through her hair. 'We might have had to drink from the toilets. Like a dog.'

'I wouldn't have thought twice about it,' I added, flipping off my T-shirt and giving it a rinse under the cold tap.

We weren't quite sure what to do next. There was no ranger, we had nothing to sleep in and life-threatening insects were on either side of us. There was no way we could sleep out in the open. It was simply too dangerous. Taking Dee's rucksack, we threw it down and sat on it just in front of the wash block. Both of us had our head in our hands, flummoxed as to what to do for the best. 'We could sleep in the showers?' I suggested. 'They were very clean.'

'I was thinking the same,' replied Dee, reaching into one of her rucksack's side pockets. 'I've just remembered we've got a carrot in here.'

'Or the beach? We could sleep on the beach?'

'What about the tide coming in?'

'Do they get tides here? Or is it like the Mediterranean? Because they don't have tides. I have no idea why. France has the Moon. It's not like there is no moon over France. Maybe there are only tides where there are shit beaches? And the beaches that are lovely and sandy are finished. So the Moon moves on?'

'You have no idea what you're talking about do you?'

'No. No I don't.'

'There,' said Dee, holding a carrot aloft. 'Do you want the thick end or the thin end?'

'Thin end, please,' I replied.

A girl was hovering in my peripheral vision. She was about nineteen years of age, had a badly done perm and was wearing oversized spectacles that swamped her face. She seemed to have a breezy disposition and was wrapping a long piece of grass around her finger. 'Hi,' she said, edging a little closer.

We looked up at her. I was chewing my carrot. 'Hello,' I mumbled, not wanting to swallow my evening supper just yet.

'Where y'all from?'

'England,' replied Dee, with a small smile.

'I saw you drinking from the taps,' she said, gesturing into the wash block.

'Yes,' Dee continued. 'We haven't got any water. We were hoping there'd be a shop but we can't seem to find one.'

'There's a store past Fort Pickens,' said the girl, pointing off into the distance. 'Can you drive there?'

'We haven't got a car, no,' replied Dee. 'How far away is that?'

'Probably three, four miles,' she answered, with a nod.

I groaned. 'We've walked miles today,' I explained. 'Oh well.'

The girl screwed her face sideways and nodded. There was a small silence.

'Say,' she suddenly announced, 'would you like to come have dinner with my family?' Dee and I shot each other an amazed sideways glance. 'It's just I saw you drinking from the taps and then you both sitting here and I told my Mom and she sent me over cos it's the Christian thing to do.'

'It's like I have always said,' I declared, standing up and beaming. 'Thank *God* for Christians.'

The Barrett Family, it turned out were Seventh Day Adventists. They believed in the imminent return of Jesus and had their Sabbath on a Saturday. There was the mom, Rachel, kind-faced and generous, a stoutly built woman with the same badly done perm and oversized glasses as her daughter. The dad, John, who had the aura of a man well fed and happy, the daughter, Susan, and her two brothers, Thomas, a quiet, brooding 18-year-old and the youngest, Michael, an overexcited 13. All of them were grinning at us. Behind them, there was a long table, laid out with table-cloth, napkins, proper crockery and covered with heaving bowls of food.

It was nothing short of a heavenly vision.

'Welcome!' announced Rachel, stepping forward and shaking us both by the hand. 'We're honoured to have you! Come! Sit down with us! Let's break bread!'

Dee and I, smiling wildly, shook everyone's hand and, after a quick round of introductions, took our place at the table. Michael had been dispatched to fetch two more chairs and we were placed in the centre so that we could be surrounded by the Barretts and enveloped in the bosom of old-fashioned Christian love. Thinking that supper had now started, I reached for a serving spoon but Dee, who was better equipped to read the situation, kicked me under the table. 'Ow,' I said, quietly and then, realising that everyone was staring at my hand holding the spoon, I gently put it back down again.

'Okay,' said John, taking the hands of both his immediate neighbours, 'let's give thanks to the Lord.' Ah! I thought. Grace. Like we had to do at school whenever the governors came. Susan and Michael, whom I was sitting between, reached for my hands; I bowed my head accordingly. John though, had not. Instead, he closed his eyes and threw his head back. I looked around me quickly.

'Sowing in the morning!' they all began singing. 'Sowing seeds of kindness! Sowing in the noontide and the dewy eve! Waiting for the harvest, and the time of reaping! We shall come rejoicing! Bringing in the sheaves!'

I shot a quick panicked glance at Dee. She pulled a small, awkward grimace and then threw herself into it. 'Bringing in the sheaves!' she kicked me again under the table. 'Bringing in the sheaves!'

I joined in. 'We shall…la, la, la, la. Bringing in the sheaves!'

The Barretts all beamed even more. I nodded back.

'Bringing in the sheaves,' we all sang. 'Bringing in the sheaves!'

'I don't quite know the next line,' I sang, jollily.

'Bringing in the sheaves!'

'Lord!' bellowed John, gripping hands a little tighter. 'Thank you for this bounteous meal! And thank you for bringing us Dee and Emma. They were lost sheep! And you have been their shepherd! Help us to welcome them with all our hearts! AMEN!'

'AMEN!' hollered the rest of the Barretts.

'Amen!' I shouted, with some gusto.

I caught Dee's eye. What in heaven's name had we got ourselves into?

'So,' asked Rachel, as she passed me a large bowl of potato salad, 'does your family have faith?'

'Well,' I began, 'it's quite complicated. My grandfather was a Baptist minister.'

They all exchanged appreciative beams. I smiled back.

'But my dad wasn't really interested in religion so he's nothing. And my mother was a Catholic. But she was ex-communicated for having a Black Mass on the altar of her school church.'

Everyone stopped what they were doing and stared at me.

'Excuse me?' asked John, leaning forward.

'She tried to summon the devil when she was fourteen. I don't think she managed it. But she was ex-communicated all the same.'

'Oh,' John and Rachel exchanged small, troubled glances.

'But it turns out we're probably Jewish. We think my great-great-grandmother was a Jew. And she's on my mother's side. So, technically, I'm a Jew.'

Dee, more astute than me, could see where I might be going wrong. 'I'm a Catholic!' she butted in. 'An actual Catholic.'

'Actually, I am too. I got christened when I was at university because it turned out my mother had forgotten to do it. My godfather is actually younger than I am. Ha!'

'So you're a Baptist Catholic Jew?' asked Susan, frowning.

'Told you it was complicated. Gosh. This spaghetti is delicious.'

We had baffled the Barretts. There was no denying it. We had sat and told them our story over supper about how we came to be in America, our struggle to find work in San Francisco and the predicament we now found ourselves in. They had sat, open-mouthed and incredulous. 'You just came to America without knowing what you were going to do?' asked Rachel, shaking her head in disbelief.

'That's pioneer spirit,' chipped in John. 'If a little foolhardy. My goodness, I can't work out whether you're fearless or just plain stupid!'

Dee and I, as a thank you for the supper, had offered to do all the washing up and as she rinsed and I wiped, the Barretts sang a few more hymns and John got out the family Bible. As we finished, he gestured for us to sit. 'So tonight, I think it's apt,' he began, opening his Bible, 'if we read something for our guests. And I thought, what could be of use to these two voyagers? And I recalled the Traveller's Psalm: Psalm 121. Would you like to read it out, Thomas?' He handed the Good Book to his eldest son, who took it, and cleared his throat.

'Psalm 121,' began Thomas, 'I will lift up mine eyes unto the hills, from whence cometh my help. My help cometh from the LORD, which made heaven and earth. He will not suffer thy foot to be moved: he that keepeth thee will not slumber. Behold, he that keepeth Israel shall neither slumber nor sleep. The LORD is thy keeper: the LORD is thy shade upon thy right hand. The sun shall not smite thee by day, nor the moon by night. The LORD shall preserve thee from all evil: he shall preserve thy soul. The LORD shall preserve thy going out and thy coming in from this time forth, and even for evermore.'

'Thank you, son,' said John, with a nod. 'Well. Life is a journey. A dangerous one at that. And we're all travellers. And we all have hills to climb.'

'Amen,' nodded Rachel, who was sitting to our left, knitting.

'And with the help of the Lord, we can surmount all obstacles. He watches over us. It is His hand that steadies our footfalls, that steers us through crevice and gully. He is the one true guide.'

'And he helps us catch the BIGGEST fish!' chipped in Michael, enthusiastically.

Dee and I were sitting very, very still. There was always a grave danger, in these sorts of situations, that either or both of us could suddenly be consumed by paralysing giggles. While I had a nodding respect for the baby Jesus, especially around Christmas, I was always slightly baffled by religion. The Bible, I had always thought, was a lovely book but until someone could prove me wrong, I was pretty convinced it was a work of fiction. Faith, that untouchable concept, had simply passed me by. Dee, on the other hand, was probably a lot more religious than I gave her credit for. She was a practising Catholic, went to mass on Sundays, and was the very essence of Christian kindness, if not quite as kind as the Barretts. Even so, I could feel her brewing up to a nervous laugh. And if she started, so would I. And so I folded my arms and frowned at my feet instead.

'And like the Lord, it's our duty to help our fellow traveller,' John was concluding. 'And this is why we are more than happy to be of assistance to Dee and to Emma.'

I nodded appreciatively, while still staring at my shoes.

'Praise be to Jesus, Amen.'

'Amen,' we all echoed.

'So,' declared Rachel, putting down her knitting. 'Would you like Thomas and Michael to help you put your tent up?'

'Ahh,' began Dee, 'the thing is we haven't actually got a tent.'

'I left it in San Francisco. It was sort of a mistake,' I explained.

'But where are you going to sleep?' asked Rachel.

'We thought the showers looked quite good,' I said, nodding back in the direction of the wash block.

'Oh no,' replied Rachel, shaking her head. 'You can't do that. John! They can't sleep in the showers!'

'Good heavens, no. Well. This is easily solved. They can have the *spare* tent. The one with the fan…Thomas, Michael! You know where it is. Let's get it pitched.'

This was nothing short of incredible. We'd been fed to bursting, sang at, prayed over and now we were being given a tent that came complete with inflatable beds and a working fan. 'Shit,' I whispered to Dee as we watched the two brothers banging in the tent pegs. 'This is amazing.'

'I know,' she whispered back. 'We're going to have to get us some serious religion. For the next three days at least.'

'Amen, sister. For a tent and some food, I'll take a vow of celibacy right now.'

Dee stood back and looked me up and down. 'Oh. I thought you had already?'

'Oh, ha ha,' I said, sarcastically. 'Just you watch me, Dee. I am going to be piety *itself*.'

*

We awoke to a dull and lifeless sky, overcast with a layer of white cloud that flattened the light. We had been stirred by the smell of bacon sizzling and had poked our heads from the tent to see the Barretts sitting at the table, boxes of breakfast cereals spread out and a packet of soft white buns that Susan was halving and buttering. Behind them, Rachel stood, gently poking at the barbecue.

'Cor,' I said, running a hand through my hair. 'Bacon butties! I haven't had one of those since I left England.'

'Bacon what?' asked John, looking up suddenly.

'Bacon butties. Sandwiches. Butties.'

'You call sandwiches *butties*? Oh my. A butt is something very different over here.'

'What a thing to call them!' laughed Rachel.

'Why would you put bacon in a butt?' asked Michael, frowning.

'So what are you girls planning today?' asked John, changing the subject.

'Well, we were going to go to the beach,' replied Dee, casting a look upwards. 'But it's not really the weather for it.'

'We can't come to Florida and not go to the beach though,' I said, taking a bun from Rachel. 'And besides, this *is* beach weather in England. I've sat on a beach in a gale before now. Determined to enjoy myself. Whatever the cost. Blimey, this is lovely. Thanks so much.'

'You're welcome,' nodded Rachel with a smile.

'What are you all doing today?' asked Dee, squeezing some tomato ketchup into her bun.

'Fishing,' answered Thomas.

'Fishing for men?' I asked, with as holy a face as I could muster. 'Like Jesus?'

Dee looked at me.

'No,' said Thomas, slightly puzzled. 'Fishing for fish.'

The beach, a long stretch of gorgeous white sand, was deserted. The clouds had darkened considerably but it was still very warm and, not having anything to change into, I stripped down to my bra and pants. The sea, which in normal circumstances would have been a bright turquoise, had assumed the murky demeanour of the skies above but that wasn't going to stop me. I was on a beach for the first time that summer and this was, lest we forget, a holiday. A group of small tern-like birds were prancing along the shoreline and as we strolled down to the water, they ran back and forth in a frenzy, much to our amusement. A few isolated clumps of seaweed dotted the edge of the surf but other than that, there was nothing. It was as perfect a beach as I had ever seen.

Shoals of silver fish flitted through the breakers, sporadically jumping as one, dazzling above the sealine like sparkling jets of water. Overhead, a few pelicans hung heavy in the air and small, translucent crabs scuttled across the sand. The water was delicious and Dee and I were quickly neck-deep into it and grinning. I floated on my back and wiggled my toes in the air. 'This is the life!' I declared. 'Even if the weather is miserable. Couldn't give a shit. Hello, sea. Hello, sand.'

Dee, who was doing a very ladylike breaststroke in a circle, swam back a little towards the shore and stood up. 'I can't get over how warm it is,' she said, scooping water over her shoulders. 'It's like a bath.'

'God knows we needed one,' I replied.

'Ow!' Dee suddenly cried out. 'Oh! My God! OW! Something's bitten me or...OW!'

I paddled towards her. 'What was it? OW! JESUS! OW! What the fuck was...OW!' Something had sent a sharp, painful shock coursing through my leg. I splashed away and peered down into a small but significant cluster of jellyfish. 'It's bloody jellyfish!' I yelled. 'We're standing in about a hundred jellyfish!' Everywhere we looked we were surrounded by large, yellowish cabbage-shaped jellyfish, pulsing away. We both screamed.

Suddenly, behind us, there was a large crack of thunder and a massive lightning bolt shattered down. Dee and I looked at each other, dumbstruck. 'What the...OW!' she cried out again. 'Quick! We've got to get out of the water! Get out! GET OUT! OW!'

We scrambled ashore, half swimming, half running through the surf. The lightning was coming down thick and fast and we threw ourselves down, spread-eagled on the sand. 'Lie as flat as you can!' yelled Dee, screaming every time another strike came searing down. 'This is because you've been pretending to be a Christian. Fishing for men, my arse.'

'My mum knew someone who was hit by lightning. She was saved because she was wearing rubber wellingtons. Have we got anything rubber? Anything at all?'

'No,' replied Dee, turning her face towards mine on the sand. 'At least I don't think we have. Hang on. The bottom of our Converse is rubber. Quick, put them on your hands. That might work.'

We both scrabbled to grab our scruffy trainers and stuck our hands into them. 'This is TERRIFYING!' screamed Dee. 'I don't dare move. Lightning always hits the tallest thing. We're the tallest things for about a mile.'

'My mum said that her friend who was hit by lightning was brilliant at maths after it.' I thought about that. 'She may have made that bit up.'

Thankfully, the whirlwind of a storm lasted only five minutes, probably due to the wind that had accompanied the unexpected squall. As I looked up, I realised that small patches of blue sky were starting to break out. 'I think that's it,' I said, with some relief. 'I think it's gone.'

We both sat up. 'Look at that,' said Dee, pointing at a large red welt on her thigh. 'Bloody jellyfish.'

'And me. Got a couple on my knee. And on my elbow. Blimey. It really stings. This is just our luck. One day on a beach, *one day*, and we manage to get stung and nearly killed.'

'Oh good,' said Dee, scrunching her nose up. 'It's starting to rain.'

'I'm not leaving,' I replied, with some defiance. 'I'm sitting here for the entire day.' I picked up my T-shirt and held it over my head. 'Never let it be said that the English don't know how to have a holiday.' And so we both sat, huddled and fending off the rain with flimsy cotton tops, for the next *five* hours.

Maybe it was because it was overcast, maybe it was because it was raining but it hadn't even occurred to me to put on any sun cream. Dee was staring at me and frowning. 'Your face is very red, Emma,' she said, as we wandered back towards the campsite. 'Very, VERY red.'

'Hmm,' I replied, 'it is feeling a bit tight. And hot. But how can that be? It wasn't even sunny.'

'Worst sunburn I ever had was on an overcast day. You forget that the beams can penetrate. Oh Emma, it's really bad. You look like an old sea-salt.'

We had walked back to the Barretts' Winnebago where I had thrown myself into a camping chair, suddenly feeling a bit dizzy and bothered. My face was sore to the touch and I could feel an intense heat coming off it, like a radiated melon. Dee rummaged about in her rucksack and pulled out a small compact case. She opened it and held it up to my face. 'Have a look,' she said, tapping me on the back of my hand. I peered into the small round mirror. Something red and livid was staring back at me, a bit like a sprayed cauliflower with some eyes sticking out of it.

'I look like John Merrick,' I replied, grimacing.

'To be honest, you looked like him anyway,' said Dee. 'Here,' she said, tossing me a pot of moisturiser. 'Rub in some of this. And have some aspirin. For the jelly stings.'

I looked again at the round red welts on my skin. 'Hang on,' I said, 'this one doesn't hurt. You don't think that one's a Lyme tick bite, do you?'

'Are you depressed?'

'Not really.'

'Then no.'

'Oh my goodness,' said a voice just ahead of us. We looked up. It was the Barretts back from their day fishing. 'Look at your face,' said Rachel, with a look of grave concern. 'You've burned up bad.'

'And we were stung by jellyfish,' I said, proffering up my knee. 'An actual jellyfish.'

Rachel bent down and peered at it. 'Not too bad. I've seen worse. John can lend you some shaving foam. Best thing for them. That or vinegar.'

'Did you have a good day fishing?' Dee asked, handing me some aspirin.

'Sure did,' said John, holding a large bucket. 'Say, didn't you say you were a doctor?'

'Going to be,' answered Dee, with a nod.

'So you're used to dissecting and stuff?'

Dee nodded again.

'Great! Well,' he passed Dee the bucket. 'You can gut the fish while we get cleaned up.'

We stared into the bucket. Six large fish were in it. 'These fish are still alive,' said Dee, quietly, handing me a cleaver.

'Why are you giving me this?' I asked, startled.

'You're going to kill them,' replied Dee, pointing into the bucket.

'I can't kill them. I've never killed anything in my life. Why can't you kill them?'

'It's against my ethical code. I can gut them, but not kill them.'

I stared back into the bucket. 'Can't we just wait for them to die of natural causes? However many years that might take?'

'All right, look,' said Dee, in a dread hush. 'We'll kill them together.'

'Why are you whispering?'

'So the fish don't hear.'

'How are we going to do it? You pick one out and then what do I do? Wring its neck?'

'That's chickens. Just hit it on the head. Or chop its head off. Whatever's easiest.'

Dee reached into the bucket and pulled out a large silver-grey fish. It was thrashing fiercely and Dee dropped it several times before pinning it down on a flat rock that was to our left. 'Quickly,' she yelled. 'Hit it. No! Wait! Open your eyes! Don't chop my fingers!'

The fish's eye was white and wild, rolling in its socket. It was putting me off, so I grabbed a dock leaf that was lying on the ground and covered it up. I took the cleaver, hovered it over the fish's head and then, with a primeval cry, shoved it downwards. A horrendous crunch hung in the air. The fish went limp. We both stared at it. 'I feel awful,' I said, 'like I've killed a family pet. I had a friend once. He had that jiggy leg thing whenever he was nervous. He went round to his girlfriend's house for tea and accidentally kicked her mother's budgerigar into the open fire. It burned to death in front of their eyes. I now know how he felt.'

There was something of the Frontier Spirit about dispatching a bucket full of fish and even though it was far from pleasant, there was something visceral about it that gave me a sense of achievement. It was the first time I'd done something right in ages. Perhaps it was a votive offering, a sacrifice that would cleanse me of my rotten luck?

The fish, of course, were delicious and as we sat, bellies full, staring into the fire the boys had made, my mind turned homewards. Here I was, surrounded by a close-knit family, all of them with a genuine sense of purpose. Yet I remained directionless. I was still no nearer to knowing or even thinking about what was going to happen to me when I returned to England. Dee would be off to Medical School and I would be left to my own devices. In many ways, this journey was our last glorious twirl of the flag, but like all parties, it was coming to an end.

Rachel had been knitting a jumper and as I sat, head hanging back, staring up at the moonlit branches above me, she gave out a satisfied sigh. 'Finished!' she declared. 'At last!' She held it up for everyone to see. It was a light blue tank top with the face of a bearded man across its front. I squinted.

'Ha!' I said, pointing towards it. 'Have any of you seen that book? *The Joy of Sex*? It looks exactly like the bloke in that. Who is it?'

There was a stony silence. 'It's Jesus,' replied Rachel, a little curtly.

'Look at Dee's hair!' said Michael, as a welcome diversion. 'It's standing right up.'

We all turned and looked. Dee, who was blessed with a bob of the finest, silkiest hair, looked as if someone had put her finger in a socket and switched it on. I laughed out loud. 'Wow,' I said, 'that's amazing. Your hair is literally standing on end. You look terrified.'

'Static in the air,' said John, standing and looking skywards. 'Dark clouds coming in from the west. Looks like we've got an electric storm coming. Might be a rough night. Will you two be okay?'

I nodded. 'We were in an earthquake in San Francisco,' I said.

'Yes,' said Dee, with a determined nod. 'And we got through that. We can cope with anything. *Anything*.'

My face, burned to a crisp, was throbbing with heat as we went to bed that night. My lips were cracked and brittle and my eyelids felt swollen and bruised. Throughout the evening I had gently rubbed moisturiser into my skin, its cooling effect temporary, but the damage was done. In a matter of days, my face would start quietly peeling off and I'd look like a leper.

'My jellyfish stings have calmed down,' I said, pointing the torch we'd been given into Dee's face.

'Mine too. How's your face? It doesn't look too bad in the pitch dark.' I swung the torch back towards me. 'Oh,' Dee added. 'I take it back. 'You look like the Phantom of the Opera. When he takes the mask off.'

'Yeah. So much for "The sun shall not smite thee by day". It smote me good. It smote me right up.' I sighed. 'What do *you* think I should do,' I asked, turning off the torch and lying in the dark. 'When I get home, I mean?'

'I think you should do something that will make you happy. I have never understood people who do the same job for forty years and hate it. What's the point of that? Everyone has something they love. Everyone. And somewhere, there's a job that goes with it. You need to work out what you love doing. Other than being an idiot.'

'I don't know if I like being an idiot.'

'No. But you're very good at it.'

'I quite like riding around on my bicycle and pretending it's a horse. Is there a job that goes with that?'

'You know, I think you need to stop worrying. You'll get back home, you'll probably go live with your parents for a bit and that'll make them deliriously happy and you'll get a job, one that'll keep you going but you won't be that into and over a period of time, you'll gradually work out what it is that you actually want to do. I think one of your problems is that you could probably do lots of different things. You're actually very lucky. Take your time. Get a job and earn some money, but work out what your What If is. Everyone has a What If – the thing that if you never try it, you'll never forgive yourself. That is what you need to know.'

'I don't know what my What If is yet,' I replied, with a small yawn.

'You will. Eventually.'

*

A quiet wind blowing through the trees and the sound of crickets softly singing in the grass had lulled us into a deep sleep. But the storm was coming, rumbling in across the Florida Keys, crackling and livid. I was woken around 1.30 in the morning by the relentless battering of rain on canvas. It was intense and insistent, like the urgent drumming of an advancing army played out to instil nothing but fear in those it sought to conquer.

Dee was sitting upright, her knees pulled to her chest. I raised myself up on my elbows and looked at her. She seemed terrified.

'Wow,' I said, rubbing my eyes with the back of my hand. 'That is some rain.'

'It's coming in,' Dee said, gesturing towards the bottom of the tent. 'We're filling with water, look.' Holding the torch in her hands she turned it on and shone the beam towards my feet. A large puddle of rainwater was gathering at the far end of the tent. 'Probably because the ground is so dry,' Dee explained. 'The water isn't being absorbed quickly enough.'

'What shall we do?' I asked, pulling the bottom of my sleeping bag up away from the encroaching pool.

'It's dry up this end,' observed Dee. 'Shift yourself this way. You won't be able to lie out. It's getting worse. If you sit up here, next to me, then we can use your foam bed to act as a sandbag. Hopefully that'll take up some of the water.'

I shuffled back towards the small square dry patch at the back of the tent. The rain was incredible, like a battery of machine-gun fire, a violent prelude to the main assault to come. The eye of the storm was fast approaching. The wind had picked up, and was whistling under the rain, a turbulent accompaniment. Thunder cracked overhead, an ear-splitting explosion followed immediately by a barrage of lightning strikes, each of which illuminated the tent briefly so that we were constantly being pitched between a strange troubling radiance and total darkness. The main offensive had begun and somehow we had to sit it out.

More thunder splintered the skies above us, lightning shattered down and over it all, the constant barrage of the rain beat on, relentless and unforgiving. The tent walls buffeted aggressively in and out as the wind howled and, with nothing to protect us other than a flimsy ground sheet, water bubbled up into the tent. If we could have got out and run for it, we would have done but the storm was so extreme we had no choice but to stay where we were and hope for the best. The lightning was coming down with such frequency that setting foot outside would have been tantamount to suicide.

I reached for Dee's hand and gripped it instinctively, like when a child finds solace in a mother's touch. I had been in storms before, but never one this violent and threatening. It was if a monster had descended from the skies, hell-bent on destruction. The earthquake had been dangerous but somehow, I hadn't been afraid. Novelty had kept fear at bay but this was like coming face-to-face with a recognisable demon. I was utterly petrified.

'Hail Mary, full of grace, the Lord is with thee,' Dee began to mumble, as she clutched my hand, tightly. 'Blessed art thou amongst women, and blessed is the fruit of thy womb Jesus. Holy Mary, Mother of God, pray for us sinners, now and at the hour of our death.'

Another piercing crack sounded to our left. The lightning was getting closer. I jumped and pushed myself as close to Dee as I could.

'Hail Mary, full of grace, the Lord is with thee,' Dee battled onwards, 'blessed art thou amongst women, and blessed is the fruit of thy womb, Jesus. Holy Mary, Mother of God, pray for us sinners, now and at the hour of our death.'

I had never given any serious thought to dying before but with the water rising, and with Dee beside herself with fear, I felt a chill grip me in the chest. I was only 22. I'd done nothing with my life. I hadn't even decided what I wanted to do, I was a blank page and here I was, at genuine risk of being permanently snuffed out.

An almighty thunder crack broke across the sky and a series of three sharp illuminations lit up the tent. 'That was close,' I whispered, my breathing sharp and shallow. 'That was really close.'

To our right something let out a deep and troubled splinter, as if something had been fatally fractured. 'It's hit the tree,' Dee whispered, holding me tighter. 'It's hit the tree behind us.'

An intense snapping noise whined through the rain, puncturing the storm with a miserable, shattering death rattle. Dee was right; the lightning had struck the large pine immediately behind our tent. 'It's coming down,' I whispered, barely able to speak. It was as if the world had come to a stop and I was seeing the last moments of my life play out in slow motion. I looked at Dee. There were tears in her eyes. There was nothing we could do. The tree was coming down.

The broken pine gave out a last shuddering moan and the sound of breaking branches filled the air. The tree, splintering in two, heaved towards the ground and with an almighty crunch, the side of the tent exploded towards us. We both screamed, clinging to each other. Thoughts of my parents coursed through me, but with the blind terror came the realisation that I was still alive. The sound of the tree falling settled, and the stubborn beat of the rain filled the void. The tree had missed us. We had been extremely lucky.

'By inches,' said John, shaking his head, the following morning. 'It missed you by inches.'

The storm had decimated the campsite and as we stared at the fallen tree, I was thankful that, for once, the fickle finger of fate had gone our way. We had been let off the hook.

We all knew how lucky we'd been. We couldn't push our luck any further. It was time to go home.

Chapter Twelve

We Are Family

$74.66

We had less than $75 between us to last two and a half weeks. The Barretts, whose hospitality had exceeded all expectations, were determined that we were going to be passed into the hands of 'good folk' and had arranged for us to stay with some second cousins who lived in Winston-Salem. 'It's on the way to Washington,' they told us. 'But not the place where the witches come from. That's the other Salem. In Massachusetts.' Not only that, but the second cousins had some obscure relatives in Pennsylvania. In theory, our passage home was guaranteed.

Given that our funds were so low, it was crucial that we didn't arrive in New York before the day of our flight. We couldn't afford to. The trick now was to eke out the journey between Florida and New York as best we could. The longer we could stay with people for free the better, but given we were relying on the kindness of total strangers it would have been foolish to assume that it was going to be straightforward. Dee was adamant that, come what may, she had to see the Edward Hopper collection in Washington. We wouldn't be able to stay there but if we arrived first thing in the morning, we could rush to the National Gallery of Art, see the paintings, and get back on the Greyhound to Pennsylvania. It was the only thing she had wanted to do. Missing it was not an option.

*

The Barretts, ever wonderful, had wanted to see us off with a decent meal in our bellies and so had driven us to the Pensacola Surf 'n' Turf, a low-to-the-ground building with the aura of a youth club that sat, rather sullenly, on a patch of large, unformed scrub. We were greeted at the door by a girl in a lobster costume. One of her front teeth was missing and she was chewing gum. She wore scuffed trainers that were poking out from a trail of lobster legs that were bunched up and hanging loose from her sides. She had terrible acne, large welts that threatened to burst at any given moment, and as I stared at her, she blew one half-hearted bubble. She was a vision of misery.

'Smokin' or non-smokin'?' she asked, eyes half-lidded and lifeless.

'Non-smokin', please,' answered John, with a smile.

The girl turned and stared into the virtually empty restaurant. 'Over there,' she said, gesturing into the space with an oversized foam claw.

The restaurant's interior was a functional affair: green tables with blue plastic chairs covered in cushions patterned with seashells. Everywhere you looked, there were pictures of cartoon crabs and shrimps and lobsters laughing merrily. 'They wouldn't be laughing if they knew they were about to be boiled alive and dipped in garlic mayonnaise,' Dee pointed out, helpfully.

We chose a table next to the window. There wasn't much of a view to speak of, just the cars and jeeps in the parking lot and one mangy dog urinating against everyone's wheels. ALL YOU CAN EAT SURFIN' FRENZY! yelled the menu: it was a buffet, hot plates heaving with giant prawns, crab legs, crab meat, whitebait, lumps of random fish in random sauces, mussels splayed open with a total lack of modesty, lobster claws, tuna steaks, tuna salads, Caesar salads, Waldorf salads,

salads I'd never heard of, French dressing, blue-cheese dressing, croutons, tomatoes, melon, mango and strawberries.
Despite the feast on offer, I wasn't in much of a mood for
eating. Anxiety was beginning to quietly gnaw at me. The
journey back to New York meant only one thing: the end of
summer, the end of my student life and the beginning of
great uncertainty.

'I feel a bit depressed, Dee,' I said, as we washed our
hands in the public bathroom.

She wiped her hands and looked at me. 'Really? Perhaps
you *were* bitten by a Lyme tick? Do you feel a bit neurologi-
cally challenged? More than normal, I mean.'

'I'm serious,' I replied. 'I do a bit. I don't want to
go home.'

'It's not that you don't want to go home. Home is great.
Your own bed! Clean sheets! I think this is about you not
knowing what it is you're going back to. You've finished
university; you don't know what you want to do as a career.
Of course you're feeling anxious. But it's not the same as not
wanting to go home. There's a difference. You'll be really
pleased to see your mum and dad won't you?'

I nodded.

'Look,' she continued, resting her hand on my shoulder,
'we've got over two weeks before we get to New York. I say,
let's go out with a bang. Make the most of it. Enjoy
ourselves. We'll never have this freedom again. Not as long as
we live. This is the last time in our lives we'll have no respon-
sibilities. Yes, we've got no money but we've also got not a
care in the world.'

'Other than making it back to New York,' I added.

'Exactly. And that's an adventure. It's not a responsibility.
The gauntlet is down. And we're going to do it. We've got the

rest of our lives to feel mildly depressed and disappointed. So why waste the time we have left fretting and feeling rubbish?'

She was right, of course, but as she spoke I began to understand what was at the root of my anxiety. It wasn't just the uncertainty of what I was going to do with my life, it was more that I realised the larger, more important thing I would be losing when I returned to England. Dee would be off to Medical School and our bond, while not broken, would never quite be the same again. I had begun grieving for our friendship. We had been together through thick and thin, not just since we'd been in America, but for the past three years. I relied on Dee for everything and we were about to be parted. I couldn't bear it.

The farewells at the Greyhound were mildly awful. The Barretts (all of them) were in tears and John, choking with emotion, had pressed $20 into my hand while sobbing, 'Take care.'

As we waved goodbye to them from the window, Dee, touched by the overly distraught goodbyes, turned to me. 'I think they genuinely think we're going to die, Emma.'

'Can't think what could have given them that idea,' I said, still waving. 'Golly they were lovely. I loved them.'

'Me too,' said Dee, with a grin.

The journey to Winston-Salem took us through Georgia and South Carolina but we had slept for most of the way, the combination of full bellies and the disruption of the stormy night taking their toll. As we disembarked, the smell of tobacco whispered on the air, a result of the large cigarette factory that dominated the city, but other than that we were in familiar surroundings: another Greyhound station in another American city.

We were met by Gayle, a petite woman with immaculate hair wound into precise curls. Her clothes were a vision in lemon and mint: crisp pleated slacks, pristine white T-shirt and a cashmere jumper tossed carefully about her shoulders. As she took us in, Dee in her crumpled flowery skirt and faded pink blouse and me in my grungy blue cotton shorts and stained Aertex top, her mouth settled itself into a fixed grin, but her eyes betrayed a small moment of panic. 'You both went to Oxford, right?' she asked, as I shook her by the hand.

'Yes,' I replied, 'yes we did.'

She visibly relaxed. 'Oh, okay, it's just…well, I wanted to make sure I had the right two English girls! Ha!'

'We've been travelling for ages,' I explained, sensing that our appearance was verging on the refugee. 'And I had my rucksack stolen so…' I gestured downwards towards my shabby attire.

'Stolen?' said Gayle, visibly shocked. 'How awful. You mean you've just been wearing the same clothes? For how long?'

'About a week,' I said, with a shrug. 'But it's fine. In many ways, I'm no different from a teenage boy.'

'They wear the same clothes for months,' chipped in Dee, throwing her rucksack into the trunk of Gayle's car.

Gayle was a stay-at-home mom, the wife of a cigarette executive, Charlie, who lived in an enormous house situated in the middle of a gated community. They had a 12-year-old son, Damian, and were, rather fortuitously, avid Anglophiles.

'We love everything to do with England,' Gayle explained, holding up a Union Jack apron and pouring us tea from a pot shaped like Shakespeare's head.

Charlie loved England so much that he'd converted the house's tornado cellar into an English pub. We couldn't believe our eyes. 'You can have a game of darts later, if you like,' said Gayle, with a smile.

We'd be sharing a room, a vision in pale pink. It was so pristine and sparkling I felt like a filthy grub that had crawled into someone's house. We had been on the road for so long and become so accustomed to making do and roughing it that I had near forgotten what being in a proper home was like. I'd been washing my pants out in sinks and under stand taps, my Converse trainers, ripened like a Camembert, had, as we liked to say 'turned', and the gusset of my cotton shorts was, on closer inspection, not long for this world. To conclude: I was a tattered shambles. Awkward then, that Charlie, on arriving home from work, declared his intention to take us to the 'smartest restaurant in town'. It was a bit like taking a pair of Victorian orphans to the Ritz.

Charlie was a vision of late eighties corporate success. He had a magnificent head of hair, heaped into an ice-cream swirl, wore a silky grey tough shouldered suit, red braces and an *amuse-bouche* of a tie, sprinkled with a tiny cigarette motif. He had a clunking brick of a mobile phone, a breeze-block briefcase and a pair of lips that swaggered into the room five minutes before he did. He had the demeanour of a danger-ous horse. He was mildly terrifying.

'Sushi!' he bellowed. 'Ever had it?'

We shook our heads.

'Oh wait!' said Dee, 'that's the raw fish thing. I've had an oyster.'

'It's not like *fruits de mer*, is it?' I asked, a stab of anxiety coursing through me. 'Because I had that once when I was little. And I became a gushing pipe of shit and vomit.'

'That's shellfish,' boomed Charlie, as we all piled into his Mercedes. 'Sushi is fish. Salmon. Tuna. Eel. Mackerel. You know, fish. Did you like your oyster?'

'Not really. It was sort of like swallowing a large, salty snot.'

'Well, you'll love this!' he declared, pulling out of the garage. 'Best Japanese restaurant in Winston! You sit round a hotplate and they cook everything up for you right in front of you. Roll the sushi, cut the sashimi, grill up the yakitori. It's great!'

Dee was sitting in the front next to Charlie, who had decided to quiz her about the six wives of Henry VIII. As he was shouting, 'So which was the one with the funny fingers?' I felt a soft tap on my forearm. I turned. Gayle was leaning towards me.

'So what was your major at Oxford?' she asked.

'We only study one subject in British universities,' I explained. 'Well. Unless you're doing English and French. What I mean is, its more usual to just study one thing in Britain. Unlike here, where it's a bit like our A Levels. So we take three A levels but then we pick one subject and that's what we read at university.'

Gayle nodded.

'So I studied English.'

Gayle's eyes, heavily made up, widened. 'Oh, I love reading,' she said, tightening her grip on my forearm. 'In fact, I just finished a book. *Bitter Blood*. By Jerry Bledsoe. Have you read it?'

I shook my head.

'It's incredible. It's a true-crime story. Happened right here in Winston-Salem. Terrible murders. This guy, Fritz Klenner, crazy guy, absolutely crazy, thought he was Jesus, thought he was a government operative, killed...well, I shouldn't say anymore. I'll lend it to you. I'd be real interested to have your thoughts.'

'Huh,' I said, nodding. 'That'd be great. Thanks.'

'Did you study many true-crime books at Oxford?'

'No,' I replied, clearing my throat a little, 'they're not really on the syllabus.'

'Oh well, great, so you won't know what happens.'

The restaurant was a vision in chrome. Instead of tables, seats were arranged around squares in which stood a chef and a hot plate. As we sat down, our chef, a Japanese man wearing a white bandana and a navy kimono, began bowing at quite a rate. We all bowed back. I went to shake him by the hand but was stopped by Charlie. 'They hate shaking hands in Japan. Hate it. It's a minefield whenever I'm abroad. You can't tip in Iceland. Did you know that?'

I shook my head.

'Totally unacceptable. Different cultures, see – the appropriate method of thanks in our culture is not necessarily that in others.'

We sat on stools and as the menus were handed out, I turned and looked around the restaurant. The lighting was low, giving the place the feel of a nightclub, the only real illumination coming from the centre of each cooking square where chefs, working up a frenzy, were tossing butterflied prawns, chopping sushi rolls and basting salt-grilled fish. I had never eaten Japanese food before so was pleased when Charlie took it upon himself to order for everyone. 'Wafu salad, edamame beans, you'll love those, spider rolls, let's get some chicken yakitori, some salt-grilled mackerel and the mixed sashimi. And for sushi, we'll get the yellow tail, salmon and tuna. How's that?'

I just nodded. 'Thanks so much for taking us out for dinner, Charlie,' I said. 'It's very kind of you.'

'Oh, no worries,' he bellowed, turning to look at me. As he looked at me, his eyes narrowed a little and he leaned in, 'Think you got something on your forehead. You might want to get rid of it.'

I frowned and rubbed my fingers above my eyebrows. The skin felt odd: crinkly yet damp. I looked at my fingertips and realised, with some disgust, that they were covered in bits of dead, burned skin. The peeling had begun. 'I got really sun scorched in Fort Pickens,' I explained. 'I'll just go to the bathroom.'

The vision greeting me in the mirror was far from pretty. Bits of my forehead were hanging off and angry pink weeping patches were moaning underneath. I looked like something that had walked out from a nuclear apocalypse. I wasn't quite sure what to do for the best. Half of it was desiccated and flaky, the other seeping. Taking the edge of one piece of flapping skin I gently tugged and watched, in some horror, as a patch about an inch across crackled off. I flicked it off my finger and then, having another close look, brushed off the flaky excesses. I looked awful. Still, it was dark in the restaurant. I hoped I could get away with it.

Back at the table and the sushi had arrived. Beautifully presented oblongs of fresh fish resting on perfectly moulded rice rectangles. In the corner of the large wooden platter there was a small triangular mound of something intensely green and next to it was a polite heap of pickled ginger. 'Go careful on the green stuff,' warned Charlie. 'It's wasabi, hot as hell.'

I took my chopsticks and reached over to pick off one of the salmon sushi but as I did so, something floated through

the air and landed, rather serenely on top of the tuna sushi
next to it. I blinked and was momentarily puzzled. What was
that, I thought, staring. I looked up, wondering if something
had floated off the ceiling but then, looking back at it again
I realised what it was. The thing that had just landed on the
tuna sushi was nothing other than the inch-long piece of skin
I had just flicked off the end of my finger in the bathroom.
Rather than falling to the floor, it had come to rest on the
end of my shirt and had been carried by a passing breeze
from my sleeve to the fish. Before I could say or do anything,
Charlie, with some gusto, clasped the tuna sushi between his
chopsticks and shoved it straight into his mouth. He was
eating an inch-long piece of my forehead. I stared in dismay.
'Oooh,' I began, 'don't...'

'What's that?' asked Charlie, chewing.

It was past the point of no return. 'Never mind,' I said,
with a small, urgent shake of my head. 'Doesn't matter.'
Something told me that serving your host your own dead
skin was not an appropriate method of thanks. In any culture.

We had been in Winston-Salem for four days. We'd spent
the time seeing the sights, going to Old Salem, eating
Moravian cookies and marvelling at the craftsmen and
women in traditional dress who baked bread, weaved
baskets and generally kept the candle burning for old-time
living. Other than that, we had read books. Dee was working her way through John Fowles' *The Magus* and I was
ploughing on with *Bitter Blood*, the book that Gayle had
lent me. It was a curious tale of family feuds, paranoia and
an obsession with revenge. It was quite heavy-going but
Gayle seemed obsessed with it. Every night she would creep
up to me and say, eyes wide, 'How much do you think Susie

really knew?' And I'd have to tell her I hadn't got to that bit yet. It was quite a thick book.

The other thing occupying our time was a video game, RC Pro-Am, belonging to Gayle's 12-year-old son Damian. It was a truck-racing entertainment requiring the players to race like a fury around an increasingly complicated course picking up points and avoiding obstacles as you went. Damian was the king of it, a fact he was more than happy to let us know.

'You suck,' he told us as he tossed off an end score of 18,450 points.

'I'm warning you now,' I said to him as Gayle took him off to bed. 'I am going to beat your score. And I am going to beat it BAD.'

'Yeah,' he answered, with a dismissive hand, 'you can TRY.'

As he left, fire in my eyes, I turned to Dee and said, 'If it's the last thing we do, we're beating that little shit's score.'

Dee was in total agreement. Damian was going DOWN.

We settled ourselves in front of the games console that was attached to a small television that sat on a round wooden table towards the back of the storm cellar. Behind us was the bar and, as everyone else had gone upstairs, I gestured towards it.

'Do you think Charlie will mind if we have a beer?' I asked Dee, who had picked up the joystick.

'No, I don't think so,' she replied, absent-mindedly, 'there's loads there. I'm sure he won't miss a couple.'

I watched over my shoulder as Dee raced through level one of the Pro-Am challenge. She won it easily. 'Good work,' I said, turning and opening the large fridge packed with bottles of ice-cold beers. I pulled two out and removed the tops using the bottle opener that was screwed to the wall. 'That's clever,' I said, nodding towards it. 'Never seen one of those before. Cool. Here you go, Dee.' We clinked bottles. 'Here's to victory.'

Four hours later and we had entered into a swirling morass of gaming madness. Having ploughed successfully through levels one to three we had entered the oubliette of level four, where oil slicks, rain puddles and a nemesis yellow lorry had entered the fray. Empty beer bottles were scattered across the floor, bottle tops lay in a heap. We had lost all sense of time or space and had barely spoken, only to shout things like 'Not the oil on the left! NOT THE OIL ON THE LEFT!' and 'FUCK YOU, YELLOW LORRY. FUCK YOU IN THE EYE!'

We had lost our tiny minds.

We had been drinking beer solidly and with every bottle, our hand-eye coordination was deteriorating. During one pass around two in the morning, we had, through sheer fluke, come within spitting distance of Damian's record, but other than that, we were nowhere near it.

'Do you want another beer?' I had slurred, crawling over to the fridge and pulling out another two bottles.

Dee cast a half-open eye at the detritus of booze that surrounded her. 'Have we had loads of Charlie's beer?' she asked, as if this was something of a surprise.

I glanced into the now near-empty fridge. There was one bottle of beer left. 'Yes,' I said, with a wobbling nod. 'Yes, we have.'

We had drunk the place dry, we were plastered and we were obsessed with beating a child. This was not a happy state of affairs by anyone's calculations. The fun had ended hours ago and we were joylessly pressing on, grunting as we crossed the finishing line again and again in second and third. It was ten to six in the morning. We had been playing the game without pause for over eight hours. I turned to Dee. 'This is the one,' I slurred. 'This is the one.' She didn't even bother replying. Her eyes were heavy and lidded, her soul crushed and withered.

The trucks were lined up. I was blue. To my left, there was a green truck (reasonable form, nippy round corners). Behind that there was a brown lorry (no threat whatsoever) and to its right the demon yellow lorry (evil nemesis). Because there was only one joystick, we had to take it in turns and between us, our attempts to vanquish level 4 now ran into the hundreds. Somehow, we had to avoid the oil slicks, water puddles, rain clouds and pop-up walls while hitting every single zipper zone which, in theory, would speed us to glory.

Over it all, compounding our miserable insanity, an electro-pop beat blared onwards. It was like Chinese water torture, the tinny cacophony poking at my eardrums like a massive annoying stick that made me want to commit real live murders. The controls, clunky and imprecise, had become my bête noire. One slight touch, and our truck was skidding sideways in the wrong direction. I wanted every single person involved in the conception, production and marketing of RC Pro-Am truck racing to *die*.

We had to complete two rotations of the track. The music sparked up, the lights went from Red to Green. Off I went, skidding round the first corner, picking up an exhaust pipe and 500 points, avoiding three water puddles and hitting the first zipper zone. I was in the lead.

Coming round the third bend I picked up a wheel, fended off an attempt to pass from the yellow truck and narrowly avoided an oil spill. Gliding through the chicane, I hit a patch of water and skidded sideways missing an essential zipper zone.

'Shit,' mumbled Dee.

The yellow truck passed me to take the first lap.

Dee, in a near catatonic state, slumped sideways and mumbled, 'Come on, Ems. For fuck's sake.'

Zooming round the tight top corner, I picked up a second wheel, went sideways around the oil slick and hit a zipper zone to pull level with the yellow truck. Dee sat up. The lorries were neck and neck. This had never happened before. Dee squealed.

Sliding into the near impossible chicane I somehow avoided three patches of water. My lorry, sliding from left to right, bumped into the yellow lorry but instead of spinning sideways, as had always happened, my lorry had the better of the knock and as they collided, my truck whispered an edge onto the final zipper zone. With a burst of acceleration, my truck shot past the yellow lorry and crossed the finishing line in first. Dee gripped her mouth and let out a thin, strangled cry.

There was a pause. The cheap, tinny music piped a triumphant blare. Up came the Trophy Room page. We had come first. Score: 18,457.

We had done it. It had taken us over eight hours but we had beaten a 12-year old-boy by seven points. In your *face*.

Without even looking at Dee, I threw down the joystick and got up but I was so drunk that as I stood I fell headfirst into a small table and stools. The table broke in half, and as I landed, two of the stools lost their legs. Beer bottles scattered everywhere, a few smashing against the wall as they fell. Undeterred, I got up, and like a marathon runner with the end in sight but with nothing but wonky legs to go on, I made my way up the flight of steps out of the basement, Dee crawling on her hands and knees behind me. We had broken Damian's record, the basement was trashed and the bar was drunk dry. We were a *disgrace*.

We woke seven hours later. I turned and looked across the room at Dee. 'What have we done?' I whispered, in horror. 'What have we *done*?'

'We need to get up right now and really apologise,' said Dee, leaping from her bed. 'Apologise as if our lives depended on it.'

We were met by stony faces in the kitchen. Gayle was preparing lunch, Charlie was sitting reading a paper. Damian, the reason for our ignominy, was playing with a hand-held electronic game in the shape of a space rocket. We stood in the doorway, awkward and ashamed, not quite sure how best to go about making amends. These people had not only put us up, they'd fed us and given us the run of the house. Gayle had lent me a book for crying out loud.

'We're both very sorry for what happened last night,' said Dee, clearing her throat. 'We got a little carried away trying to beat Damian's score on the RC Pro-Am. It sort of felt quite important at the time. It ended up taking eight hours.'

Damian looked up. 'I beat it back again. First time.'

I shot him a short, incredulous stare. 'You broke it back again?' I began. 'In the first go?' Dee nudged me in the side.

'Anyway,' continued Dee. 'We're truly very sorry. And if there's anything we can do. We'll give you some money. For the beer.'

'When are you leaving for Washington?' asked Charlie, not looking up from his paper.

'Well,' said Dee. 'We can leave today actually.'

'Great,' said Charlie.

'Can I have *Bitter Blood* back,' added Gayle, slowly chopping some celery. 'Before you go.'

'Oh. I haven't actually finished it but...'

'He blows himself and everyone else up in the back of his truck,' snapped Gayle, still chopping. 'Susie knew everything. That's what happens.'

I nodded. We all stood in silence. This was, without a doubt, *very* awkward.

Given the extent of our shame, it was a massive relief to be back on the Greyhound. We were terribly hung-over and we both sat, our heads in our hands, feeling wretched. 'When we get back to England,' Dee mumbled, 'and we've got some money, we need to send Gayle the biggest bunch of flowers ever.'

'Wonder how long that will take us,' I burbled back, eyes closed. 'I've just remembered I owe the bank manager three hundred and fifty pounds when I set foot on English soil. Interesting. I told him I'd be back with pockets stuffed with gold. Ha! Now I've had my rucksack stolen, I haven't even GOT any pockets. Take that, Mr Bank Man!'

We drifted off into a thick, uneasy sleep. We had caught the evening bus that would get us into Washington the following morning. We had left $30 for the beer, way beyond what we could afford, but such was our guilt that we were prepared to leave almost half of our available funds. We now had a grand total of $40 to see us home with nine days to go.

Washington was going to be a whistle-stop. The only reason we were getting off the Greyhound was to satisfy Dee's long-held ambition to see the Edward Hopper paintings in the flesh. He was her favourite artist, prints of his work had been pinned to her walls at college: *Chop Suey*, *Nighthawks*, and *Office At Night*, all of them focused on a quiet, intimate moment. But it was his solitary female paintings filled with regret and isolation she loved the most. Hopper had scraped back the brashness of American living and revealed the sadness underneath. She thought he was wonderful.

According to a woman at the Greyhound left-luggage deposit, we weren't that far from the National Gallery of Art, no more than a ten-minute drive, but if we didn't know where we were going we should take a cab. 'It'll be about five bucks,' she told us, as she heaved Dee's rucksack onto a rack and handed her a docket. 'And you shouldn't walk round this area. It ain't too safe.'

Even though five dollars was a massive dent in our already dwindling budget, this was a treat for Dee and I readily agreed. The gallery, after all, had free admission. In the ever-turning carousel of our fortunes, it would all even itself out.

Immediately outside the Greyhound station there was a group of men hanging around cars, none of which looked particularly like standard taxis. Some were bent over bonnets, others were leaning against open doors but all of them looked like sharks waiting to pounce on soft, unsuspecting prey new to the capital. One man, holding worry beads and ostentatiously showing off a large Rolex, jerked his head towards us.

'You wanna taxi? I can take you, come on,' he said, opening the back car door and gesturing into it, 'get in. I'll take you wherever you wanna go.'

Three months ago, Dee and I would have taken one look at him and walked in the opposite direction but we were now so immune to catastrophe that he could have been dressed like the Child Catcher, had dead body parts hanging out the boot and we *still* would have got in. 'Wow,' he said, taking a good look at us. 'You girls are *hairy*.' I frowned. What was he talking about? I looked at Dee, she raised her eyebrows and gave a silent shrug.

'National Gallery of Art, please,' I said and sat back.

'You from Australia?' asked the man, staring back at us while driving.

'No, England,' I replied.

'Right, right,' he nodded, still looking at us. 'Cos you got that Australian vibe goin' on. Rough-looking. Like you could fight a kangaroo.'

'Can you watch the road please,' I asked, choosing to ignore him.

'So rude,' mumbled Dee, shaking her head.

'Seriously,' he persisted. 'You been livin' rough or something? You smell kinda funky.'

'National Gallery of Art, please,' I said again.

Ignoring me, he launched into a random monologue about English women and how he'd heard Europeans don't wash and all have nasty teeth. As he spoke, he kept gently touching the sun visor above the steering wheel and I realised, with some horror, that there was a gun wedged into it. I quickly scanned the dashboard. There was no meter. 'This is going to cost five dollars, right,' I asked, with some insistence. 'That's what the lady at the Greyhound told us it should cost.'

The driver looked away and sucked his teeth. Before we had left the Greyhound building I had had a quick scan of a map of the area. The gallery, I had ascertained, was on Constitution Avenue at the bottom of which was the iconic Lincoln Memorial. We were being driven down 2nd Street. I could see the Supreme Court ahead of us and remembered from the map that Constitution Avenue would be to the right, yet as we approached the Court building he took a sharp left. I looked back over my shoulder and could clearly see the long green expanse of Constitution Avenue receding behind us. 'Umm,' I said, 'isn't the gallery that way?'

The driver said nothing. He was clearly taking us on a circuitous route. Dee, who had already had quite enough, piped up, 'Let us out here please. Now.'

'But we're not there yet,' he protested.

'Pull over. Now,' barked Dee. We had stopped at some traffic lights where, rather fortuitously, two police officers were chatting. As the car came to a halt, Dee nudged me and pointing to the door said, 'Get out, Emma, get out now.' We bundled ourselves onto the pavement.

The driver, leaning over towards his open window held out his hand and said, 'Forty bucks.' His other hand, I noticed, was hovering over the sun visor. I stood back and looked over my shoulder to check where the two police officers were.

'You must be joking,' said Dee, reaching into her bumbag. 'You'll get five dollars. I've only got a twenty-dollar bill. I want fifteen dollars' change. Do you understand?'

The driver looked at her and shrugged. 'Yeah, yeah. Pass it over.'

Thinking we had come to a deal, Dee handed over the twenty-dollar bill but as soon as it left her hand, the driver put his foot on the accelerator and was gone. We stood, incredulous. We had been fleeced. And in one fell swoop, our survival fund was halved. We gasped and stood open-mouthed. Dee shook her head. 'I hope his cock drops off, Emma. Actually drops off. Or is eaten, in his sleep, by a penis louse.'

'Is there such a thing as a penis louse?' I asked.

'No. But I wish there was.'

'We've got twenty dollars to get to New York,' I said, staring blankly after the departed taxi. 'Oh, hang on, what's that I can hear?' I added, cupping a hand to my ear. 'Oh yes. It's the bells of doom.'

As always, we weren't going to let adversity set us back. We walked the rest of the way to the National Gallery of Art, past the Supreme Court building and the mighty white dome of the Smithsonian Institute. The National Gallery itself was as grand as they come; mighty Corinthian columns made of pink Tennessee marble lined the front portico that stood, majestically, at the top of a long flight of steps. Everything about it was crisp and clean and certain, a fitting backdrop for Dee's date with destiny.

The Hoppers were in the East building, a spectacular edifice connected to the main body of the gallery by an escalator cut into a vast wall of granite. Sunlight poured down through glass pyramids above us while waterfalls, trapped behind glass, cascaded down around us. It was fair to say this building demanded our attention.

Dee had entered into a different plane of consciousness. Despite our recent setback, her dream was about to come true. Beatifically calm, and glowing with an expectation of what was to come, she gave me a quick potted analysis of Hopper so that I could better enjoy his work. 'Look out,' she began, 'for pictures where lone figures stand doing things. It's all about distraction and isolation. Everyone's distraction is different and everyone's distraction is isolating. It can be anything. Reading a book, getting dressed in the morning, reading an envelope in an office – every action is a distraction and automatically isolates the individual. Hopper is very preoccupied with loneliness. Empty streets. People on their own. Oh, Emma, I'm very excited.'

We passed a small sign on the wall with a list of artists on it, HOPPER being the pertinent word. A small, discreet arrow pointed to a room at the far end of the corridor. As we came nearer the only sound were our own footfalls on the polished floor. No one else was around. Dee had drifted ahead of me slightly as I had stopped, momentarily, to look at a marble nude so when I caught her up I was puzzled to see a small expression of alarm.

'That's not possible,' she mumbled, shaking her head.

'What isn't? I asked, joining her.

She pointed towards the door of the side gallery. It was shut and from its handle hung one single sign. '"Hopper exhibit temporarily closed,"' I read. '"Collection currently on loan."' My hand involuntarily went up to my mouth. 'Oh no, Dee,' I mouthed, the words barely making themselves heard.

The Hoppers were not there.

I knew, as soon as I took in the disappointment on Dee's face, that this was one blow too far. Dee, the backbone of our adventures, was broken. Her strength and perseverance, qualities that had carried me through all our adversities, had, at last, failed her.

We sat on the steps of the gallery staring out at the passing cars of Washington. We were in the capital of the modern world yet all the power on earth couldn't make our day any better. Dee, other than a five-minute string of expletives, hadn't really spoken since we discovered the closed room and was now hunched and filled with sorrow. I looked at her, thinking what I could do. She had helped me so many times, picked me up when I was down, dusted me off and sent me skipping out ready to fight another day. I had to step up to the plate. It was my turn to be the best friend.

'You know,' I began, softly. 'In a way, you don't need to see his paintings. They're all etched into your memory. You're carrying them in your head. That's the best place for them isn't it?'

Dee shrugged.

'What was that one you told me about the other day? *Cape Cod* something?'

'*Cape Cod Morning*,' replied Dee, quietly.

'Yes, that one. Tell me about it. Describe it to me.'

Dee let out a small, frustrated sigh. 'It's the one where a red-haired woman in a pink dress is leaning on her hands looking out of a window into a wood. She's standing by the bay window. The painting is divided into two. House on the right, trees and sun-scorched grass to the left. A very intense light is bouncing off the house's white wooden slats.' She stopped, and scuffed at the step below with her foot. 'This is stupid.'

'No, it isn't. Tell me about another Hopper painting. I want you to tell me.'

Dee pursed her lips in thought and looked out over the avenue below. The sun was high, the sky cloudless and as she squinted into the light, she looked lost in thought. Then, with a small decisive heave of her chest, she turned back to me. '*New York Movie*. A woman with shoulder-length blond hair, it curls at the bottom, in towards her neck, is standing in the corner of a movie theatre. She looks subdued. She's wearing a dark navy blue trouser suit. The trousers are flared, tight fitted at the waist and have a red trim running down the side. She has one arm crossed over her, the other is held lightly touching her face. She looks preoccupied in thought. Some bright red curtains are immediately to her left, tied open. They reveal a staircase. We don't know where it goes.'

'Tell me another.'

'*Office at Night*. You know that one. It was on my wall. A man and woman are in an office. The man is sitting at his desk, looking at a piece of paper. Remember what I said about distractions and isolation?'

I nodded.

'He's absorbed by it. To his left there's a woman standing at a filing cabinet. She's got a massive arse.'

I laughed.

'She's looking at him but he doesn't notice. It's a brilliant painting. There are pieces of paper scattered throughout it. There's the paper he's reading, a piece of paper on a chair just behind the woman, a piece on the floor. It's sort of saying that even when he's done reading the piece of paper in his hand, he'll never have time to return her gaze. It's beautiful.'

Dee told me about the paintings of Edward Hopper for an hour. And I was in no mood to stop her.

As we got back onto the Greyhound later that evening, we were in a sombre mood.

Despite my best efforts, there was a listlessness to Dee that hadn't been there previously. Somewhere inside her a light had been switched off. America had been nothing we had expected it to be and it was difficult not to feel a tinge of disappointment. We had come for the time of our lives but it

had been a tough struggle and only naivety and blind optimism had kept us from going under. The leaves on the trees
were turning, late summer was presenting its final calling card
and autumn was on its way. The end was in sight. We just had
one more final race to run.

POTTSVILLE, PENNSYLVANIA, yelled the sign. Built on seven
hills, like Rome, Pottsville was the gateway to coal but for us,
it was the place we had to stay, come what may, for the next
seven days. 'One hill for every day,' said Dee. 'We shall have
to tick them off.' We had got off the Greyhound in
Philadelphia but because the bus to Pottsville was going to
cost us fourteen dollars, 'She's fifteen,' said Dee, nudging a
thumb in my direction, we saw nothing more of that great
city than the terminal. As we sat on the bus, Dee got out our
remaining six dollars. 'Well,' she said, staring down at it.
'That's it. We're now on less than a dollar a day.'

'We could live on gummy bears,' I suggested. 'At least
their chewy smiling faces will lift our spirits.'

We were picked up from the station by a woman in her mid-
twenties. Cherry had very long, straight hair and was severely
boss-eyed. She was one of the daughters of our hostess,
Marlene. 'There's eight of us,' she said, narrowly avoiding
hitting a parked car. 'But only me and my brother still live at
home. Well, that's not quite true. Sandy lives in the basement. But we don't really talk about him.'

Dee and I exchanged a short, puzzled look. Shall I ask, I
thought? No. Best not.

The house where we would see out the end of our
American adventure was on the corner of a maple-lined
street. It was a tall, wooden structure, with a porch that had

seen better days and, unlike the gleaming white houses either side of it, the paintwork was grey and peeling, the windows smothered in grime. The front yard was overgrown and a car with no wheels sat abandoned in the driveway. As Dee pulled her rucksack out from the truck, I looked up. 'Have you seen *Psycho*?' I muttered. 'It looks just like the house from *Psycho*.'

We were taken round to the back of the house where we picked our way around large piles of browned paper in bundles and boxes filled with empty bottles. Cherry pushed open the fly door and yelled, 'Ma! They're here!' We were in the kitchen. Dark, stained linoleum covered the floor, the walls a dusty brown. An aged and battered-looking oven stood, rather forlornly in the centre of the far wall while, to our left, a host of shelves were covered in a maelstrom of blackened pots. Dee went to put her rucksack down but stopped, realising she was about to plant it firmly in a small, still steaming, turd.

'Oh,' she said, staring down.

'Poop!' yelled Cherry, lunging at a small, hairy dog darting across the floor. 'Come here! Not again. Sorry. He shits everywhere. And Peep. Though she mostly just pisses. This is Poop,' she added, holding up the guilty canine. 'And that one, the one behind you, that's Peep.'

We turned and looked. Something that may have once been a spaniel stared up at us. It was the fattest dog I'd ever seen and had the look of a drug addict. I bent down to give its head a stroke. 'I wouldn't touch her right now if I were you,' warned Cherry. 'She's got fleas.'

I straightened up. A woman appeared in the doorway through to the dining room. She was small, quite fat and was dressed in a bright lemon velour tracksuit. Her face looked as if it had been smashed roughly from granite and her hair, an indefinable russet, was cropped short and had been styled by someone who may, or may not, have been drunk when they cut it. 'Jeez Loueez!' she yelled, seeing the dog shit quietly stewing on the kitchen floor. 'Get rid of it, Cherry! What a welcome! Hi. I'm Marlene. So I hear you've had some cash trouble?'

'That's putting it mildly,' I said, stepping forward to shake her hand. 'We've got six dollars to last us till New York.'

'Yeah, well,' said Marlene, with a dismissive wave. 'I'll be keeping you busy. I've arranged for you to do some...stuff. You can make yourselves useful.'

Behind us, the fly door gave a small bang and we turned to see a man in a check shirt and baseball cap. His face, slightly swollen about the edges, was defined by the presence of one, massive monobrow. It was as if someone had glued a handful of caterpillars onto his forehead and painted over them with creosote. We all stared at each other. Without a word, and after a quick glance at us, the man put his head down and wandered past us to a door in the far corner of the kitchen. He opened it and disappeared down a flight of stairs.

'That was Sandy,' said Marlene, as the basement door banged shut. 'Just ignore him.'

Dee and I exchanged another quick, puzzled glance.

'So you two are in the sitting room. That's through there. Bathroom's over there. That's all you need to know. Okay. I'll make eggy bread.'

As Marlene sparked up the stove, Dee and I wandered through to the sitting room to make up the sofa bed. There was always an awkwardness involved in first encounters, especially when you are totally reliant on other people's goodwill, and as we pulled on pillowcases and flicked out the sheets it was obvious how much of an imposition our staying was going to be. The sitting room, the only communal room in the house, was small and our sofa bed now took up most of it. 'Push my TV chair so it's at the bottom of your bed, will ya?' yelled Marlene from the kitchen.

The room was decorated with floral wallpaper, long faded, and one picture hung on the wall. It was a portrait of a girl, terribly done, but going on the fact that one of the girl's eyes was totally cock-eyed, I had to assume it was a picture of Cherry. Only one other thing of note was in the room, a large television in the corner blaring out a rolling shopping channel. A woman in astonishing pink was declaring the virtues of a jewellery range called 'Tears of the Angels'. We watched it in silence.

'Come get your eggy bread!' came a call from the kitchen.

When you only have six dollars in your pocket, there is one immutable fact etched into your consciousness: you'll take what you're given and you'll like it. As I stared down at the eggy bread I'd been handed I wasn't quite sure what to think. A large doorstep of white bread seemed to have been fried in something so black, it may have been axle grease. We took our forks and returned to the sitting room where, rather uncomfortably, we both sat on the edge of the sofa bed staring down at the plates in our laps.

I cast a glance towards Dee. She was pressing into her eggy bread with her fork only to see thick, black, anonymous treacle oozing out of it. She shot me a small, despairing look. I went for a mouthful and bit down, its suet-like slippery texture blubbering over my tongue. A greasy warm fat filled my mouth as if the bread was simply there as a spongy conduit for oil. I stared down again at my plate. The eggy bread was congealing and waxy lumps of fat were starting to gather at the edges. I pressed into it again with my fork but it slid away, skidding across the plate on its own hovercraft of lard leaving a dark slimy slug trail of grease as it went.

It took us over an hour to eat it.

I wouldn't have thought it was possible to be emotionally broken by a solitary piece of fried bread but, looking at Dee, slightly green, head in hands, I realised it was. Marlene had been chatting non-stop about anything and everything: her friend Letitia and her no-good husband Todd; her neighbour Roberta's bowel problems and her daughter Tania's close encounter with a lesbian. 'I said to her, Tania, trust me, the woman is a lesbian and she wants more than your recipe for shortbread.'

I sat, nodding and making appropriate noises in the gaps, of which there were few, occasionally pushing away the grease-congealed plate that was still wafting its deadly oleaginous spores in my direction.

There was a noise from the kitchen and a woman, her brown hair piled high on her head and oversized tinted glasses up on her forehead appeared in the doorway. She was wearing a short-sleeved jumper emblazoned with stars tucked, rather stubbornly, into a set of high-waisted stone-washed jeans and had phenomenally fancy fingernails. 'Hi Marlene,' she drawled as she chewed gum. 'You the kids from the UK?'

We nodded.

'Come on, then,' she said, gesturing back towards the kitchen. 'Let's go.'

Marlene thumbed in her direction. 'That's Letitia,' she

explained. 'You're going with her today.' Dee and I looked at each other. 'Up and at 'em,' urged Marlene. 'Hop to it.'

Letitia lived a ten-minute drive away in a condo with her husband Todd whom, on the evidence presented in the car on the way, was a 'fat, lazy son of a bitch.'

'I mean what is the point,' she rattled on, 'of being married to someone who a: eats all your food; b: never lifts a finger, and c: hasn't given me an orgasm in five years? He's worse than a dog. In fact, it's an insult to dogs to call him a dog. He's a heel. He's lower than a heel. He's scum.'

Dee and I sat very, very quietly.

'So you tell me,' Letitia asked, shoving her tinted glasses up her nose with one snazzy talon, 'is it acceptable to invite all your buddies over without asking, get blind drunk and sit about watching pornos? Don't get me wrong. I'm no prude. But on Easter Sunday? During lunch?'

I coughed.

Letitia lived in the upstairs apartment of a house that sat on a square of parched grass and had the air of a small, boutique motel. The house was on three levels – below was a covered but open garage space while above, a set of stairs led to a railed gangway behind which sat three flats and then another set of steps that led up to the top floor. To the left of Letitia's front door there was a small heap of decorating equipment: a packet of brushes, two rollers, two trays, four tins of paint and a large, folded-up dust sheet. 'Grab those,' she said, nodding downwards.

'Okay,' she said, showing us into the kitchen. 'Do you want the radio on while you work? I can put that on for you if you like?'

'Sorry,' said Dee, putting the pots on the floor. 'While we're what?'

'While you're doing the painting. You're painting the kitchen. Didn't Marlene say?'

'No,' replied Dee, trying to hide a small expression of surprise. 'I haven't actually had any experience of painting and decorating. Is that a problem?'

'No,' answered Letitia. 'I just want the whole thing spruced up. You'll do fine. Watch the tiles. Don't get paint on them. How long do you think it'll take you? I have to go out.' She looked at her watch.

'Not really sure,' said Dee, chewing her bottom lip.

'Well,' said Letitia, throwing an arm in the air. 'I'll be back around four. Let's say four. That gives you, what? Five hours? That's doable. I'd say that was doable.'

Dee and I stared and said nothing. So there it was. We were painting a stranger's kitchen.

To be honest, I thought we'd done quite a good job considering. We'd finished just before four and had spent the ten minutes before Letitia returned dancing round the kitchen to John Denver and Billy Joel. As the door opened we were singing gustily to 'Allentown', happily providing all the mechanical accompaniments. We stopped and looked at Letitia. She looked aghast. 'What the hell?' she said, shaking her head.

'We've finished,' I said, grinning. 'Didn't get any on the tiles.'

'No, no, no,' she continued, head still shaking. 'I wanted peach on the walls and white on the skirting board. Not the *other way round*.'

'Hmmm,' said Dee, screwing her nose up.

'You've put *gloss* on the walls,' wailed Letitia, gesturing at our handiwork.

'Did we really?' I asked, picking up the pot of white paint and looking at it. 'Oh. We did.'

'Hmmm,' said Dee again.

'Well,' said Letitia, with a sigh. 'I suppose you get what you pay for. But I ain't paying the full amount. No way.'

Dee shot me a puzzled look.

I was woken at seven the following morning by the television blasting something about a revolutionary new cleaning system. I opened one eye and peered over the top of my blanket. Marlene was sitting in her chair, legs up, in a spotted nightgown, drinking tea and writing down shopping numbers. I had tried to maintain a soft doze but the television was loud and insistent. I rolled over and saw that Dee was awake.

'I'll make some coffee,' I mumbled. 'Do you want one?' She nodded.

Since losing my rucksack, my nightly attire had been courtesy of Dee's own wardrobe and after a short period of negotiation, we had settled on a pair of pink elasticised shorts and a yellow T-shirt. Giving my eyes a rub I swung myself upwards, letting out a small groan as I did. 'Crikey,' I said, stretching out my back. 'I'm really aching. Must have been the painting.'

'Morning,' said Marlene. 'I'll fix you some breakfast when I'm done with my tea. Just let me get a couple more of these numbers down. It looks real amazing.' She gestured towards the shopping channel.

I wandered bleary-eyed towards the kitchen. Still a little unfamiliar with my surroundings I looked around for something half resembling a kettle but then noticed that there was a coffee machine on a counter opposite the door.

Running my fingers through my hair, I shuffled towards it but as I stepped forward I felt something soft and warm seep up through my toes. I looked down. I had trodden, barefooted, into a massive dog shit. Poo had squeezed up between every toe. My foot looked like the edges of a black forest gateau.

'Oh no!' I yelled. 'No! Dee! Oh no!'

Dee, on hearing my whelps, and after a considerable and lengthy guffaw, helped me hop to the bathroom. Given that we were dealing with dog shit, it didn't seem appropriate to use a facecloth or a towel. Neither did I want to stick my foot in the bath or shower until I had got rid of the lion's share of shit. 'Jesus,' I said, staring at the mass of poo stuck to my foot. 'What the fuck has it eaten? A vat of *glue*?'

'I know,' said Dee, steering me towards the toilet. 'It's practically concrete now. Right. Stick your foot in the toilet bowl and I'll flush.'

Hoisting my leg into the toilet, I lowered my foot into the water. 'Well, this is a first,' I muttered, as Dee flushed.

'Hasn't quite come off,' said Dee, peering into the bowl. 'We'll wait till the cistern has filled up and have another go. Wriggle your toes. Maybe I'll have a scrub at it with the toilet brush as well.'

Three flushes later and the majority of the poo was gone. 'Clean it with soap,' said Dee, as I lowered my foot onto the bathmat. 'Put your leg in the shower. You can do it there.'

I reached over and pulled the shower curtain to one side. Dee let out a blood-curdling scream. There, sitting in the shower tray, was a massive six-foot python.

'Not again!' yelled Marlene, coming up behind us. 'Sandy!' she barked. 'Sandy! Your goddamn snake is out again!' And with that, she gave it a quick thump with a loofah.

*

'We are staying in a *madhouse*,' muttered Dee, later, as we were dispatched to a house three doors up the street. 'It's like *The Waltons* gone very, very wrong. And what the fuck is going on with that bloke who lives in the basement? I mean, why don't they just hang a big sign up that says "Serial Killer This Way" and have done with it?'

I didn't really know what to make of all this. I was in a daze. Apart from the fact that we seemed to have found ourselves in a Dickensian hellhole, there was something highly fishy going on. We were on our way to a neighbour's house, Roberta of the watery bowels, where we were to walk her Great Dane, Thunder, because she was having a 'bad spell' and couldn't 'go five steps without filling her pants'.

Having said that, Roberta, on first impressions, seemed in utterly fine fettle and as we stood on the doorstep I eyed her suspiciously. She was petite, her dark hair drawn back into a ponytail and had the sort of face you wouldn't trust with even the most basic secret. Her eyes, an insubstantial green, stared out from unnaturally tiny sockets while her pinched nose and her lips, painted London-bus red, combined to present a vision of cold cruelty.

'He likes to run,' she said, reaching for a lead that was hanging from a hook inside the porch. 'I can't really walk him anymore,' she added. 'Not since I broke my arm.'

'How did you do that?' I asked, taking the lead.

'Walking Thunder,' she replied. 'He's in the backyard. Just go round the side. You'll see him. Oh and I better give you this, for Marlene,' she added, reaching into her purse for a $20 bill. 'Let her have that when you're done.'

The dog was massive. As we rounded the house, there he was, standing on his hind legs, paws resting on the gate, looking for all the world like a tall, brown man with an unfeasibly large nose. 'Hello, Thunder,' I said, approaching him slowly. 'I'm Emma, this is Dee.'

'It's a dog, Emma,' said Dee. 'You don't have to do introductions.' She was standing just behind me and was staring at the $20 in her hand. 'Do you think,' she began, slightly ponderously, 'that we're being hired out by Marlene for money? I mean, yesterday we painted a kitchen. Today, we're walking a dog. And each time we've been given money to give to Marlene.'

'Good boy,' I said, clicking the lead onto his collar. 'Perhaps it's just a coincidence?' I said, handing Dee the lead as I went to undo the gate. 'Perhaps they just owed her money?'

Dee was about to answer but as I unhooked the latch from its catch, Thunder burst through the open gate and galloped off, yanking Dee behind him. It happened so fast, I had barely time to shut the gate before realising they were already halfway up the street. 'Heel, Thunder, heel!' I could hear Dee yelling in the distance. I tried to give chase, but Thunder, clearly knowing where he was going, had dragged Dee, stumbling as she ran, around a far corner.

With a stitch gnawing away at my right side, I ran after them, every now and again, hearing a plaintive 'No, Thunder!' floating somewhere ahead of me. Not knowing where I was, it was difficult to know where to turn, but by a fortuitous twist of fate, I had taken a left and could see Thunder crashing towards me. Dee was hanging on for dear life. As the lumbering Dane approached, I threw myself into his path and the three of us collided. I went over his back, Dee tripped and landed on her belly.

*

'Here,' said Dee, twenty minutes later, handing the $20 to Marlene. 'Roberta asked us to give you this.'

'Thanks,' said Marlene, stuffing it into a jam-jar on a shelf in the kitchen. 'I cooked some supper. It's in the oven.'

She pulled two plates out from the stove. They had eggy bread on them. I smiled weakly. Marlene wandered off to watch a 'great hour on casuals' and left Dee and I standing in the kitchen.

'I can't eat this again,' whispered Dee. 'What shall we do?'

I looked down. At our feet sat Peep, the swollen dead-eyed dog. Dee didn't need a word of encouragement. She took her eggy bread by its corner and threw it to the floor. 'Whoops,' she said, raising a hand to her mouth. Peep, ever ravenous, was on it in seconds, wolfing down the oil slick of a meal. I was about to do the same with mine but Peep, having swallowed the greasy treat in some haste, looked up, wagged his tail a bit and then, shoulders dropping, promptly threw the whole thing back up again. We looked at the sick at our feet.

'Well,' said Dee, cocking her head to one side, 'it looks better than it did.'

There was no doubt about it. Marlene was hiring us out as cheap labour to friends.

Over the coming days we creosoted a fence, supervised a children's birthday party, replanted a garden and folded 2,000 weight-loss leaflets into envelopes. Every time, without fail, we were handed money that was to be given to Marlene. By our reckoning, she'd made about $120.

It was our last night in Pottsville. We'd had a barbecue and I'd helped Dee pack her rucksack in preparation for leaving in the morning. We'd spent the day shifting rockery for a woman who claimed to have a bad back but was perfectly happy to leave us to it while she went off to a Jane Fonda workout class. We didn't mind. It was $30 for our gang-master Marlene, our top wage yet. Because the day had been quite physical and the weather still warm, we had gone to bed relatively early and had fallen asleep to the sound of Marlene and the television droning on at the foot of the bed. I had drifted off, thoughts of America floating past, excited and nervous that tomorrow was our final farewell.

I don't know what time it was when I woke up, but it was still dark. I was lying on my back, my blanket loosely covering my chest and as I opened my eyes I was startled to see one, heavy monobrow staring down at me. It was Sandy. He was standing by our bed, watching me sleeping. He was wearing a T-shirt with a stabbed serpent on it. And he wasn't moving.

'Hello, Sandy,' I mumbled, clutching at the blanket.

He stared back at me, not blinking. 'Do you want to come and watch a movie in the basement?' he whispered.

I looked over at the digital alarm clock that was on a sideboard. It read 3:18. I looked back at him. This is the sort of situation in horror films where the first victim goes down, I thought. This is how it starts. The killer stands over your bed and asks you to go into a basement to watch a movie and then he kills you, probably with some sort of idiosyncratic, slightly unexpected weapon, like a spoon and then, after he's killed you and is wearing your skin as a hat, he comes up from the basement and kills everyone else in the house. This is how it is.

'Yeah, okay,' I said.

I followed him through the house to the door in the kitchen. He opened it and said, 'Mind the third step down, it's a bit wobbly.'

It was.

The basement was barely lit. There was a small, single bed over in one corner, a tank in which I could just make out the shape of the python and to its left, a rifle and a fishing rod leaning up against the wall. There was a bookshelf filled with videos, the walls were covered with posters that I couldn't quite make out and there was one armchair, battered and brown, sitting squarely in front of a TV and video player. He gestured towards it. 'You sit there,' he said, picking a video from a tall stack. 'I'll watch from the bed.'

I wonder what the film will be? I thought. Something light? Frothy? A rom-com? Or a gritty police drama that involved a tart with a heart? No. None of the above. We watched *The Texas Chain Saw Massacre*. The most notorious, violent horror film known to man. It involved hanging women from meat hooks. And cannibalism. Neither of us said a word. At the end, I simply stood up, said, 'Well, thank you for that, Sandy,' and left.

'Where've you been?' enquired Dee, waking up as I returned.

'Don't ask,' I said, puffing up my pillow.

In a way, it was a fitting end to our grand adventure, an inexplicable event to cap off four months of baffling fortunes. I can't say I wasn't glad to leave Pottsville but even so, the gratitude we both felt for the kindness we had received was immeasurable. People had, quite simply, taken our breath away. We had been dogged with misfortune at every step of the way, but simple acts of gentle benevolence had kept us afloat. America, it turned out, was a nation of Good Samaritans and as we were driven towards New York, sitting in the back of an open-topped truck that belonged to a friend of Cherry who had offered to take us, I resolved there and then that when I returned to Britain I would for ever live by the maxim that one good deed deserves another. I had left for America with thoughts of nothing but myself but I would be going home with a thorough appreciation of basic human decency.

'I'm going to do favours for people for evermore, Dee,' I said, as we stared up at the sign for JFK airport.

She turned and looked at me, throwing her rucksack up onto her shoulder. 'Be careful, Ems,' she smiled. 'You're sounding like a grown up.'

Chapter Thirteen

The Long Way Home

$5.10

We had arrived at the airport in good time. Our flight was at three but with two hours to spare we were yet to check in. We had done it. We had made it back to New York with $5.10 in our pockets. It was a triumph.

'I think we deserve a drink,' said Dee, nodding towards a small bar to our left. 'Let's get a cocktail. And share it.'

'Great idea,' I replied, grinning.

The barman was in his early twenties, tanned with a good square jaw, and as we hopped up onto two tall bar stools, he smiled and placed some paper drinks coasters in front of us. 'Hi,' he smiled, flashing a set of perfect teeth. 'What can I get you?'

'Can we have a cocktail that costs less than five dollars ten please?' Dee asked. 'That's all we've got. Oh and two straws please.'

He blinked, his grin widening. 'Sure thing. I can do you a Margarita for five dollars?'

'Perfect,' Dee replied, dropping her rucksack to the floor.

'Frozen? Salted?'

'However it comes,' I answered, leaning forwards onto the bar. 'Just make it so it lasts us ages.'

It was an extraordinary feeling. Against all the odds we had crossed a continent on a shoestring and fended off everything fate had flung at us. I let my head drift downwards into my upturned hand. I felt battle weary but content, as if a job had been not quite well done but certainly accomplished. 'Can't believe we've made it,' I muttered. 'I just can't believe it. We couldn't get a job in McDonalds. God. I thought we were going home there and then.'

'Ugh,' replied Dee, screwing her mouth sideways, 'that was grim.'

The barman poured the mixed cocktail into a long glass and threw two straws into it with a flourish. 'There you go,' he said, moving both our coasters so that they were between us, 'one Margarita. I've put it in a tall glass. So it'll last longer,' he added, with a wink. 'That'll be five dollars.'

Dee reached into her bumbag and pulled out our last five-dollar bill. She held it up and looked at me. 'Well, this is it. The last of our money. We're down to a dime.'

'We can phone home now and tell our parents we're coming back.'

'No, Emma, we can't,' Dee replied. 'We still don't know how to use the phones.'

I smiled and leaned forward to take a straw. 'Here's to us, Dee,' I said. 'Cheers.'

'Cheers,' said Dee, with a nod.

The Margarita was delicious: bitter, hint of salt, sharp citrus kick and we sucked our straws slowly so that we could savour every mouthful. We deserved this. We may have been foolish, we may have been blundering but we had crossed America with hope in our hearts and that had never been diminished. 'Never stop persevering,' I mumbled. 'Do you remember?'

'Your old English teacher?'

'Yes. Mrs Graebe. She'd be proud of us.'

'Maybe,' answered Dee, with a small sigh, 'although I'm
not sure if we had any other option. People who give up are
people who have the luxury of choice. We had none. We had
to keep going. If we'd given up we'd be dead. I'll be honest.
When we were in the Grand Canyon and I realised you had
totally miscalculated our travel fund I could have happily
killed you. Actually killed you with pine cones.'

I winced. 'I am shit at maths, Dee. It was criminally negli-
gent giving me that job. You only have yourself to blame.'

'I know. That's why I couldn't be cross with you. Oh!'
she suddenly exclaimed, throwing her head back in a vision
of ecstasy, 'I'll be in my own bed tomorrow. My *own* bed.'

I thought about my own room back at my parents'
house: the pin board that was a treasure trove of small
triumphs – tickets to concerts at the Milton Keynes Bowl; a
bronze disco-dancing medal embossed with a suited John
Travolta, one arm aloft; a row of School Colours and a
prefect badge. Then there were the posters on the walls: Phil
Oakey from the Human League, a collage of cut-out fashion
shots from my mother's magazines, photos of school friends
I no longer saw and a giant poster of Superman. The lips
were worn away because I'd practised kissing on it for years.
All of it, a tomb to my youth. I was going back to something
I no longer recognised but far from being disconcerted,
sitting here in the comfort of the airport bar, I relished the
challenge ahead. I would have to re-invent myself as a grown-
up, work out what I was going to do and where I was going
to live. Going back to that room didn't really feel like an
option anymore. I looked at Dee. She sat, chin in hand,
gazing out into the maelstrom of people wandering past us.
She seemed relaxed, at peace. Her grand adventure was over
and tomorrow she would see her family, rest for a few days

and then pack her bags again to go to London and begin the rest of her life. She was ready for it, excited. That's what I needed to find. The spark of something that would keep my interest.

'It's going to be weird you going to another college,' I said, taking another sip of the Margarita.

Dee turned to look at me, her bright blue eyes sparkling. 'I know,' she said, softly. 'I'm looking forward to it though. It'll be quite nice to meet a new bunch of people.'

I nodded and fingered the paper coaster in front of me, a small knot of sadness gathering in the pit of my stomach. I wasn't stupid. Dee and I would always be friends but once parted, the intensity of our alliance would slowly diminish. It was as if Dee was in a rowing boat built for one and I was standing, holding her hand from the shore. She would quietly let go of my grip and drift away with neither fanfare nor fuss. This was the way life would turn. Significant people burn brightly for their allocated time and then fade, only to be replaced by others.

As we sat there, quietly contemplating the past four months, I knew that this was my letting-go moment. As soon as we stepped off the plane in London, the giddy whirl of Oxford, America, Dee and I was over. It had been a phenomenal party but it was time to clear up.

'I'm going to miss you, Ems,' said Dee, putting a hand gently on my forearm. 'What a time we've had.'

I could feel a lump mustering in my throat, so I played it safe and didn't say anything.

'There's never a dull moment when you're around,' she continued. 'Who will I muck about with now?'

I shrugged and picked at the edge of the coaster.

'Maybe you'll move to London?' she suggested. 'We

could have a hilarious flat share. Although, having said that, neither of us has got any money.'

'I'd have to live down the back of a sofa,' I mumbled. 'I haven't got a job or anything.'

'You'll get one,' said Dee, and then, screwing her nose up, added, 'can't think what though. What do you think you'll do?'

'Who knows,' I said, throwing my arms in the air. 'Maybe I'll be a lawyer!'

Dee blinked and then threw her head back and guffawed. 'Can you imagine? You? A lawyer? People will come in, plastic bags stuffed full of documents, rant on at you for an hour, livid as hell, and then you'll just look at them, shrug and say "Let it go".'

'Yeah,' I laughed. 'I'll be like – "Why are you getting so wound up? It's not worth it. Just forget about it." I'd be a rubbish lawyer. I'd forget to charge people for a start.'

'I can't even imagine you in an office.'

'I was in an office at L'Aroma, Dee. I had stickers that said "See me for more info".'

'Emma, any office where the boss deliberately sets out to get you drunk before lunch doesn't count. I mean a proper office. Where you have to mind your Ps and Qs.'

'What is a P and a Q? That's one of those things that everyone always says but no one knows what it means. Like Sweet FA.'

'That's sweet fuck all, that one's easy.'

'Ahhhh!' I said, lifting a finger, 'but it's not. It's actually from Sweet Fanny Adams. And Fanny Adams was a little girl back in the 1800s that was murdered and eviscerated. So yes, there was sweet fuck all. Because there was nothing left of her.'

'That's awful. I say that all the time. I shan't say it anymore. Poor Fanny Adams.'

'I know. My dad used to call my front bottom a Fanny Adams.'

'We called it a hoohah.'

'My mum called it a Mary.'

'Mary?' Dee laughed, 'Why did she call it that?'

'I asked her and she said, "I had an Aunty Mary. She was a complete cunt."'

Dee bent forward and let out a long, joyful hoot. I grinned. I loved making Dee laugh. 'Still don't know what a P or a Q is though. I suppose it just means to be watchful. Talking of which, what's the time?'

Dee looked at her watch. 'Twenty past one,' she replied, still laughing. 'We've got ages.'

I nodded and turned on my stool to look out at the airport. How different I felt now to when we arrived just four months ago. Wide-eyed, not a scrap of sophistication about me, yet here I now was, sitting on a barstool like a gnarled lion ready to bat away the cubs. If two English girls had come up to us there and then, I would have been able to give them *advice*. The concept was inconceivable. 'If we could go back in time, Dee,' I began, 'and meet us coming off the plane, what would you tell us?'

'You'll need change,' said Dee. 'And don't forget the tent.'

'Ahh, the tent,' I nodded. 'Our lovely unused tent.'

'In a way though,' added Dee, 'I'm glad we forgot it. Think of all the people we met because of it. And the scrapes we got into. This is what living is all about. I've had loads of lovely holidays where nothing went wrong. Can I remember one thing about them? No. This trip is going to be ingrained on my memory for ever.'

Dee was right. I sat thinking about all the people we never would have met had it not been for that one moment of forgetfulness: the lesbian rabbi, Rhoda; Tuesday the Goth; the lovely Barretts; the oversexed midget. It was amazing how one tiny twist can alter a course irrevocably. Fate and free will, decisions of the past rippling through to the present. People were hurrying towards check-in desks while others, just arriving, were sauntering out. Everyone was on his or her own adventure. If there was one thing I had learned on this trip, it was to go with the flow. Sometimes, you have no control over what happens and rather than kick against it, it is far better and rewarding to embrace every stone and pitfall that crosses your path.

I sat back in my barstool and lifted the Margarita to take my last sip, leaving just enough so that Dee could have the last mouthful. 'There you go,' I said, handing her the glass. 'You finish it. That was lovely.'

As Dee sucked up the last of the cocktail I glanced again out into the concourse. I heaved a deep sigh. My time in America had been both horrendous and wonderful. And I wouldn't have changed any of it. It had been the making of me and I knew it.

And then I saw the clock. And frowned.

'That's funny,' I said. 'That clock's wrong. It says it's two thirty.' I pointed.

Dee looked towards it and cast another look down at her watch. 'I've got one thirty.'

I looked around again. I saw another clock. It also said two thirty. 'Dee,' I said, slowly. 'When was the last time you changed your watch?'

Dee blinked. 'New Orleans.'

I turned to the barman. 'Excuse me,' I asked, with a sense of some urgency. 'Is New York in a different time zone to New Orleans?'

'Yeah, we're an hour ahead.'

'Shit. Fuck. Shit. Fuck. Fuck. Shitty shit. Fuck!'

I don't think we had ever run faster in our lives. We made the gate with three minutes to spare.

We were quiet on the flight home, both lost in our own thoughts. Dee, as usual, fell into a deep sleep and I stared out the window at the vast expanse of blue. In a way, I felt more nervous going home than I did when I arrived in New York. Back then I had been filled with cocky confidence but now reality had set in and I was fully aware of the challenges that faced me on my return. But the difference now was that I wasn't afraid. I still had no idea what I wanted to do but I understood that if you want to enjoy your life, then patience and determination will see you through. I didn't know what life held for me in Britain but I was ready for it.

Landing back in Heathrow, I was awash with mixed emotions. I was really looking forward to seeing Mum and Dad but I was also saying farewell, not just to my youthful exuberances but to the best friend I ever had. Dee would be leaving for Medical School within days and I knew that, bar the odd get together, I would never spend the same amount of time with her again. It was time for us both to move on.

As we came through Customs and approached the big double doors into Arrivals my heart began to thump in my chest. We had both, instinctively slowed almost to a standstill and with the doors in sight we came to a mutual dead stop. We looked at each other, said nothing and embraced.

Through everything that had been thrown our way we had survived and without one single cross word between us. Our friendship was a miracle.

Pushing our way into Arrivals marked the end of it all. It was the full stop, the line to be drawn under our fabulous escapade. As we saw our respective parents and peeled off for the inevitable clasping, we exchanged a small, lingering look that in many ways was our own goodbye. Dee was the person on whom I had depended. She had never lost her temper with me and had stood by me come what may. She was my buddy, my soul mate, and my dearest friend. And I loved her.

When it came to it, it was almost as if we didn't want to acknowledge what was happening. There could have been wailing and minor scenes of hysterics but given everything we'd put up with over the last four months, it would have been a disservice to what we'd been through. Instead, Dee, ever the lady, looked at me, gave a short, wry smile and said one thing, 'Now go and find your What If.'

Epilogue

Much to my father's delight, I've been living at home for the last six months and have had a couple of jobs working in London: at a publishing company as an assistant editor and a short stint in recruitment. It's not what I want to do but I'm earning a wage and I've managed to pay off my bank loan of $350. It's a Thursday night and I've arranged to meet Dee after work at the Royal Academy on Piccadilly. I haven't seen her in ages and I'm really looking forward to it.

She is leaning against the corner of the Palladian entrance, *Evening Standard* in hand, reading, her light bob blowing gently in the sharp April breeze, wearing the same battered leather jacket that she'd been in when I first met her.

'Hello, you,' I say, flinging my arms about her. 'I'm so glad we're getting to do this.'

'Me too,' Dee replies, as we pull apart and turn to walk into the courtyard. 'Who would have thought? We went all that way and we could have waited six months and seen them here.'

We are here to see the Edward Hoppers.

We walk through the entrance and Dee hands me my ticket. 'Are you still working at the same place?' she asks. 'Oh, do you want a brochure?'

I shake my head. 'I don't think we'll need one. I've got you. And no, I left. I don't think recruitment is my bag.'

Dee nods. 'No. You need to do something with a bit more of a thrill.'

'Well,' I say, as we hand our tickets over to be torn. 'I've got something to tell you. I've made a decision.'

Dee turns, looks at me, and raises an eyebrow.

'I've been doing work experience at a law firm. I've got a secretary called Madge. They've offered me articles. I'm off to Law School, Dee. I'm going to be a lawyer!'

And at that, she stops in her tracks, throws her head back and laughs. I grin. 'Let the world beware!' she declares, smiling broadly. And, with that, we disappear into the gallery.

Acknowledgements

As always, there are many people to thank. Firstly, massive gratitude needs to be chucked in the direction of the editor of *Cosmopolitan*, Louise Court, who allowed me to rummage through their back catalogue to find the edition I needed. Everything from chapter three comes from the June 1989 edition of *Cosmopolitan* from which the following people are quoted: Junius Adams who wrote the quiz, Eve Cameron who wrote 'How to Have Lovelier Legs', Isobel Morgan who wrote "Do you have Career Charisma', Irma Kurtz, the phenomenal agony columnist and Quentin Lamb, who provided the horoscopes. I'd also like to thank James Ward who provided me with exemplary stationery advice and the wonderful Jennifer Ehle who went beyond the call of duty in her determination to avail me of every known fact about the Appalachian mountains to the west of Winston-Salem. I would also like to thank my amazing editor, Jake Lingwood, and everyone who works so hard for me at Ebury. Your efforts are greatly appreciated.

I'd also like to shower voluminous thanks in the direction of my wonderful agent, Sheila Crowley at Curtis Brown. She is amazing.

On a personal note, yet again, I have to bend over backwards to thank my parents, Brenda and Tony, who were constantly on hand to remind me of small incidents and conversations but greatest thanks of all goes to Bernadette, without whom this book would have been entirely impossible.